ABOUT
LOVE

ABOUT LOVE

REINVENTING ROMANCE FOR OUR TIMES

ROBERT C. SOLOMON

HACKETT PUBLISHING COMPANY, INC.
INDIANAPOLIS/CAMBRIDGE

For permissions and other inquiries, please address:

Hackett Publishing Company, Inc.
P.O. Box 44937
Indianapolis, IN 46244-0937

www.hackettpublishing.com

Cover design by Christina Kowalewski
Printed at Versa Press, Inc.

Library of Congress Cataloging-in-Publication Data

Solomon, Robert C.
     About love : reinventing romance for our times / Robert C. Solomon.
          p.   cm.
     Originally published: Totowa, N.J. : Littlefield Adams Quality
Paperbacks, 1994.
     ISBN-13: 978-0-87220-858-2 (cloth)
     ISBN-10: 0-87220-858-3 (cloth)
     ISBN-13: 978-0-87220-857-5 (pbk.)
     ISBN-10: 0-87220-857-5 (pbk.)
          1. Love   I. Title
BD436 .S6 2006
128'.46—dc22   2006046580

The paper used in this publication meets the minimum requirements of
American National Standard for Information Sciences—Permanence of
Paper for Printed Library Materials, ANSI Z39.48–1984.

FOR KATHLEEN,
my patient teacher

Now, I think love is becoming an abstraction. . . . The soul has become a department of sex, and sex has become a department of politics.

If our society is going to recover, we must recover this idea of love. But we can't go back to the early platonic and Christian ideals of love, because biology and modern science have changed things. Poets, artists, musicians, men of imagination have to find a new image of love, and that is the most important thing. If we don't find this, life is going to be a desert. We must reinvent love.

—O C T A V I O   P A Z, Newsweek *interview*,
November 19, 1979

What follows is an essay, a personal "attempt," not a scholarly study or a scientific investigation. It represents a struggle, not laboratory research or sociological theory or moral lobbying. I have tried, no doubt without complete success, to avoid glibness, cleverness, cuteness, ostentatious scholarship, extensive philosophical argument, and other such distractions, though I confess that I feel a bit naked without those familiar supports. My conclusions, too, are personal and practical, not scholarly or scientific, though I do develop a theory of love along the way. My thesis is, in a nutshell, that love is in fact even more profound and basic to our being than most of our talk about it would suggest, that love is best when cultivated from friendship rather than propelled with great force from some initial explosion of passion, and that love actually gets *better* with time, rather than waning as we so often fear. In finishing this book, I am struck most of all by the enormous expenditure of intelligence, experience, emotion, and bad judgment that it has taken me to reach these conclusions.

Many friends and authors have contributed to the thoughts in this book, but deserving of special mention are Angela Cox, Betty Sue Flowers, Carolyn Ristau, Paul Woodruff, Susan Tyson, Shari Starrett, Irving Singer, Jane Isay, Phyllis Green, my editor at Simon and Schuster, Laurie Lister, and her assistant, Scott Corngold, and especially all the students in my 1985 Humanities seminar, and to the Monotones, wherever they are.

CONTENTS

3. "Falling in Love"

4. The Self in Love

5. The Dynamics of Love: Making Love Last

INTRODUCTION: REINVENTING LOVE

There is only one
serious question. And that is:
. . . how to make love stay?

—TOM ROBBINS,
Still Life with Woodpecker

This is a book about love—romantic love. It is an emotion much celebrated, often mocked and criticized, desperately looked for and longed for and—consequently—much misunderstood. But misunderstandings in thought and expectation breed disappointment and tragedy in practice. We have cultivated a paradoxical view of love and, consequently, we find lasting love elusive, difficult, even a "mystery." But we *define* love in such a way that it could only be a transient experience, and then we wonder—sometimes bitterly—why love doesn't last. We insist that love is a "feeling" and then complain when something so effervescent bubbles away. We say that love is a "passion" and then are disappointed when something so passive passes away. We identify romance with novelty and then object that the new becomes old, and we celebrate "young love" then wonder why it is that we have trouble about love later in life. At the same time, we idealize love in such a way that lasting love is all but impossible. For example, we are taught that love should be completely selfless when in fact there is no emotion that has more to do with the self. Then, too, there is a very real conflict between the values that attract us in love and the virtues that make love work, leading to an image of romance and romantic attractiveness that is antithetical to love that can last. And perhaps worst of all, we are taught that love is eternal when in fact it is something invented—and reinvented—throughout history. So we get the sense that love, once truly found, is virtually guaranteed when the fact is that love is always an open question, a matter of individual responsibility.

How are we to make love last? It is the thesis of this book that love is an emotional process that not only takes time but also reaches into the future and builds its own foundation. It is not a momentary feeling or passion and it should not be conceived in the limited terms of initial attraction and youthful first love, nor should it be overly domesticated or idealized. Love doesn't last because we misunderstand it, lose interest in it, take it for granted or suffocate it with careers and routines. Love lasts when it recognizes itself as primary, when it faces up to its own difficulties, when it understands itself as a process rather than a passion. This is a book about how love lasts, but it must be, first of all, a book on what love is.

Love is the most exhilarating—and sometimes the most excruciating and destructive—experience that most of us have ever had, or will ever have. Love has long and with some justice been celebrated as a religious experience, but so, too, the nature of "true" love has become as thorny and as theological as the notion of true religion. Ever since Plato elevated a vulgar domestic deity called "eros" to divine status and distinguished it sharply from ordinary human love, there has been an unresolvable tension between the excessive idealization of love and the more mundane and less ethereal facts about sexual relationships and their vicissitudes. Love is too often praised as "divine," and its extravagant nature is explained in terms that reach far beyond—if not infinitely beyond—the boundaries of mere human desire and emotion. Today our ideas about love are even more torn between realism and idealism, between our sense of the natural and ordinary availability of love and the rarity and difficulty of "true" love. We want a miracle, and we expect it as a matter of course.

And yet it happens—all the time. Every evening, in America alone, 6,000 teenagers are newly initiated into the act if not yet the art of love. Every day in America, 6,000 people are divorced, their love legally terminated (figures from Tom Parker, *In One Day*, 1984). That is a statistical correlation that should bring us up short. This twin statistic strikes home in that peculiar election-poll and batting-average language in which Truth in the twentieth century is exclusively captured. What should strike us is not the mystery but rather the very familiarity of love, its overwhelming ordinariness. It is not a rare emotion that strikes an occasional Romeo and Juliet. It is a feeling shared by millions, most of whose families, happily, are not so doomed, and whose love, accordingly, may be far more comfortable and comic than tragic. Ironically, it sometimes seems to be those most suited to love, and most thoughtful and conscientious about it and most successful in life in general, who have the most trouble finding love and making love last.

The problem, the irony, is that in our obsession with love we have lost touch with what love is, and we have stopped thinking carefully about what it should be. Love, like happiness, may make itself more available to those who don't press it too hard, who don't expect too much, who aren't too impatient to see it through. We pack so many expectations into the beginning of love and we are so insistent on "the real thing" that we are bound to be disappointed. We fall in love and, even if it ends in disappointment after seven weeks (or seven years), this provides the proof that love is possible—the exhilaration, the whole-hearted devotion, the mutual excitement and trust, the wonder of sharing, really sharing, with someone. But all too often love doesn't last or, even more often, it never gets off the ground. And the result is not just disappointment but bitterness and disillusionment, a sense of betrayal and the precipitous conclusion that love itself is an illusion, that it is only fantasy, that it is propaganda or a device or a conspiracy. Or, more ideologically fashionable but more destructive too, the conclusion is that love is okay but "men [women] are just no good"—frustration elevated to the status of widsom, infantile rage raised to the level of politics. But such indictments never stick, and a few weeks or months later we are hoping or looking for love again. But what are we hoping and looking for? And is what we have been taught to look for what we *should* be looking for? This is not to say that there is some authoritative conception of love that everyone ought to accept, but, quite the contrary, it is to suggest that love is now private and personal, so that each of us contributes to its reinvention according to our own needs and circumstances.

There is no ultimate answer to such questions as "Which is better, a series of several exhilarating, awe-inspiring romantic affairs or a single, stable, happy marriage?" There is no authoritative reason to condemn the couple that thrives on verbal battling, the romantic who prefers unrequited love to love returned, the couple that uses sex to hold together an otherwise impossible relationship, the couple that prefers calm and chastity to excitement and sexual passion. What I have tried to do here is to explore the factors and underlying structures that make such pluralism not only possible but necessary.

The central theme of this book is that love is essentially a matter of ideas. It is, as the novelist Laurie Colwin writes, "an amazing product of human ingeniousness, like art, like scholarship, like architecture." The promptings of love may begin with the libido but the structures that aim it, guide it and define it are not libidinal but conceptual. Desire may (or may not) be "natural," but *whom* and *how* we desire is something cultivated and conceived through a culture and its ideas. But there are good ideas and bad ideas, creative ideas and self-destructive ideas, obscure ideas and clear-headed ideas, ideas that tell us what to look for and ideas that make it impossible to find our way, and all of these enter into love. One bad idea, for example, is the idea that love is a feeling, a feeling that "hits" us unawares, that one must wait for, perhaps look for, rather than a complex emotional process that takes attention and effort as well as decisive action. Another is the disastrous idea that love falls into two distinct parts, the initial, exciting romantic part and, what follows, working it out (this part perhaps hidden from the first by the promise of "happily ever after"). This bad idea raises the troublesome question of "How to make love last"—as if love were an intrinsically transient experience that quite naturally tends to run out of fuel. But does it make sense to see love that lasts as nothing but a residue, a leftover from the original passion rather than as "the real thing"? It is only in the luxury of modern self-indulgence that "falling in love"—as opposed to *being* in love—has warranted any attention at all, but neither does it do the case for love any good to simply reject that initial enthusiasm with an unflattering theory (Scott Peck—"infantile regression") or an ugly word (Dorothy Tannov—"limerance"). The truth is that the two should not have been distinguished at all, except in the innocent sense that every story needs a beginning.

It is a product of that same modern misunderstanding and our infamous impatience that we insist that love just happens to us, all at once and from the very beginning. The suggestion that love takes time is anathema to us. It doesn't fit in our busy schedules. The idea that one might spend years with a person one does not love is viewed as a tragedy (think of Gershwin's song "How Long Has This Been Going On?"), and the suggestion that one should grow to love someone over time strikes us as barbaric, a throwback to the arranged marriages of our ancestors. Similarly, we expect love without doing anything about it, except, of course, looking good and being in the right place at the right time. ("But where is it?") We take responsibility and pride in everything else in our lives, but when it comes to love we want to deny that love is something that one chooses rather than simply finds or walks into. In our proud independence we deny that what one chooses is not just a companion or a feeling or a relationship, an accessory to success, but a life, a life shared, a life altered, a life in which one is, no matter how independent, inextricably tied to and dependent upon another person. We have lost the idea that love takes time, that love is a process and not just an experience, that love is a lifelong development and not something found and enjoyed, ready-made. A diamond mine is the right place to look for diamonds, but not if you are expecting to find a stone already cut, set, polished and fitted, just for you.

THE FOGGERS AND THE FACILITATORS

We will be attempting to examine the unexaminable and to know the unknowable. Love is too large, too deep ever to be truly understood or measured or limited within the framework of words. . . . Love is a mystery.

—M. SCOTT PECK, *The Road Less Traveled*

Why does love seem like such a "mystery"? Part of the blame must be placed on those who have so long tried to "explain" love to us, who have sung its praises so obscurely or reduced love from a grand emotion to a matter of mere management, a domestic science. I call such theorists the Foggers and the Facilitators, and between them they have turned love into a muddle. The Foggers confuse critical thinking with pious reverence and hide love—perfectly ordinary day-to-day sexual love—behind a cloud of false promises and the proud, vain display of their own ethereal sensitivity. The Foggers tell us how wonderful love is, but they don't tell us *what* it is. They often tell us how rare true love is, but they rarely tell us the truth about love—that love is in fact quite ordinary, less than cosmic, not the answer to all of life's problems and sometimes calamitous. What they give us, in other words, is edifying fraud.

This is the trademark of the Foggers, that love itself is an unqualified good and any problems or complexities are a sign of incomplete, immature or inadequate love rather than part of the structure of love itself. It is a degrading view of love that may be as old as Plato, though it was expanded to monstrous proportions through many years of confusion between religious love (agape) and ordinary human sexual love (eros), which, needless to say, suffered enormously in the contrast. That same demeaning tradition is now continued, ironically, by psychiatrists who begin by assuring us that love is indeed the answer to life but then accuse us of being too selfish, too narcissistic, too immature and too obsessed with sex to realize this. One thinks, for example, of Rollo May, Dr. Fromm and, more recently, doctors Peck and Gaylin, all of whom diagnose the problems we encounter in love as "neurotic," attack what they (falsely) claim to be the contemporary separation of love and sex and typically conflate erotic love with parental and family love, betraying a crippling dependence on Freud (whose own lessons on love were far from edifying). Like the medieval priests whose tradition they follow, the latter-day love pundits demeaningly juxtapose our everyday, ordinary, sexual love against an unreal and abstract ideal, currently accessible, it would seem, only to God and certain best-selling therapists. But it is time to get over our tendency to moralize about love and medicalize it in clinical terms. We are not a society that neglects but rather one of the societies that has invented love. We are not the first society to separate sex and love but one of those who try to bring them together. It is not our conception of love that is fraudulent but rather the pompous pretense that love itself is something ideal and beyond our grasp. We are in the process of reinventing love, and the moralizing of the Foggers obscures rather than clarifies that task.

The Facilitators, by contrast, have turned love into a set of skills—negotiating, expressing your feelings, asking for what you want, sharing the housework, planning time together and working out sexual incompatibilities. Even as we try to edify ourselves with sermons by the Foggers, we ingest equally stultifying quantities of advice from the Facilitators. While the Foggers make love more mysterious, the Facilitators make thinking about love facile. Love is something quite simple, a commodity to be acquired much like a new job or a more flattering style of dress. Love can be won and maintained through consultation, "communication" and games. The Facilitators bombard us with exercises and prefabricated exchanges with such cute titles as "The Emotional Garbage Can," "The Artichoke Test" and "Co-piloting the Relation-ship" (these titles from *Making Love Work,* Wanderer and Fabian). Monthly magazines provide a favorite forum for the Facilitators ("How to Tell Him What You *Really* Want" and "How to Keep the Spark in Your Marriage!"). The demand for new techniques to catch and keep a lover seems to be unlimited. The precariousness of our intimate self-knowledge seems desperate ("How Good a Lover Are You?" and "Are You in Love? Ten Ways to Know for Sure"). While the Foggers play on our idealism, the Facilitators cash in on our insecurities. But in the process love gets lowered to just another skill, an achievement, a game with secret rules but "proven" strategies for winning.

For the Facilitators, love is "useful"—for avoiding loneliness, for setting up a home, for assuring regular and dependable sexual satisfaction, for overcoming one's "natural" inhibitions concerning commitment to another person. Love is considered just one more way of "having fun," as one thoroughly serious magazine editor recently insisted to me. Love is made into an excuse for foolish or irresponsible behavior ("crazy in love") or an excuse for disrupting established if unrewarding patterns of behavior, marriages and careers. And, worst of all, love is conflated with "relationships"—whose banality is reflected in the vacuity of the word itself. The triviality of "relationships," however, is not merely verbal. A "relationship" is just that—the more or less stable juxtaposition of two separate and self-contained entities. Love, on the other hand, is an explosive fusion. The parts of a bomb do not stand in a mere "relationship" to one another.

It is important to see the current bloating and obscuring of love by the Foggers as just the other side of this diminished and demeaned conception of love. To say that love is perfectly ordinary and not at all rare is not to say that it is just one more commodity in the life well-lived, an acquisition or the fulfillment of some particular search or desire. The vulgar reduction of love invites an equally vulgar inflation of love, and so we get those heaps of extravagant praise without a hint of danger, as if love were always good and not sometimes stupid, even fatal, as if the virtues of love were "sweetness" and calm rather than exhilaration and violence of the soul. It is all well and good and perhaps even poetic to call love "divine" and "the answer," but as love becomes more abstract and idealized, it loses touch with the realities of passion and our everyday fears, desires, hopes and expectations. Idealized love is not more "true," it is only vacuous —and unrelated to any genuine human emotion.

A THEORY OF LOVE

To take a hard look at love is not thereby to become cynical and "against love." A theory of love need not be pessimistic. It need not say or hint that love is illusory, evasive or not worth the trouble. And yet the truth is that much of what we say and believe about love is sheer garbage, not romantic garbage but the kind of garbage that clogs up the emotions and renders them ridiculous. Romantic love is, in truth, quite intelligent and insightful, even if it is sometimes misguided and made to seem stupid by the wrong kinds of theories. Love is not just a dumb feeling, and it is not an empty abstraction. Love is a particular set of insights, a process that is motivated by passion and focused with affection. Indeed, it is rather what we praise as "reason"— the esoteric rationalization we supply to our emotions—that is often "blind," childish and sometimes fraudulent, disguising if not denying the profound insights of our emotions. Paraphrasing Pascal, the heart has its reasons which reason is too stupid—or too proud—to appreciate.

What reason tells us—most unreasonably—is that we are each self-contained, self-defining individuals. Our philosophies assume this. Our individualist pride endorses it. Our therapies confirm it. The truth is, however, that the self is a social construct, mutually defined with and through other people. And if this is so, love is not a mysterious "union" of two otherwise separate and isolated selves but rather a special instance of the mutually defined creation of selves. Who and how we love ultimately determines what we are. A theory of love, thus, should tell us how we become who we are. It is, accordingly, primarily a theory of the self, but a *shared self*, a self mutually defined and possessed by two people. What a theory of love should *not* do is to let us lose sight of ourselves in a conceptual fog of supposed "selflessness" or allow us to distract ourselves with the mere details of love.

The theory I want to consider in this book is in fact an ancient one, dating back (at least) to Plato and his friends. It is that metaphysical view of love as a "merging" or a "union" of two souls. It is a view that has permeated much of Christian and romantic philosophy, but its classic statement is to be found in the speech by the playwright Aristophanes in Plato's great dialogue the *Symposium*. There he suggested that love is nothing less than a shared self-identity, a desperate lifelong attempt by each of us to find "one's other half." A writer of comedies, Aristophanes presented this view in comic form: we were all once double creatures, filled with hubris (ancient chutzpah) and consequently split in two by Zeus, "like apples." Ever since, he concludes, we have been looking to make ourselves whole again. The story is nonsense but the conclusion profound. It is the task of this book to make sense of it, and to make new sense out of "love" through a literal rather than metaphoric sense of the "fusion" of two souls.

The key to that interpretation is the idea that love is fundamentally the experience of redefining one's self in terms of the other. But it should be noted that, despite the inheritance of that ancient metaphor, the invention of romantic love presupposes a very modern set of concepts concerning the individual, sexuality, marriage, the family and the personal nature and privacy of the self. Romantic love is, in short, a modern invention, to be found only in the past few centuries and only in certain parts of the world. Of course there are some obvious exceptions to this claim, examples of romantic love that are far from modern. It would be hard to find a sensibility more romantic, for instance, than the soul of Solomon back in biblical times. But the rare emotion of one or two exceptional individuals (typically kings or queens or otherwise very privileged persons) hardly points to a general conception. Indeed, such exceptions prove the rule—that romantic love is an emotion that presupposes two autonomous individuals, the dramatic freedom of choice enjoyed formerly only by a king or queen (but which we take for granted) and the freedom to enjoy love in leisure apart from the economic and social demands of marriage and family considerations. (It is worth pointing out that such ancient romances were often the subject of tragedies or, at least, comedies or condemnation.) On the other hand, it should not be glibly supposed that any and all sexual attraction, attachment or fondness is to count as love. Sex, perhaps, is indeed indigenous to all cultures, but sexual enthusiasm is something short of love. When I insist that some cultures have "invented" love I do not mean to say that they invented sex; rather, they invented a very special meaning for sex, presupposing a host of other ideas and concepts as well. So, too, when I say that we must "reinvent" love, I do not mean to say that there are no pre-given elements or emotions in love, or that love can be anything that one wants it to be, or that we can ever free ourselves from the historical, conceptual and emotional contexts in which we find ourselves and which we have not ourselves invented. Nor does each individual or every couple invent their own ideas about love. There are variations and important decisions (most important, the choice of one another) but there is nevertheless the given context and established conceptions through which these variations and decisions are made possible.

Most of all, it should be made clear that virtually all of the concepts I will be describing here are in a constant state of tension—or more properly constitute a *dialectic*—in which one claim makes sense only against the pull of another. Thus, my most central claim—that love is the experience of reconceiving of oneself with and through another—must always be balanced by the appreciation of the importance of that individual identity and autonomy that is the presupposition of romantic love. It is this dialectic that produces the powerful feelings and the familiar excitement of love. It was Maxwell, I believe, who invented the electric generator by discovering that it was the *movement* of a magnetic force through a coil that generated electricity, not its mere insertion. Closer to the current topic, it is the movement of bodies that generates the excitement and exhilaration of sex, not the mere presence or pressure of skin against skin. So, too, it is the movement of two dialectically opposed conceptions of ourselves—as individuals and as a fusion of two-into-one—that generates the passion of love. What I am calling shared identity —and consequently love itself—is always a process, not a state. A flat-footed statement of either polarity alone ("Love is shared identity") will always seem like a stupid mistake, the sort of mistake that leads the Foggers to proclaim that love is always good, when the obvious fact is that it is sometimes disastrous. But then again it is the same flat-footedness that prevents the Facilitators from appreciating just how powerful and marvelous love truly is.

A theory of love is (as it must be) a theory grounded first of all in personal experience, but it is also (as it must be) supported by science, by history, by cross-cultural anthropology and by literature through the ages. It is a theory that—like everything about love—has been anticipated in the titles of a half dozen country ballads and a thousand Sunday sermons. It is a theory that, if true, should strike every reader as familiar—not familiar in the dull sense of "I've heard all that before" but because it suddenly makes sense out of a wide variety of perplexing experiences— why good love can go so bad and how it can get better, how one can tell infatuation from "the real thing," why love is so exhilarating and why "breaking up is so hard to do," why the unusual burst of creativity and how love can be so "liberating" when there is nothing in life that ties us down so thoroughly. To theorize about love is to pay special attention to personal experience and understand it as the product of cultural, conceptual and historical forces without losing our sense of its intimacy. It is not to reject the idealizations and the petty, daily details but to understand them, to see them in a larger context. Love is both personal and abstract, real and ideal, which is why it is so easily reduced to the logistics of "relationships" and at the same time blown to cosmic or comic proportions. Social psychology provides valuable insights and helps us see beyond our own emotional blinders, but psychology alone is not enough. It provides the distance, the broader view, but a theory of love has to be personal and farsighted at the same time without losing hold of either. It is being in love, ultimately, that is the only adequate grounding for a theory of love.

Love depends on ideas, and ideas change through the years. An idea though once functional may become an anachronism, and an idea once liberating may become a self-imposed prison. Sometimes an old and seemingly discarded idea may present itself as a revelation. Such an idea is the simple idea that love takes time. And the idea that love is something that is cultivated and grows rather than simply found or experienced when it explodes upon the scene. And the ancient idea that love involves an actual fusion of selves, a kind of mutual indispensability rather than mere mutual attractiveness and enjoyment. But these good old ideas have been smothered with too much piety and too much moralizing, and they have been starved with too little tolerance and too little thinking. They have been eclipsed by too many demands, too much impatience and desperation, too many political diagnoses and too much bitterness. The simple truth is that love is readily available and quite ordinary even though it is the most extraordinary experience in life. But we have to reinvent love. It is time to reconstruct the rules of romance in line with the new independence and equality of men and women. Most of all, however, it is necessary to open up that ancient question "What is love?" and come up with an answer that is something more than mere feeling, physical attraction and the desire for constant companionship, a renewed concept of romance that is appropriate for our times.

1

. . . .

THE ELUSIVE
EMOTION

"Charlie, are you in love again?"
"Naah, this time it's the real thing."

—EDGAR BERGEN AND
CHARLIE MCCARTHY, in conversation

"What is love?" This is not a quest for an abstract definition but for concrete clarification. It is the answer expressed in that wonderful song from *Fiddler on the Roof*, "Do You Love Me?" There the response is, "What do you mean, I've cooked your meals and washed your clothes for twenty-five years." The question gets repeated: "Yes, but, do you love me?" And the answer is once again a list of acts of lifetime service and devotion, which do not seem to add up to love but, in another sense, far surpass and more than prove it. No one who has been married for a lifetime could miss the poignancy of that question and the fact that love can be most in doubt when there seems to be nothing to doubt. How often does a partner in a long marriage, a good marriage, consider walking out, not because anything is wrong but just because love is in doubt, "something is missing." They still have fun. They still get along, and they have talked for so many years that it is almost as if they no longer have to. There is unlimited concern and caring and neither can imagine existing without the other. But whether it's love, romantic love—that question can become all-absorbing, obsessive.

THE CRITICAL QUESTION

I watched with a voyeur's fascination as the couple in their eighties slowly seated themselves in the rural Wisconsin Holiday Inn coffee shop for Sunday breakfast. I was on tour, alone, and I began to spin a writer's story: the brief courtship in a rural Wisconsin junior high school, a small-town wedding overflowing with family, all now long gone, a few weeks of sexual frenzy before settling down into a lifelong marriage filled with kids and duties and traumatic month- or year-long fights, routine sex with no expectations, silent evenings and unchivalrous tenderness. I thought, "But is it love?" Is it what I want, what I'm looking for? I'm charmed by what I see, but I would not tolerate the well-traveled road to get there. And yet, here (I could imagine) was real companionship, a literal union of souls, two frictionless surfaces ground to a perfect fit after decades of banging and rubbing against one another, now inseparable by force of time and continuous cohesion. Is this the love that we dream about? If it is, aren't we already far, far too gone for it? And if it is not, then what is?

Consider that young man and young woman who have recently met. They are still "dating," to use that already antiquated euphemism, but they are in a perpetual state of frenzy—expressed but not necessarily limited to virtually nonstop sexual desire and activity. They can't get enough of each other—though they try. He doesn't really know her, or she him, but they feel as if they would give their lives for each other. They both feel ready—though they have not yet done so—to blurt out "I love you." But the future is so uncertain; emotions are so unpredictable. And to keep it going they both would have to take serious personal risks and make considerable sacrifices. So they must ask the critical question "Is it love?" They've exhausted the stock evasions, "special," "wonderful," "how much I enjoy being with you," etc. But it's not just timidity that prevents each of them from saying the magic formula "I love you." They know how much is at stake with these three words, how fast obligations and expectations will multiply. Each isn't sure; "do I?" How can they tell? What should they look for? And does saying "I love you" simply describe the state of mind that each of them feels— or does it *make* something true? Is love what they feel—or is love what follows? Is love the excitement and the desire—or is it the satisfaction and its duration?

This is the critical question. One might complain that looking so closely at love spoils the magic, but love is a pretty cheap trick if mere looking will spoil it. One might object to the analysis of love or insist that love is not sufficiently precise, but our own experience shows that we demand just such precision and understanding. Indeed, the fine distinctions we make and the extent to which we worry about them are remarkable: a young woman, rejecting the overtures of a desperate friend, consoles him by saying "I love you but not that way." What way? (And what consolation?) A young man's friends all insist "You don't really love her. It's only infatuation." But what's that difference, and how would he know? An adolescent creeps carefully from "I like you" to "I like you a lot" to "I *really* like you" before daring to use the word "love." An adult who has been through this before cautiously insists that she loves but is not "in love." Counting angels on the head of a pin was never quite so precise.

An older woman has been with an admirable man for seven months, a happy and productive period following an extremely unhappy and destructive divorce. She admires him and enjoys his company. She can imagine spending the rest of her life with him and being happy. The sex is good and they have much in common, but, she says with considerable sadness, "I just don't love him. . . . I wish I did, but I don't." What does this mean? What should she do?

Or what about a man, thirty-eight, married once and resolved not to settle down. After dating for a month or two, he reels out the prepared speech that every woman knows and rightly despises: "I don't want to be committed" or, the pathetic version, "I'm afraid of commitment." The woman he is dating knows better, that he just isn't willing to commit himself *to her*, but she prefers to believe what he tells her, coupled with the false generalization "Men are afraid of committing themselves." But having used this little speech a number of times, he rightly worries whether he is "incapable of love" and, consequently, whether he is—as one of his friends reminds him—wholly human. He tries to make himself feel better by telling himself how much he is enjoying his bachelor life and that love isn't so important after all. But nagging doubts remain, and four months later he is married.

And what about the one who says "I still love you" but it's been four years since he first announced that he would leave his wife to marry her. (He's still not packing his bags.) Is he lying? Can love play second fiddle and still be love?

A friend is devastated in a divorce and within months meets and marries a woman who more than resembles the wife who dumped him. Does he love her? Or is he getting back at or still in love with his wife? Change the case. A man is devastated in a divorce and within months meets and marries a woman who could not be more different from the wife who dumped him. Same questions again.

A young woman is "swept away" by a man who is charming, seductive and, in bed, the most exhilarating and overwhelming partner she has ever even imagined. But she doesn't particularly like him. She finds him "too smooth" and not particularly entertaining or intelligent. He isn't very dependable or considerate either, and he is occasionally almost cruel. She tells herself that this is "all wrong" but finds herself drawn increasingly to him, bursting out with "I love you" in moments when she "can't control myself." Does she love him?

And then, Othello loves Desdemona so much, he flies into a rage and strangles her. This is love?

The critical question does not always look forward; sometimes it looks back. After six years the love affair ends in disaster. She begins to doubt and asks, "Did I ever love him?" It is always hard to recapture previous feelings, especially when they have been washed over with suspicion and bitterness. One tries to remember the good times, block out the fights and misunderstandings, imagine tender moments, but the doubt does not go away. One is tempted to say "What does it matter? It's all in the past." But how could this be an empty question? The meaning of one's whole life turns on the answer.

"I LOVE YOU"

What we call "love" is a social invention, a construction of concepts that serve a very special function in our society. What we call "love" is not a universal phenomenon but a culture-specific interpretation of the universal phenomena of sexual attraction and its complications. Love may begin in biology, but it is essentially a set of ideas, ideas that may even turn against the biological impulses that are their source. The history of romantic love is the history of a special set of attitudes toward sex, even where sex is never mentioned, and if love seems so elusive that is in part because sex is so obviously tangible. Love is, as Willard Gaylin keeps telling us, "so much more" than sex, but it is that "so much more" that is so elusive, and the reason is that it is our own doing and it changes even as we are looking at it.

"Love" is first of all a word, a word we are taught to honor, a word that we are urged to use. It is not long after "dating" that one feels compelled, as one has been taught, to describe what one feels as love. The timing is essential: unless you are exceedingly confident and/or resistant to humiliation, one does not proclaim love at a first meeting. One should be cautious about first saying it during sex; it may not be taken seriously. Waiting too long does not increase the impact but reduces it, like the climax of a movie gone on too long. But it is our saying "love"—not feeling it—that is responsible for the existence and importance of love in our society. How many people would be in love, wrote the writer and aphorist La Rochefoucauld two centuries ago, if they had never heard the word? The answer is "none of us," for to love is not to experience a natural sensation but rather to participate in one of the great ongoing innovations of modern Western culture.

It should not surprise us then that the definitive moment in love is not the moment of meeting, the first longing look or the initial touch or caress. It is not making love or the feeling of love but the word "love"—or rather "three little words," one referring to self, the third to the other and the verb tying the two together in a novel and perhaps terrifying complex of intentions, obligations and social expectations. To be sure, love involves desire and feeling, but if love were just a desire or a feeling, there would be no need to announce it or even put a name on it, much less identify it as the most important event of our lives. We would not worry about the possibility of getting it wrong or wonder about whether or not it was "true." We would not feel so compelled to write poetry about it. There would be little cause for anxiety or embarrassment, much less sleepless nights and endless confusion. If love were, as the cynics say, nothing but "ignorance and deprivation" (Kingsley Amis in *Lucky Jim*) or "lust plus the ordeal of civility" (Freud), it would be hard to imagine why it should be so important, why it should matter so much *whom* one loved, much less whether one is loved in return, why it would be anything more than an itch in need of a scratch easily satisfied or forgotten. It would not be clear why the desire for love to last—not for a while but "forever"—should be so essential to the emotion, nor would it be at all evident why the emotion should be so desirable in the first place.

To say "I love you" is not to report a feeling and it is not just the expression of a feeling. It is an aggressive, creative, socially definitive act, which among other things places the other person in an unexpected and very vulnerable position. The question may involve a long period of deliberation and shy hesitation. We might just blurt it out without any preparation at all, surprising even ourselves. It may follow months of passion and companionship or it might come immediately upon meeting, following a strangely long, hypnotic "hello." It is not so terrible, of course, if he or she is willing and ready with the one acceptable response, namely, "I love you too." But nothing else will do. No excuses are appropriate. One cannot say "How interesting" or "How curious, I'm in love with someone too." "You'll get over it" is outright cruelty, and silence isn't much better. But from that moment on, nothing will ever be the same. From that moment on, there is no going back. (Imagine saying "I love you" to someone by mistake, and then trying to explain how it was that you "didn't mean it.") From that moment on, there will be the need to keep saying it, day after day, year after year.

Why is the phrase so significant? Because it signifies a decision and presents an invitation, perhaps a dilemma, which may well change the whole of one's life. The phrase, like the emotion, is at its very heart *reciprocal*, not that it cannot be rebuffed (it often is) but in that it is essentially a plea, even a demand, for a response in kind. It is the signal that changes a delightful friendship or a casual relationship into something much more—or, if it misfires, something much less. "I love you" is not just a phrase or an expression. It is not a description of how one feels. It is the opening to an unknown future, an invitation to a new way of life.

"I love you" does not always have the same meaning, and this, too, should tell us something about the elusive nature of love. The first time it is always a surprise, an invasion, an aggressive act, but once said, "I love you" can only be repeated. It is unthinkable that it should not be said again, and again, and again. When one has not said it for a while, this may itself precipitate a crisis. ("Now why haven't you said that in all of these months!") On the other hand, "I love you" can also serve as a threat ("Don't push me on this; you might lose me"), emotional blackmail ("I've said it, now you have to respond in kind"), a warning ("It's only because I love you that I'm willing to put up with this"), an apology ("I could not possibly have meant what I just said to you, *to you* of all people"). It can be an instrument—more effective than the loudest noise—to interrupt a dull or painful conversation. It can be a cry, a plea, a verbal flag ("Pay attention to me!")

or it can be an excuse ("It's only because I love you. . . "). It can be a disguise ("I love you," he whispered, looking awkwardly askance at the open door). It can be an attack ("How can you do this to me?") or even an end ("So that's that. With regrets, good-bye"). If this single phrase has so many meanings, how varied and variable must be the emotion.

But "I love you" is not a universal language. There is nothing like it in most societies, and so no emotion quite to compare with it. Some sort of sexual desire might be universal, but the set of ideas, demands, rituals and expectations that are synthesized in the words "I love you" are very special and, anthropologically speaking, quite rare. Love is elusive because we are trying to define a creative act in the making, trying to catch fully formed that which can be ours only in time, insisting on proof and assurances when it is in fact up to us whether "I love you" has any meaning at all.

LOVE AND RECIPROCITY

If love begins with a word then love is elusive in part because of the abuse of that word. We are a vulgar people when it comes to the word "love," using the same exhausted verb to express our enthusiasm for music groups, for McDonald's french fries and for the person with whom we want to spend the rest of our lives. There is obviously a distinction to be made here that our language does not make for us.

If a theory of love is to have any meaning at all, it must be restricted to that special form of love that is the love of a lover. It is not, as Erich Fromm argues in *The Art of Loving*, the love of humanity or a generally loving attitude. That noble emotion (sometimes called "agape") may in fact be the passion that can save the planet, as religious leaders often tell us, but it is not at all the same or even related to romantic love, which is wholly particular and aimed just at one special person. Romantic love is also exclusive. A mother with several children may love them all equally and without any sense of conflict, but if one can love more than one person romantically, it will certainly be a source of conflict, even in the most enlightened circles. The love we are discussing is not the love of inanimate objects, no matter how ecstatic or excited. As Aristotle put it 2,500 years ago, ". . . of the love of lifeless objects we do not use the word *philia*, for it is not mutual love, nor is there a wishing of good to the other. It would surely be ridiculous to wish wine well; if one wishes anything for it, it is that it may keep, so that one may have it oneself" (*Nicomachean Ethics*, VIII, 2). Nor is this love the love of God, no matter how devout or passionate, and it is only the failure of English, which does not include the distinctions made so clearly in Latin and Greek, that makes these appear the same. (The quasi-romantic passion of St. Thérèse is here something of an exception, if not a conflation, of two very different kinds of love.)

What we mean by "love" is the love of a person, the *exclusive* love of a *particular* person. Don Juan, whatever else might be said of his affections and prowess as a lover, does not love. It is said too glibly that "he loves them all," but Albert Camus is much closer to the mark when he says (in *Myth of Sisyphus*) that what Don Juan loves is *woman*, writ large, the abstract set of women and not women themselves. Love requires specific focus, not global perspective or random aim. It is not a fund of affection which we can distribute as we will. In legal terms, one would say that lovers are essentially non-fungible—they cannot be replaced with another of the same style and make like a broken toaster or a worn-out Oldsmobile. It is important to add, however, that this particularity does not demand or entail what is usually referred to as "commitment." Commitment can sometimes lead to love, and love can be a very good reason for commitment, for example the commitment of marriage. But the idea that love is based on commitment is, I believe, fundamentally wrong and underestimates the power of love itself. The devotion and particularity of love are such that commitment is quite unnecessary, although it may well present itself as an expression of love.

It is not enough just to say that love involves one particular person; it is also a question of how we relate to that person. Love has long been thought to be a kind of desire, or else the admiration of one's lover. Thus Plato describes love as the admiration of and desire for beauty, and Spanish philosopher Ortega y Gassett describes love as "a gravitation toward the desired object." But love is not a desire for nor an appreciation of any "object," no matter how beautiful or charming he or she or it may be. Love is the emotional need for another *subject* who also has emotions and attitudes and, in particular, has emotions and attitudes about *us*. We might think the face delightful and the body beautiful but what concerns us in love is what that face and that body have to *say* to us. Perhaps it was Freud, most recently, who taught us to think in the psychodynamics of the "love object." But by treating the person we love as the "object" of love, he forced himself and many others to think in terms of an isolated self reaching out to possess or win over another being. It is as if the image of the love object suggests a piece of porcelain on the shelf—or on a pedestal—to be admired or looked at but not to be touched, much less talked to. Freud sometimes even suggests that the person (object) loved is no more than a vessel filled (cathected) by our own psychic energy, perhaps just a fantasy, not a real person at all. Not surprisingly, Freud then gives us insights into how love may have neurotic and unreal origins, how love can be an illusion and sublimation. But the picture itself is faulty as the basis of an analysis of love. What gets lost in the "object" image of love is the notion of love as a complex emotional attachment between two people. On Freud's model, narcissism becomes the norm instead of the exception, and successful love becomes a psychoanalytic mystery if not a logical impossibility. But this is not just a recent error. Even in Plato's much celebrated image of love as the divine love of Beauty, the matter-of-fact love of everyday life gets short-changed and corrupted. The love of Beauty does not define a relationship between two people, and, however glorious those Socratic images may be, this is not the emotion that we are concerned with here.

Love, in other words, is necessarily *reciprocal.* It is the love of a particular person and it is love that we want returned to us. Romantic love is never just desire, never merely an attitude toward the other person. Too much of what we call love is only admiration at a distance, anonymous appreciation or perhaps even abstract lust but without the real possibility of rejection or recognition. It is more like loving an odalisque by Velázquez, which we enjoy precisely for its human qualities, but we do not expect her to turn and wink back at us—nor would we welcome this if it were to happen. Too many people think of love in terms of desire and/or admiration instead of reciprocity. Some feel mutual admiration and respect and may even say that they love one another but, in an important sense, resist that reciprocity, a fact that may be disguised with clichéd phrases about the lack of "communication." Love may begin as desire but it is love only when it demands return. To love is not just to admire a person's beauty or charm or intelligence or anything else but rather to want a certain kind of response. It may seem like an obvious point, but many of the greatest thinkers in history, from Plato to Freud, have neglected its centrality.

It is often said that love is "selfless" and "unconditional," but we can start to see from the above why this cannot be so and why we should give up these saintly ideals of love as pure giving, expecting nothing in return. Such love may be imaginable for most of us in brief intervals, and for a few for substantial periods of time, but there are always conditions, and there is always the danger of disappointment and betrayal. We are rarely selfless, and when we are in love—which is the height of self-awareness —the self is indelibly written into one's every gift and gesture. This is no vice, unless we begin with some impossible notion about what love should be. Love is reciprocity, and to talk in terms of selfishness and selflessness is to obliterate the reciprocity that is essential to love. Indeed, it might not be going too far to say that to love is to want to be *indispensable* to the person who is already indispensable to you. (Thus the inevitable power struggle in love, but more on that much later.)

ROMANTIC LOVE

"I do think," he said, "that the world is only held together by the mystic conjunction, the ultimate unison between people—a bond. And the immediate bond is between man and woman."

—D . H . L A W R E N C E, *Women in Love*

We are getting closer to our goal of pinning love down, removing the "mystery" and in its place supplying some concrete understanding of what love is, how it works and how it can last. We began, innocently enough, by removing two prevalent obstacles to understanding—the honorable but nevertheless misleading temptation to think of love as a general attitude of loving instead of a particular passion that focuses—necessarily—on an individual person, and the mistaken idea that love is some form of admiration or desire, which treats the lover as an object rather than as a subject who might return one's affection. But this much is true of all forms of personal love, mother for a child, a brother for a brother, a friend for a friend. Romantic love is a certain kind of love, inappropriate or perverse between mother and child or between brothers, and it is quite distinct from friendship too. Our traditional paradigm of romantic love is a young, single man and woman "falling in love." But it is certainly not essential that they be young, or single, or be a man and a woman, or for that matter "fall" into anything.

Romantic love, unlike any form of family love, is distinguished by three features: (1) It is sexual in origin and motivation, no matter how otherwise inhibited, chaste or sublimated; (2) it is spontaneous and voluntary, a matter of will and not just circumstances; and (3) it is an emotion appropriate only between equals, Cinderella and Lady Chatterley notwithstanding.

The first essential structure of romantic emotions is sex. Romantic love isn't *about* sex (a common fallacy) but it depends upon sex, thrives upon sex, utilizes sex as its medium, its language and often its primary content. Whatever else it may be, romantic love begins with the inspiration and exhilaration of sexual attraction (sexual performance is secondary and in many cases actually a distraction). Sexual attraction is not "just physical," of course, and it is not to be confused with the bodily fetishism and Hollywood charms that we too often confuse with attractiveness. But whatever else it may be, sex is bodily and sexual desire engages us as embodied creatures for whom "looks" and the blessings of nature are at least as important as the egalitarian insistence that we are all, "deep down," essentially the same. This suggestion has often offended the Foggers, with their idealized notion of spiritual love, and throughout the history of the subject theologians have struggled for an idealized concept of love that dispenses with sex altogether. (In just the last century American philosopher Ralph Waldo Emerson speaks rhapsodically of "a love that knows no sex," a refrain to be found over and over again since the beginning of the last millennium.) But as we have degraded friendship in favor of love, so, too, have we degraded sexuality. Sex is a spiritual impulse as well as a physical one. Sex, too, is part of the self, even the soul. One's true self-identity is something more than the honors, success and status that are conferred fully-clothed in society: It is rather to be found in our emotional nakedness. Nietzsche remarks, sarcastically, "The body has the audacity to act as if it's *real!*" and, indeed, that is where our reality is to be found. There can be romance without "consummation," of course, for a dozen moral and medical reasons. But the fact is that romantic emotion is as intrinsically sexual as gourmet sensibilities are tied to food. "Man ist was Man isst" writes Feuerbach ("We are what we eat"). So, too, what we are is revealed by desire.

The second essential feature is the centrality of personal *choice* in love. On the one hand this is obvious, but at the same time it is so remarkable that only with a bit of distance from ourselves can we fully appreciate how much it sets us off from most of the world. To understand romantic love is to appreciate that peculiar sense of time and spontaneity that makes "love at first sight" and love between strangers possible. In societies where marriages are arranged, or, less formally, marriage is dictated within an established framework of social, religious and economic expectations, there is very limited room for choice and, consequently, very little room for romantic love. Most forms of love, we should note, are "prescribed," set by one's situation. One does not choose one's (literal) brother or sister; one finds oneself in a family and makes the emotional best of it. Brotherly and sisterly love take years to develop. Motherly love, on the other hand, may begin at the child's birth, but it, too, has been gestating for nine months or much more, and the mother in any case (except in adoption) does not *choose* the recipient of her motherly affection. But we *look for* romantic love, or it "finds us" in the most unexpected of places. Love in general takes time, but romantic love can begin all at once. And though romantic love may "deepen" and become enriched over time, it need not—as we all know too well—increase in either intensity or significance. It is sometimes most intense *before* it has had time to develop, and some authors deny that old, established love can still be "romantic" at all, just because it is no longer a matter of choice. Social significance, knowledge and the long habits of domesticity have their undisputed value, but it has been said that they are more antagonistic than compatible with romantic love just because they are not spontaneous, not exciting, *not new*. In our culture, the tie between romantic love and marriage is virtually sacred, but if love is to last it must remain a matter of choice, a continuous decision. Love is the justification of marriage, not the other way around. In other cultures, love between a married man and woman may be possible and even desirable, but it is not the sine qua non of the relationship. In such societies, romantic love holds a low priority—if it is permissible or intelligible at all. Where choice is not available, romantic love will appear only as an aberration, even as a crime, in certain circumstances and societies.

The third, often neglected (or rejected) structure of romantic love is a powerful form of egalitarianism, not as a social or a political concept but concerning equality between two individuals. It is often remarked that love is a great "leveling" device, bringing the powerful down to the ordinary and raising the otherwise down if not out up to acceptable if not exceptional status. Romantic love not only requires equals, it, as the French Romantic Stendhal tells us, *"creates"* them, whether it be the scullery maid Cinderella becoming Prince Charming's Princess or Lady Chatterley visiting the gardener's hut. Indeed, it is for this reason that romantic love, originally a distinctively aristocratic emotion, now finds its greatest popularity in self-consciously egalitarian societies, an antidote to, a conspiracy against, class stratifications. The heroes of Harlequins may still be nobility, but romantic love itself is unabashedly bourgeois.

And yet it is often charged that romantic love is a structurally inegalitarian emotion, casting the woman in a subservient role.

This has been asserted as a right by certain macho males (represented somewhat paradoxically by George Gilder in *Sexual Suicide*) and as an offense and an outrage by a good many feminists. This, I want to argue, is an abuse and a misunderstanding of the nature of romantic love. Equality is a complex business in most love relationships and, in Orwellian phraseology, we might well point out that at any given time "some lovers are more equal than others." To insist that romantic love requires equality is not to deny that there are still gross injustices and institutionalized inequalities between the sexes; it is rather to point out that love presupposes a radical conception of privacy in which the public dimension is suspended, in which personal choice is definitive, in which equality is determined by two individuals and not by a structure that encloses them. Love is a democratic emotion, despite its aristocratic origins. It is clearly to be distinguished, in any case, from those brands of love in which domination or authority of one partner is essential, as in parent over child, as in beloved country over dutiful citizen, as in lover of pâté over pâté. Love of God, no matter how personal, is certainly not love of equals. (The very suggestion is what the Greeks called "hubris.") Romance is the vehicle, not obstacle, for equality. Cinderella could not remain a scullery maid once she had met her prince.

These three features begin to account not only for the differences between romantic love and other forms of personal love; they also give us some preliminary explanation of why romantic love should be such a powerful and celebrated emotion in our society. The sexuality of romance is already explosive, especially when it is forbidden, abused or denied. The egalitarianism of love assures a continuing struggle for equal shares and status, a constant tension between demands, expectations, and sacrifices, not to mention the creation of a fertile field for envy and resentment. But most of all, the drama of love, the drama *in* love, is the result of spontaneity. Love appears unannounced, suddenly, often inappropriately, even disastrously. It is an emotion that is curiously severed from and even antithetical to our ordinary civil routines. It is an emotion—coupled with our vanity, pride and obstinacy—that thrives on opposition and implausibility. But spontaneity does not mean passivity, and suddenness does not mean unpreparedness. We are never mere victims of love. It is always our choice, our vanity, our achievement, our embarrassment, our tragedy or our comedy. Romantic love is essentially a decision—or a series of decisions—no matter how hard and arbitrary it seems to "hit" us. What's more, it is an emotion that has been publicly cultivated and encouraged—obsessively so—for the entirety of our lives, just so that—suddenly—it may seem to come out of nowhere.

Do we now have a "definition" of love? We are not even close. We have not yet said anything about the caring that is so essential to love, or the companionship, the compassion, the good times together. We have not said anything about time—the time love demands, the time it takes to let love grow. But most of all, we have not truly addressed what makes love *love*, as opposed to sex and friendship and companionship and caring and living together and shared interests and all of the other things that are familiar in but wholly possible without love. That central, definitive characteristic, I want to show, is a special conception of personal identity, a redefining of ourselves in terms of another. To make things more complicated, the terms of this redefinition vary enormously. Love is a historical emotion, a product of particular cultures and a special set of cultural circumstances. It is not a phenomenon that can be defined as such but rather a process that gets redefined and reinvented in every culture. There is no cross-cultural definition of love. Rather love is defined by a narrative, a culturally defined story (or set of stories) that weave our culture's sense of individual choice and autonomy, our natural sexuality and our political and personal sense of equality into the familiar process of "falling in love" and its consequences. What sets romance off from all other love is—as the very word tells us—the sense of drama and plot development, the way in which, no matter how unique our love, we are following in the footsteps of millions of lovers before us who also thought their passion utterly unique and individual. To understand love is to understand this narrative of shared selfhood and how peculiar as well as exciting it is.

Perhaps the very special and peculiar role of romantic love in our lives may be summarized in a recent response of the thirteen-year-old daughter of two of my friends. During a conversation concerning the possibility of her dating one of the boys in her class, she replied, shocked, "Not Jimmy! He's a *friend!*" That reply seemed to cut so deep into the fabric of emotions and judgments that define our ideas about love that I call it, after the young theorist in question, Becky's Theorem. It shows how naive we are when we cozily collapse love, friendship, familiarity and even marriage into the same gentle stew. Becky's Theorem makes explicit our strange obsession with an emotion that conscientiously severs itself from assurances, knowledge and the comforts of established relationships and then proceeds to define much of what we think of ourselves. It is a kind of love dramatically different from all other affections.

OTHER CULTURES

In premarital relationships, a convention of love-making is strictly adhered to. True, this is a convention of speech rather than action. A boy declares that he will die if a girl refuses him her favours, but the Samoans laugh at stories of romantic love, scoff at fidelity to a long absent wife or mistress, believe explicitly that one love will quickly cure another. . . . The composition of ardent love songs, the fashioning of long and flowery love letters, the invocation of the moon, the stars and the sea in verbal courtship, all serve to give

Samoan love-making a close superficial resemblance to our own, yet . . . romantic love as it occurs in our civilization, inextricably bound up with ideas of monogamy, exclusiveness, jealousy and undeviating fidelity does not occur in Samoa. . . . Even a passionate attachment to one person which lasts for a long period and persists in the face of discouragement but does not bar out other relationships, is rare among the Samoans. Marriage, on the other hand, is regarded as a social and economic arrangement in which the relative wealth, rank, skill of husband and wife must all be taken into consideration. . . . As Samoans lack the inhibitions and intricate specialization of sex feeling which make marriages of convenience unsatisfactory, it is possible to bulwark marital happiness with other props.

—M A R G A R E T   M E A D , *The Coming of Age in Samoa*

So long as we think of love as something "natural," as a phenomenon as universal as hunger or mutual dependency or sexual impulses and appetites, we cannot possibly appreciate the extent to which romantic love is culturally defined and, consequently, the extent to which we are responsible for determining the rules and the context in which we love. Now, on the one hand, it would be ridiculous to overdo the claim and insist that we alone (perhaps with the French and a few other decadent European societies) believe in romantic love or even understand what it is. Quite obviously there have been stories that strike us as clearly romantic even in ancient times—in Sophocles and The Tale of Genji, in the Song of Solomon and the legend of the Taj Mahal. But to so expand the notion of romance that it includes every form of sexual obsession in every society and every desire to marry the girl or boy in the next house or hut obliterates all the distinctions worth making and ignores the very special conditions and demands of love that we take for granted in our society but are rare exceptions in most others. Our examples of famous lovers in the past and other cultures almost all find themselves in extremely fortunate circumstances. It is not just our luxurious notion of "romance" that leads us to look for love only among royalty and the aristocracy, for only such rare individuals had the leisure or the freedom to indulge in the luxury that we call "love." We, on the other hand, take the freedom, comfort and comparative leisure of our individualism for granted, not realizing that our common ability to see ourselves as individuals capable of love is the product of 5,000 years of history and an exceptionally benign set of social circumstances —however much we may find to bitch and complain about.

It is this same lack of individuality, freedom of choice and leisure that explains the preponderance of cultures without love as we might define it. It is not that these people lack an essential emotion, and it is certainly not the case that they are any less caring, less compassionate or less sensitive or tender in their relationships. It is not the case that they are any less sexually excited or satisfied; indeed, one of the most self-consciously romantic periods in modern Western life—nineteenth-century Victorian culture—used love as something of a substitute for sex. While it celebrated and encouraged marriage based on romance, it notoriously condemned the idea that married couples should enjoy sex together. The proper loving wife was advised to "close her eyes and think of England." It is perfectly desirable and clearly possible that two people living their lives together in an arranged marriage should come to love as well as honor one another, but such love does not strike us as "romantic." Two teenagers on some exotic South Seas island might dream of running away together, but such childish fantasies are not deemed worthy of more than amusement in such societies. Such love is not an end in itself, much less an emotion to be coveted. Sexual experimentation and enthusiasm may be fine, but marriage, especially, is considered far too important to depend on such whimsical factors.

All societies have sex, and given the consequences of sex, all societies have rules and practices that delineate the circumstances in which sex is permissible and in which it is not. And despite the perennial warnings against our "permissive society," ours is far from the most or the least tolerant where sexual promiscuity and fidelity are concerned. Margaret Mead's classic description of sex in Samoa makes it clear (as did the voyeuristic descriptions and fantasies of earlier male explorers) that sex as such is plentiful and "no big deal." What we call "love" was considered by the Samoans as a relatively rare and amusing neurosis. Marriage had nothing to do with love not because it ignored love but because love as we think of it simply was not part of the equation. So, too, the great anthropologist Bronislaw Malinowski writes in his *Sexual Life of Savages* that many societies lack what we call romantic love because such idealization of a single person occurs only where there are substantial obstacles to erotic satisfaction, a theory more recently advanced by Philip Slater in his polemical diagnosis of love as the result of making sex an artificially scarce commodity *(The Pursuit of Loneliness)*. Where several possible sex partners are always available, so the argument goes, the intensity of romantic love seems quite beside the point. Of course teaching that sex is a sin is an effective way of restricting the acceptability if not the availability of many sex partners, and we should not be surprised to find that romantic love tends to flourish in societies that have been Christianized (as observations of recently converted societies in Africa and the South Pacific make quite clear). But it is not just sexual restriction that makes Christian societies particularly receptive to romantic love; the Christian emphasis on individuality and equality are at least as important, and we should not be surprised that the development of romantic love in Europe closely parallels some of the more dramatic changes in the conception of Christianity, for example the rising attention to the Virgin Mary in the twelfth century, at just the time when the status of women began to improve enormously, making courtly love—a precursor of romantic love—possible.

One of the factors making romantic love possible or impossible is the presence and importance of privacy. Now, on the one hand, virtually every society has some sense of the importance of privacy (Barrington Moore, *Privacy*, 1986), and most societies —from ancient Greece to the Fulani tribe in Africa and the Hopi in the American Southwest—insist that the sexual act be private, even if they exhibit enormous tolerance concerning sexual activities as such. But more important than such physical privacy is the conception of personal privacy in such matters as individual rights and personal choice and, we shall see, in the concept of personal identity, that form of self-identity that is defined not by our roles in society but rather in our personal relations. In most societies this conception of the private and the personal does not exist; one's identity is solely defined by one's place in the society. In such societies it is to be expected that marriage too will be a matter of social determination. Romantic love has nothing to do with it and, consequently, has nothing to do with the life of such a society.

Another essential factor in romantic love, we noted, is equality. This alone explains why so few societies recognize romantic love, and why the few examples from ancient times typically involve women of the very highest social standing, queens like Guinevere and Sheba, for example. In most societies the unequal status of the sexes makes romantic love unthinkable, and marriage is mainly a matter of domination and submission. In our own past the ancient Hebrews had no concept of romantic love. The roles of men and women were thoroughly defined and unequal. Marriages were arranged rather than by choice, and arranged marriages strike us as the very antithesis of romance, even leaving aside the awkward question about whether such marriages are in general as successful as romantically based marriages (the evidence suggests a clear yes). In Japan, too, marriage has never been romantic, not just because marriages were arranged but also because the role of the woman is so submissive, because she is discouraged from all of those talents that would make her an equal and interesting partner instead of a devoted and, in many cases, abused servant. As if to prove the point, the one place in Japanese history that romantic love did seem to flourish was in the "floating world" of the Tokagawa Shogunate. Those luscious depictions of mutually enjoyed intercourse in the classic art of the Shunga do not depict married couples but, for the most part, merchants and courtesans. The "floating world," built by a clever shogun to distract the rich but status-less merchant class from politics, was the one place in class-defined Japan where well-educated women could meet men on a more or less equal basis, and many love stories emerged as the result. Sexual freedom was a presupposition, but a more important foundation was equality, an equality not to be found in loveless marriage. We might note that such inequality in sexual matters is not necessarily a distinction between the sexes. In ancient Greece, where men and women were also distinctively unequal, homosexual relations too were asymmetrical and therefore not romantic. The standard relationship was between a man and a "youth." Their roles were different and so were their feelings: the man was the mentor and admired the beauty of his beloved; the youth was expected to be grateful, but not enamored. (There is an ironic twist in Plato's *Symposium*, where the youth Alcibiades turns this tradition upside down in his love for Socrates, his teacher and "beloved.") Romantic love demands, if not presupposes, equality.

The perennial debate in anthropology and in discussions of "human nature" generally has to do with the relative importance of human differences versus cross-cultural similarities. What, in other words, is a matter of culture and what is a result of biology or "the human condition." With respect to romantic love, there are features of love that can be found in all societies—the importance of sex and the culture-bound preference of some partners as more desirable than others. But those features that constitute romantic love are quite specialized and can be found only in a small number of societies (though the number is rapidly growing). Yet lest we draw the moralistic conclusion that our romantic society is somehow "better" than those cultures without romance, let us remind ourselves that we have a long way to go before we can praise our invention for its contribution to social harmony or stability, much less happiness. Most of the world looks upon our romantic fantasies as a source of social chaos and irresponsibility, as the cause of much unhappiness and, to say the obvious, the reason behind our appalling divorce rate and the enormous numbers of older women, especially, who find themselves abandoned in a culture not particularly sensitive or responsible. Our emphasis on romance encourages vanity instead of camaraderie, seclusion instead of community, whimsicality instead of responsibility, emotional excitement instead of social stability. The result seems to be a culture that is fragmented, frustrated and lonely just as much as (and because) it is romantic. Until we reinvent a form of romantic love that answers such charges, we should be humble about our enthusiasm indeed.

THE HISTORY OF LOVE

The Western concept of love (in its heterosexual and humanistic aspects) was—if not "invented" or "discovered"—at least developed in the twelfth century as never before. Only at that late date was man able to begin thinking consecutively about ways of harmonizing sexual impulses with idealistic motives, of justifying amorous intimacy not as a means of preserving the race, or glorifying God, or attaining some ulterior metaphysical object but rather as an end in itself that made life worth living.

—I R V I N G   S I N G E R , *The Nature of Love, Vol. II*

We have said that love is historical, and what this means is that we can understand it only by understanding its history. Many of love's virtues represent the proudest achievements of our civilization—the respect for the individual and our protection of individual choices, the equalization of the sexes and the destruction of class distinctions in society, the delicate balance between sexual desire and expression and the need for privacy, subtlety and limitation, the pursuit of happiness. At the same time the long evolution of love means that we still carry with us much of the baggage of the past, including residual sex roles, inhibitions, and an overidealization that tends to confuse love with religion.

Love has developed through five thousand years of history, reaching fruition as "romantic" love only in the past century or so. Sexual desire may seem like something of a constant through history, but the objects of desire and the source, nature and vicissitudes of that desire vary as much as societies and their philosophies. Romantic love is built out of those very modern ideas about the status of the sexes, the importance of sexual relations, the significance of marriage, the nature of personal identity and the meaning of life as well as the perennial promptings of biology. Strictly speaking, there is nothing in Plato's *Symposium* about *romantic* love. It takes modern thinking to feel modern love, and however rich the insights of the ancients or dazzling their poetry, the understanding of love is now up to us.

Romantic love is an amalgam of primitive, ancient, medieval and modern ideas about sex and its significance. Sexuality "fits" into different societies in different ways, and conceptions of love and marriage vary accordingly. However necessary heterosexual intercourse may be to the preservation of every society, sexual desire is virtually never limited to this reproductive end. It is almost always tied to a network of philosophical ideas, whether the Platonic conception that all desire is ultimately a desire for Goodness and Beauty, the medieval doctrine that intimacy represents the union with God or the late Romantic philosophy that sex is the life force of the universe flowing through us all. What distinguishes romantic love is, more than anything else, its importance for its own sake—not as a means to have children, not as a celebration of God. It is the emotion itself (not the sex which prompts it) that is important, quite apart from its role or consequences in society. To celebrate love for its own sake meant giving primary attention and trump status to personal preferences and feelings, even when they were irrational and self-destructive and contrary to the good of everyone. How many societies have had the luxury of letting sex and marriage be determined on the basis of individual desire, satisfaction, emotion and enjoyment alone?

The history of romantic love begins to take form with the Greeks, with Plato in particular. Never mind that the relationships celebrated by the Greeks were strictly between men and excluded women or that erotic relations were typically unequal. What Plato added to the more primitive conceptions of the importance of sex was the concept of *idealization*, not only the idealization of one's lover but of love itself. Plato is often criticized for overidealizing love but, in retrospect, we can see that without that sense of idealization, we would not have a concept of love that was so much more than sexual desire; we might still be enamored of just a beautiful body rather than a beautiful person, and we would not care that the feeling last, as Plato says, "forever."

Christianity is not always considered a romantic religion, mainly because of the several centuries during which the church attacked sexual desire as such in all of its forms and expressions, even within marriage. But the history of erotic love has been determined not only by the fact that Christian thought demeaned sexual love but also by the Christian emphasis on the "inner" individual soul and the importance of such emotions as faith and devotion. The genius of Christianity was that it virtually invented the "inner" self and raised certain emotions to divine significance—think of Saint Augustine's *Confessions*, for example. But following Plato, Christianity also co-opted erotic love and turned it into something else, still the love of one's fellow man and perhaps the love of one's wife or husband, but no longer sexual, no longer personal, no longer merely human. In its positive presentation, love became a form of idealization, even worship, an attempt to transcend not only oneself and one's own self-interests but also the limited world of mere human relationships. The Christian conception of love aimed always "higher," toward not just virtue or happiness but perfection itself. It is with Christianity that love becomes literally "divine"—not just exhilarating but an absolute in itself. But on the negative side, it must be said (and often has been) that the Christian conception of love could be brutal and inhuman, denying not only our "natural" impulses but even the conception of a loving marriage as such. Saint Paul's advice, "Better to marry than to burn," was one of the more generous sentiments governing this revised concept of love. Tertullian was not alone in insisting that even to look on one's wife with lust was a sin. Indeed all such desires become antithetical to love, not an expression of it. To Nietzsche's observation that Christianity is Platonism for the masses, we might add that because of Christianity, we now have psychoanalysis.

Christian theology may have encouraged and revered love above all else, but it was not erotic love that flourished. Alternative names for love—"caritas," "philia" and "agape"—may have clarified the scholarship but not the phenomenology of the emotion. When one looked lovingly at another, who could say whether the feeling was divine caritas or nasty eros, except that one knew that one *should* feel the former. An entire literature grew up, from which some of our favorite first-date dialogues are derived, distinguishing loving from sexual desire as if these were not only always distinguishable but even opposed. By the fourteenth century this confusion had become canonized as Platonic love, for which Plato (or at least Socrates) is indeed to blame. Platonic love substituted Christian faith for pagan wisdom. Love had become even more idealized than Socrates had urged, but what had been gained in spirituality was lost in the denial of the erotic passions and the importance of happy human relationships for their own sake.

It was in reaction to this insensitivity to human desires and affections that courtly love was directed in the twelfth century. Romantic love is often identified historically with courtly love—which is rightly recognized as its significant late medieval predecessor. But the two are quite distinct, as Irving Singer has argued in his *Nature of Love*. The two are often conflated, and courtly love in particular is often reduced to the ridiculous image of the amorous but frustrated troubadour singing pathetically before the (very tall) tower of some inevitably fair but also unavailable lady. But the point of courtly love was not frustration. It was a renewed appreciation of the beauty and importance of sex, but although the sexual consummation of love was the explicit goal of courtship, this was not, in an important sense, its purpose. Courtly love was an aspiration for perfection, using sex as its prod, encouraging good manners ("chivalry") and courage, articulateness and poetic creativity. The troubadours and other courtly types followed Plato but integrated much of Christianity as well (though the church took a dim view of the practice, considering it nothing more than a heretical rationalization for sex). Indeed, the paradigm of courtly love began not as chaste and frustrated (if poetic) desire but as secret, adulterous and all-embracing illicit love (Lancelot and Guinevere, for example). Socially, courtly love was a plaything of the upper class. It was as much talk (and crooning) as action, and, perhaps most important, it was wholly distinct from, even opposed to, marriage. It is not at all surprising that the texts and theories of the male troubadours—Andreas Capellanus, especially—were typically drawn from the adulterous advice of Ovid. But their female counterparts—Eleanor of Aquitaine, for example—didn't take love and marriage any more seriously (in part because they were almost always already married).

Much of the history of our changing conceptions of love has to do with the effort to bring together and synthesize the idealization suggested by Plato and Christian love with the very real demands and desires of a couple in love. The virtue of courtly love was its effort to carry out this synthesis and at the same time introduce some sexual and aesthetic satisfaction into a world of arranged marriages based wholly on social, political and economic considerations. It is courtly love that also introduces the essential romantic conception of erotic love as good in itself, a conception that one does not find in the theology of the *Symposium* and certainly does not find in Christian concepts of love. In his study, Singer formulates five general features of love that characterize the courtly: (1) that sexual love between men and women is *itself* an ideal worth striving for; (2) that love ennobles both lover and beloved; (3) that sexual love is an ethical and aesthetic achievement and not merely sexual in the narrow sense; (4) that love has to do with courtesy and courtship but not (necessarily) with marriage; and (5) that love involves a "holy oneness" between man and woman. The first feature signals a radical challenge to the traditional Christian view of love, while the third is a rebuke of the vulgar view that love is nothing but sexual desire. But it is the last feature listed that is perhaps most important for our contemporary conception of love. With its roots in Christian mysticism but ancient mythology too, this idea of a "union" between a man and a woman would become the central but most difficult (and therefore often "magical" or "mystical") theme of the romantic period.

Romantic love as such is part and parcel of Romanticism, a distinctively modern philosophy. It presupposes an unusually strong conception of self and individual autonomy and passion combined with a dramatic metaphysics of unity—of which sexual unity in love is a particularly exciting and tangible example. The great German philosopher Hegel advocated a vision of the universe as a single unity, which he called "love." The romantic poet Shelley described two selves in love as "one soul of interwoven flame." Romantic love takes as its premise the idea of the expansion of individual self to include another—hardly necessary in those societies in which citizenship and other memberships provided all of the shared identity one could possibly imagine. It is the culmination of the notion of the "inner self," again not a virtue that would have been understood in less psychological or individualistic societies. In essence, romantic love came of age only when newly industrialized and increasingly anonymous societies fostered the economically independent and socially shrunken ("nuclear") family, when women as well as men were permitted considerable personal *choice* in their marriage partners, when romantic love novels spread the gospel to the multitude of women of the middle class (whereas courtly love had been the privilege of a few aristocratic heroines) and, philosophically most important, when the centuries-old contrast between sacred and profane love had broken down and been synthesized in a secular mode (like so many ideas in the Enlightenment). Romantic love depended on what the historian Robert Stone has called "affective individualism," an attitude to the individual and the importance of his or her emotions that did not and could not have arisen until modern times.

What is also particularly modern is the linkage between love and marriage. The two have not always been linked so essentially as "horse and carriage," as one popular song would have it. In Plato, for obvious reasons, the question of marriage did not even arise in considerations of eros. Ovid considered love and marriage as opposites, although the marriage of one's intended did provide a challenging obstacle and thereby an additional source of excitement. The long history of marriage as a sacrament has little to say about sexual love and sometimes has much to say against it, and by the time of courtly love, courtship typically provided an *alternative* to loveless marriage rather than a prelude to marriage or—almost unheard of—the content of marriage itself.

In fact, the history of romantic love would seem to indicate that love has its origins not only independent of marriage but as a rebellion *against* marriage. The classic chivalric romance of Camelot was not the story of Arthur and Guinevere but of Guinevere and Lancelot—illicit, illegal, clandestine and doomed. Tristan and Isolde were each married to someone else, and most of the romance in European literature has consisted of stories of mistresses and adultery, not successful marriages. The twelfth-century troubadours encouraged love outside of marriage as an escape valve for women trapped in loveless political marriages. Indeed, one French historian, Denis de Rougement, has insisted that the whole history of romantic love is one of pathological rebellion and self-destruction, quite opposed to that quiet, faithful form of marital love that he calls "conjugal." It is not until the seventeenth century, in Shakespeare's comedies, for example, that we start to see some synthesis of the ideals of love and marriage, the latter typically supplying the culmination of the former (as well as conclusion of the play). But Montaigne, Shakespeare's near contemporary, and Stendhal, the great nineteenth-century romantic, both thought that love and marriage did not mix, and given our current emphasis on the thrills of early love and the hassles of marriage, one might well conclude that the modern reconciliation has not yet taken effect either.

What we know as romantic love is the historical result of a long and painful synthesis between pagan eros, idealistic Christian love and modern philosophy. It is not just sexual, or even primarily sexual, but an idealistic updating of the pagan virtues of cultivation and sensuousness, Christian devotion and fidelity in the modern context of individual privacy, autonomy and affectivity. To think that romantic love is just a "natural" reaction of one person to another is to ignore the whole historical development that lies behind even the most ordinary love affair.

LOVE AS IDENTITY

Love is the expression of an ancient need, that human desire was originally one and we were whole, and the desire and the pursuit of the whole is called love.

—A R I S T O P H A N E S , in Plato's *Symposium*

It is time to introduce the central ingredient in love, the conceptual nucleus that holds all the rest together—the sex, the companionship, the "natural" tie to marriage, the grand importance of the passion and the devastating impact of its loss. That central ingredient is personal self-identity. It would be best to begin by restating the most powerful if also frivolous statement of the identity theory, the speech by the playwright Aristophanes in Plato's *Symposium*.

In response to the request that each of the symposiasts give a speech in praise of love, Aristophanes invents a tale that, though intended to be humorous and a lighthearted escape from some of the pompous and self-important pronouncements preceding, strikes a chord of profound familiarity. The story is that we were all, "once upon a time, " roly-poly impressive double creatures, bounding around the earth and having a jolly good time. Our shapes then—as opposed to now—were nearly perfect, which in Greek geometry meant the shape of the sphere. Two faces gave us total vision, four hands and four feet made us excellent tumblers. We were much smarter, much bolder and filled with hubris, so much so that we were a challenge to the gods themselves. In defense, Zeus humbled our pride and split us in two, diminished in strength and increased in numbers. Apollo saw to it that the anatomy of the remaining halves was rearranged into the odd and incomplete forms in which we now find ourselves, and we have ever since wandered the earth, "each of us but the indenture of a man, and always looking for our other half." Here is the power of love, not just sexual desire nor any sort of mere admiration but the desire to be whole again. We want to be unified, not so much finding somebody else as finding *ourselves*. Sex is a ready vehicle for doing so, but it is only a partial success, and then very transient, and Aristophanes is very clear that sex is not the goal of love: "For the intense yearning which each of them has toward the other does not appear to be the desire for intercourse, but of something else which the soul desires and cannot tell, and of which she has only a dark and doubtful presentiment." That desire is for unity, and Aristophanes suggests that if Hephaestus, the blacksmith of the gods, could literally weld our two halves together—body and soul—there is nothing that we would want more. In other words, against the cynics, we should not try to understand love in terms of sex but rather, perhaps, the power of sex in terms of love. "So ancient is the desire of one another that is implanted in us, reuniting our original nature, making one of two, and healing the state of man."

What are we to make of this? In the *Symposium*, Socrates dismisses it as ridiculous, and modern scholars have objected to it as "barbaric and unphilosophical" (J. A. Stewart, *The Myths of Plato*). The history is as absurd as the anatomy, and whatever it is that touches us, in addition to amusement, cannot easily be credited to an understanding of love. But what Aristophanes has given us, I want to show, is an ancient model for understanding modern love. It is a model that is often reiterated in Christian accounts of love as a "merging" of souls in the mystical "union" of marriage, and it is an idea that is still repeated today, for example, by Willard Gaylin in the form of an unexplained "fusion" of two people.

If we can interpret this notion of shared identity without the false historical picture of an "original unity," if we translate the metaphor into a real psychological mechanism, if we can understand the unification of two selves, only in part through sex, without the absurd mythological correlates, then we shall understand what love is, why it is so important, why it so often appears as comedy, and tragedy, and why it centers around that "infinite longing" that goes so far beyond sex without ever leaving sex behind. And we will be in a position to appreciate how love lasts, why it does not naturally fade or wane but rather endures. What we have to understand is how we can and do literally "merge ourselves" in love, for this, and nothing less, is what love is.

THE PARADOX OF LOVE

Love is a drama of contradictions.

—FRANZ KAFKA

A paradox is an idea that is irresistible but seemingly impossible at the same time. Romantic love is a paradox. The paradox of love begins with the very idea that two people can become one, that two independent and very different personalities can not only "fit" together without friction and disharmony but form a coherent and seamless unity. There is no doubt that people can make "arrangements" and share time, pleasure and an apartment. They can cooperate and live together, perhaps even enjoy a lifetime of friendship, companionship and shared desires and interests. They can form an alliance, even that lifelong legal alliance called "marriage." But love, that's a different matter altogether. Aristophanes, in the *Symposium*, suggests that love is looking for one's other half, but the truth is that we weren't once together. Indeed, we've grown up quite separately and differently, with divers experiences, fears and expectations. We've polished our independence and our ability to be "on our own" to a fine art, and the very idea of merging two such established and full-grown autonomous individuals into a single harmonious and nonexplosive entity seems to be a logical impossibility. And yet we try it all the time.

It is tempting to suggest an unromantic analogy: the fusion of two independent atoms to form a molecule. The atoms retain their identity as atoms of a certain element but, at the same time, they together form a new substance with quite different properties. But we know that the dynamics of chemistry can be explosive, and atoms, like individuals, may show a dramatic resistance to bonding, especially when they are stable on their own. Bonding takes energy—a great deal of it—and the truth is that an element in a compound no longer retains its original nature and cannot easily bond again. But the analogy hides as well as illuminates the paradox of love: how can two very different people, two quite independent and stubborn individuals, form a union? The bonds that hold a molecule together exhibit an explosive complex of attractive and repulsive forces. We should expect no less of love.

Here is the paradox: the independent individual is the presupposition of love, and this independence is just what love wants to overcome and deny. The individual insists on self-definition; love demands mutual and shared definition. The individual occupies his or her own space and time, but love breaks down all distance and denies the integrity of the isolated body. Love invades and occupies the body, subverts it with its own needs. Time is redefined as time together.

We sense the paradox in every conversation, in every caress— the touch that lingers too long or not long enough, the word that jars. We are one, we think, but there is always that awareness that we are still two. I can't imagine your leaving me, but I know that you could. Making love is a desperate and temporarily successful attempt to be one, but we are painfully aware, even in our most satisfied moments, that there is still an abyss between us. And so we always want more, love being not satisfaction but desperation, for the true end of our desire is never satisfied.

It would be wonderful, we might think, if we could simply be identical (the two-peas-in-a-pod imagery of unimaginative to-getherness), or if we were complementary and simply "fit" to-gether like Aristophanes's two halves. But then it wouldn't be love, for love, unlike similarity and complementarity, presup-poses differences to be overcome, conflicts and contrasts. We don't just "fit" together. Love is a process, not a serendipitous discovery—although it is clear that some processes are more difficult and implausible than others. The story of love takes as its essential plot a sequence of misunderstandings, underestimat-ings, disagreements and miscommunications which, sometimes, get resolved. It is a tale of coordination and compromise, not the idyllic image of perfect harmony and "happily ever after." The successful man or woman who expects love to run as smoothly as a well-run office is probably looking for the wrong emotion.

How does an independent isolated self ever reach out to merge with another? One unsatisfactory answer is that true love does not reach out at all, but stays self-contained, even "unrequited." D. H. Lawrence opposes Aristophanes with the image of two polar stars, holding each other in orbit but nevertheless indepen-dent and unmerged with each other. More extreme is the claim that love is always spoiled, not just by marriage, but by relation-ships as such. What is important about love, the argument goes, is the desire, the fantasy, not the reality—which is impossible. The troubadours are often taken as representatives of this per-verse view, but they stressed the importance of prolongation and inspiration, not frustration. Not so Stendhal, who seemed to believe that love is better without the other person to muck it up. Or as Goethe put it, bluntly, "If I love you, what business is that of yours?"

It is often suggested that this "union" is not real, only a tem-porary self-delusion. Kingsley Amis writes (in *Lucky Jim*) that the essential ingredients of love are "ignorance and deprivation." The alleged unity is an illusion, its apparent harmony based on mutual unawareness, the overwhelming desire based on frustration or inexperience. The suggestion, accordingly, is that knowledge and sexual satiation will get rid of love just as surely as limeade will quench a thirst. So, too, the great comedian W. C. Fields insists that love is a combination of "lust, possessiveness and confusion." Again, the idea is that the supposed merger of souls is nothing but a poetic fantasy, whose reality is nothing so poetic or spiritual. In place of Aristophanes's metaphysical unity, the cynics suggest instead epistemological error and sexual discomfiture. This resolves the paradox by dissolving one of its terms: there is no spiritual union, only two irrational individuals. But then, of course, there is no love.

Such cynicism is embodied in much of our practical common sense. Why is it that love so often fades with knowledge and protracted intimacy? Why is it that the sexual desire that was once so breathless and insatiable slowly, even unnoticeably, dwindles to a routine or even indifference? If we are so often disappointed, isn't it plausible to suppose that the identity that is so celebrated is itself a delusion, a poet's image rather than a real possibility? An acquaintance of mine—a French Canadian—recently married a Japanese woman. She spoke neither English nor French. He spoke no Japanese. They were the ideal couple —loving, attentive, totally passionate, apparently the paradigm of Oneness. But then she started to learn English. Now they fight all the time. They are getting to know one another. And the sex isn't so good anymore either. What once was a lusty mutual mystery has turned into mutual resentment and resistance. The bond between them was based upon ignorance. There was no "union"—only a desire to possess what would normally be out of bounds.

The paradox gets discussed by Plato by way of the question "How can one desire that which one already has?" There is a contradiction between desire and attraction, on the one hand, and fulfillment and unity on the other. Love is the latter, not the former, but love seems empty, even bankrupt, without the former. Moreover, the very features that make us attractive (e.g., strong-willed independence, self-confidence and "cool") may be those that make harmonious unity impossible. The fantasies and needs that give rise to desire may be those that make fulfillment most difficult.

The paradox of two-into-one cannot be dismissed as a delusion. What we have to understand is the nature of the self, so that it can be "merged." But what we must also understand is that the self is such that this form of merger can never be complete. Love is always a tension of opposition between the ideal of a perfect union and the equally unyielding ideal of an autonomous and independent self. Those with a strong sense of self and independence will therefore find love particularly difficult, and be tempted by the temporary delusion that "falling in love"— completely yielding control—is the only way to do it, like going limp when diving into cold water instead of wading slowly in. But once in the water, one has to swim, and once in love, one's self demands its usual attention.

Love is also the paradox—the contradiction—between friendship and sex. We would like to imagine that these are the same, or that one is just a subset of the other. Indeed, when we think about what we want in a lover, friendship surely appears near the top of the list, and what could be more fulfilling in a friendship than love? Love and friendship have so much in common, in terms of both presuppositions and ideals. Both require some radical sense of equality and mutual concern. Both are matters of individual choice and preference. Historically, it should not surprise us that in the twelfth century, the time of the appearance of courtly love, there also appeared cults of friendship— friendship as a Christian virtue, not just as a secular comfort. The social contexts, however, were different: courtly love was confined to the courts, the cults of friendship mainly to the monasteries. (The theorists of courtly love read raunchy Ovid; the defenders of friendship tended to read the more philosophical treatises of Aristotle and Cicero.) And going back several centuries more, the Greeks didn't really distinguish between love and friendship. (Our reading of "eros" and "philia" is far more a reflection of our distinctions than theirs.) But for us, love and friendship are not the same, and not easily fused. (Remember Becky's Theorem: "Not Jimmy; he's a friend!")

Perhaps most of all, the paradox is male and female, masculine-feminine, not two sexes or two genders or two bodies or even two minds but two cultures, two histories, two contradictory views of life. Simone de Beauvoir once wrote that men and women have different concepts of love, and that's why they fail to understand one another. I don't doubt that this is true, even if it is changing. Women still write about being in love and its disappointments while men preach about the divine nature of love and write books as experts—deep thinkers, psychiatrists or holy men—never just as men. One wonders how they so often manage to get—and stay—together. One wonders how—or if—love is possible.

2
. . . .

GETTING CLEAR
(ABOUT LOVE)

Helas! je sais un chant d'amour
Triste ou gai?—tour à tour.

(Alas, I know a love song,
Sad or happy?—each in turn.)

—OLD BRETON LOVE SONG, *Anonymous*

If love is a matter of ideas, then wrong or inappropriate ideas will distort or undermine both our theories about love and our experience of love itself. The belief that love appears out of nowhere, for example, leads us to wait instead of look for love, to expect that love will "happen" to us when in fact it is a readiness that must be conscientiously adopted. The belief that love guarantees happiness similarly leads to that overconfidence and inattention that lets love grow indifferent and even sour. The idea that love will last forever makes us overly self-critical and quite confused when love ends. The idea that love is always good allows us to rationalize some truly horrendous relationships, while the idea that love is an illusion leads us to dismiss some quite workable romances that might just turn out to be magnificent.

The fact that love is a cultural construction means that most of us—as natives of that culture—should get it right. We have been spoon-fed since birth with romantic stories, images, movies, novels and gossip, indeed so much so that we mistake what we have been so thoroughly "taught" as strictly "natural" and universal. (The erotic misadventures of those who have been raised in other cultures are amusing, accordingly; what is harder for us to appreciate is that our attitudes when exported are no less amusing and ludicrous.) But much of what we have learned about love belongs to the past rather than the present, and entrenched beliefs about love may be more appropriate to an age going through the breakup of feudalism or the first experiments with the nuclear family than to the late twentieth century, with its tremendous mobility and flexibility, its breakdown of traditional social roles and responsibilities, its problems of overpopulation, its near perfection of birth control, its enormous urban centers with their hustle and anonymity, its unprecedented ambition and greed, its consequent chaos. What will always remain is the necessity to continue procreation in some form and to establish intimate ties of some sort, but from these minimal demands one is not entitled to infer the necessity of romantic love, or even heterosexual intercourse, or the need for families— much less the nuclear family, which is an experiment less than two hundred years old and may be declared a failure by the next century. History moves quickly, and though our ideas about love are embedded in our culture, our culture has changed and is changing so dramatically that we must be particularly critical of those ideas and fantasies about love which no longer have meaning for us now.

Our ideas about love are a blend of religion, biology and sociology, coupled with a thousand themes from movies and romantic novels (invented in the eighteenth century to encourage domesticity among young women). The old image of romantic heroism is a hangover from the days of chivalry, when a lover had reason to be good with a sword and possess a solid set of armor. It is hardly appropriate today, when social success is more likely to involve a good sense of the stock market and a business suit. There have been attempts to save and update the idea of the hero in modern times, in Montaigne's quaint bourgeois notion of the "hero of everyday life" and, much more recently, in the extreme notion of the anti-hero, the "bad boy" rendered charming, the Belmondo/Burt Reynolds set. But the virtues of modern society are rarely heroic; they have more to do with such bland moral merits as being a "good person" and having integrity, sensitivity and sympathy. And the sad truth is, there are just not enough heroes to go around, which is why movies must provide them for the millions. So, too, the idea of the woman in the passive-receptive role of "beloved," an advance over her role as economic chattel in medieval times and a necessity given her social and physical vulnerability in a violent age, no longer applies in this society of increasingly equal opportunities and sporadic violence against which a male "protector" would be of little avail. From medieval marriage we inherit the asymmetry of our traditional marriage vows, now often replaced by young couples with original ceremonies. The oath of "obedience" is no longer acceptable in love or marriage and the vow "for richer or for poorer" is no longer taken seriously. A spouse who abandons a marriage in hard times may be criticized for "using" the marriage or lacking consideration, but not for the violation of a sacred obligation.

Early church attitudes toward sex have been the source of rebellion since the days of the Gnostics, and much of the history of Christianity—as well as the history of love—has been defined by changing attitudes toward the acceptability of sex and sexual enjoyment. No longer is love considered sinful for its sexuality, and the residual rejection of the importance of sex in love is more often a symptom of neurosis than a sign of spirituality. The troubadours considered themselves good Christians when they tried to synthesize even adulterous sex with such Christian virtues as fidelity, and part of Martin Luther's rebellion against the Church was his attempt to sanctify sex in marriage. Edmond Leites has recently argued persuasively that the Puritan rebels opposing the established Church of England practiced a sexually passionate form of marriage—quite the contrary of our current notion of "puritanism." In general, the emphasis has turned from sex and sexual enjoyment as a Sin (especially for women) to sex as a *right*. Indeed, whatever else the "sexual revolution" established, it set once and for all the acceptability of sexuality even within the most conservative confines of Christianity (Ehrenreich et al., *Re-Making Love*).

Before we can proceed to understand exactly what love is, it will be necessary to say something about what love is not, and about the illusions that make love so easily misunderstood. I want to deal with six general misconceptions—by no means an exhaustive list—that systematically distort our theories and our practice of love. Some of them are part of our inheritance, from centuries of thinking about and experimenting with love. Some have their origins more in fantasy than in actual practice, but, in retrospect, it is not always possible for us to clearly see the difference. Some are more recent, the product of modern psychology. All of them are sufficiently damaging to require special attention in our attempt to reinvent love as an emotion appropriate for life today.

The six misconceptions are:

1. that love is a feeling;
2. that understanding love is the same as understanding the dynamics of a relationship;
3. that love is good in itself and "all you need is love";
4. that love is or should be like our love stories: "once upon a time . . . happily ever after";
5. that love is essentially bound up with the beautiful;
6. that love is for the young.

IS LOVE A FEELING?

It's not at all unusual for love to remain for a lifetime. It's passion that doesn't last.

—TOM ROBBINS, *Still Life with Woodpecker*

It is absurd to think of love as a feeling and then complain that it doesn't last. Feelings don't last. The thrill of being swept away in sex might last an hour or so. Excitement might last a full day or two at most. A feeling of euphoria might last several months —but this is still a short span of time in the calendar of love. Of course one might object that the word "feeling" does not necessarily refer to such dramatic and physiologically disruptive sensations; there are also those feelings of "being comfortable" with a person, feelings of respect and loyalty, but now the word "feeling" has lost all specific meaning and seems to refer to any mental attitude. Indeed, using the word "feeling" when talking about the mind is about as helpful as the use of the word "thing" when talking about objects: it covers virtually everything and accordingly helps us to understand nothing.

There is, for example, that palette of feelings that we call sensations, quite specific, tied to the senses and fairly easy to pin down to physiology: flashes of color, the sound of middle C produced by pressing a single piano key, the taste of maple syrup, the feeling of a single fingernail tracing its way up the inside of one's thigh. Then there are complexes of sensations, still specific but structured and no longer simple and no longer accountable in terms of innervation and nerve endings alone: the "impression" of a Monet water lily or a Delacroix lion, a Mozart melody, the taste of a Cabernet, the sense of warmth and affection while being hugged and held by one you love. Such structures already involve taste and interpretation, value judgments and estimations of significance. They are not only pleasant or unpleasant, successful or unsuccessful, but *meaningful*. Some "feelings" dispense with sensation altogether, or in any case they consist of those "inner" sensations that, though still in some sense bodily, seem to have no real connection with the five physical senses, no precise source or localization, a feeling of queasiness or repulsion, the exhilaration of joy or delighted surprise. Some such feelings might be easily explained—the effect of hormone secretions, for example, but most such feelings are more than this, involving judgment and perception as well as bodily awareness. And then there are those feelings that might better be called "intuitions" or "inclinations" or even "thoughts," for they have about as much to do with simple sensations as the idea that the feeling of the apocryphal apple hitting Isaac Newton on the head was the same as his insight that the fall of the apple could be explained by the same force that would explain the movements of the stars. Such "feelings" encompass some of the greatest thoughts in the history of science and mathematics as well as the feelings of insight, illumination and confidence that we all experience, but this is hardly what anyone means when they claim that love is a feeling.

When love is said to be a feeling, it is that relatively dumb and aimless feeling of exhilaration and excitement, that "warm feeling all over" that is getting confused with love. So, too, many emotions (and in some psychological theories, all emotions) are conflated with the physiological feelings that accompany them, but in virtually every case this is a serious mistake. Emotions are not so dumb or aimless, and though to be sure every strong emotion—especially romantic love—is bound to be escorted by some strong bodily reactions, the emotions themselves are much more than the feelings and over a long period of time might persist with very few outbursts of feeling as such. Indeed, even the feelings are subject to the interpretation of the emotions they accompany. Whether they are pleasant or unpleasant, for example, depends upon the emotions they are bound up with—the same tingling sensations will be delightful in love, upsetting in unwanted fear. Emotions are not feelings, even when emotions are bound up with feelings. The emotion itself is a form of intelligence, a set of judgments, a way of seeing the world. As such it can last for years—even a lifetime. And quite the contrary of a feeling, which is exceedingly limited in its duration, a true emotion rarely lasts for only a moment. Real love, like real hatred and real anger, has its will to endure built right into it; it is intractable, stubborn, demanding. Unlike a feeling, it is not merely a felt physiological episode; it does not just intrude into consciousness. Love, like all emotions, is a product of the will, and in the willfulness of love the idea of fleeting romance is all but unthinkable.

There is a second and in some ways more profound problem with thinking about love as a feeling, and that is that "feelings" may turn out to be a distraction from love rather than express its essence. Paying attention to the warm and bubbly sensations of early love can too readily bewilder our attention from the strategy and obligations of love, which is why Jean-Paul Sartre suggests that romantic love is essentially an escape from responsibility. Furthermore, the feelings involved in love are, as we all know, exhilarating and inspiring, the best natural "high" that most of us know. But this (along with the chemistry that is its cause) can be seriously addicting, and we can thus understand why it is that some very "romantic" people prefer the continuous "fix" of a series of truncated love affairs to the sustenance of love as such. Feelings are not the essence of love, and the feelings of love, ironically, can lead away from love.

In a long and rightly famous discussion of the role of pleasure in our lives, the great Greek philosopher Aristotle argued long ago that to think of our activities as aimed at enjoyment was both vulgar and misleading. It was vulgar because it ignored or degraded the "higher" aims of life—reducing them to nothing more than means to pleasure, and it was misleading because it misdescribed and misunderstood the nature of pleasure itself. With the exception of a few possible and unusually distinct sensations, pleasure is not a particular feeling at all; indeed, on analysis it might seem to be nothing at all. The pleasure of orgasm is perhaps the most dramatic exception, but even this is subject to dispute. We all know how hard it is to "remember" the power of an orgasm—even soon after the fact. What such powerful sensations mean, even at the time, depends wholly on the context in which they occur. A spontaneous orgasm in the middle of a medical examination is not a pleasant experience; an orgasm induced by rape is an extremely painful experience. In today's performance-minded sexual context, an orgasm in the course of sexual intercourse may be pleasant mainly because it is an accomplishment, because it is expected, or because it proves that one is a "real" man or woman. In love, an orgasm may truly signify the "union" hypothesized by Aristophanes and the total selflessness urged (in different contexts) by the Christian saints, but here, too, it is not the intrinsic pleasure of the sensation that is enjoyed but its context and meaning. Pleasure and enjoyment are not experiences in themselves but the accompaniment, the "completion" of activities that we happily engage in, according to Aristotle. To enjoy skiing is not to engage in a rigorous and slightly risky activity with the aim of producing some sensation of pleasure; rather one's enjoyment of skiing is inextricable from the actual doing of it. To put it plainly, one does not ski in order to get the pleasure; one gets the pleasure from enjoying the skiing. Indeed, to concentrate on the pleasure of skiing is a good way to wind up around a tree. So, too, the pleasures of love are in the loving, and there are few worse lovers than those who celebrate the feeling instead of the beloved, like those who see orgasm as the goal of making love instead of the physical culmination of an activity that is thoroughly endowed—from first caress to morning coffee—with meaning and significance.

This confusion of enjoyment as an end in itself instead of part and parcel of the activities we enjoy is very much like the confusion of the more obvious feelings of love—the excitement and exhilaration—with the love itself. We mistake the excitement for that which we are excited *about*. This is not to deny the place and importance of exhilaration in love but only to put it in its place, as a faithful companion of love but not love itself. Lovers may enjoy this feeling (though many do not), but the excitement as such is not the measure of their love. Indeed, excitement in many cases is the measure of the *difficulty* of love and, accordingly, its improbability. Exhilaration is a physical sense of overcoming, but in some "ideal" relationships the "fit" between two people is so exact and easy that there is little to overcome. Such love will resemble a warm bath more than a volcanic geyser, but it is still thoroughly romantic. Exhilaration is at most a symptom of love; it is not love itself and is not necessary for love. In fact, some recent theorists (Tannov, Peck) have argued that the initial thrill is pure pathology and the very antithesis of love. This goes much too far in the opposite direction, turning all of love into something inevitably lukewarm and denying the more dramatic instances which keep romantic love alive, but the view is correct in its rejection of the excessive attention often paid to the secretions of the brain and their short-lived, disruptive (if inspiring) effects.

We too easily tend to conclude that great feeling constitutes love, and the greater the feeling, even if incapacitating, the greater the love. But this is dangerous nonsense. Feelings follow, they do not lead the psyche. They are the body's attempt to keep up with the mind and its intentions. Feelings are not the whole nor even the measure of love. Indeed, one way of understanding *infatuation* is to suspect that it consists of just the feeling of excitement, perhaps indeed quite overwhelming, but with none of the other structures of love—no caring or compassion, no sense of mutual identity, perhaps not even strong sexual desire. One just finds oneself enormously excited in the presence—or even at the thought of—another person. The feeling may be quite pleasant. (It can also be debilitating.) But it has little to do with love.

The emphasis on feelings in love is itself worth emphasizing, however, not just because it has served so often as a wrong-headed account of love but because of its importance in the cultivation of love in the first place. The intensity of our inner awareness is itself part of the phenomenon of love as a deeply self-reflective emotion. One reason why love is not just a feeling, why it is peculiar to such self-absorbed and intellectually sophisticated cultures as our own, is that love could not exist without our obsession with it, our need to know whether we love or not, our attention to what it is we feel and why, our concern with our inner states of consciousness instead of just our actions and our status in the world.

It is the self-awareness of love that explains love's variability and its tendency to change under examination and criticism.

Even sensations, which get their meaning from their context and the significance we give to them, have the perplexing habit of altering under examination, shifting perspectives, changing their meaning. Consider, for example, how different a momentary chill appears depending on whether one interprets it as a sign of fear, or romantic anticipation, or a first symptom of the flu. Sensations shift with our awareness of them and emotions even more so. Think of how hard it is even to get a perceptual grip on —much less describe—a simple pain to a physician. And most to the point, try to describe the "feelings" one has in any emotion —shame or embarrassment, envy or jealousy—or love. There is no description, however clinically exact or poetically elegant, that even begins to capture love, not because our medical or literary talents are inadequate but because love is not a feeling and does not involve any specific feelings—except for that one grand "feeling"—which is much more than a feeling. Love is nothing less than an opening up of ourselves, not to the world, but to a single other person, struggling to redefine ourselves in his or her terms. It is a process—not just a feeling—of discovery, of development, of growing together. The thrill of love is our reaction to this process of self-transformation, approaching but never reaching that ultimate union.

LOVE AND RELATIONSHIPS

I believe that we all should wise up and recognize that a marriage is a small business and that married couples are business partners.

—DAVID HOPKINSON

In the days of courtship, before live-in lovers, before affairs in which sex comes first with feelings (perhaps) to follow, it was easy to hold on to the idea that romantic love was one thing, a relationship another. Love was the state of mind that desired nothing more fervently than a permanent, formal bond with one's intended. What we now blandly and vaguely call the "relationship" was then a legally defined, unambiguous contractual agreement called "marriage." Today a relationship can be anything from an irregular dating pattern to a Platonic roommate arrangement. Love may precede the first sexual encounter by a few hours or days or so, but just as often the sexual encounter comes first on the basis of the mere possibility of a "meaningful relationship," and love, if it arrives, will probably appear somewhere in the middle. Indeed, it is not always easy to tell whether love really arrives at all or whether the word "love" just gets used to declare the happy fact that the relationship is working. That is why it is important to clarify and distinguish the two, to insist that love is the experience, a relationship the medium (together with mind) in which love develops.

Love is an emotional process, whether it is that stage filled with frenzy and despair that may mark the early days of uncertain love or the calm comfort that comes after years together. A relationship is an objective fact, a social arrangement that involves working out the daily problems of life and enjoying the advantages of a life (or part of a life) together. Love can continue after—even long after—the end of a relationship, for instance following the death of a loved one. The love doesn't terminate just because the objective fact of being together is no more; it is enough that the survivor still remembers, and feels, and imagines, and, no doubt, wishes that it were otherwise. Love has its psychological dynamic; relationships have their interpersonal and social dynamic and, of course, the two affect each other at every step of the way. Nevertheless, it is important to distinguish the two, not only because they occupy two different realms— the subjective and the objective—but because they have different advantages and drawbacks. To put it bluntly, a great many people who claim to be looking for love are in fact searching for a relationship and would in fact be quite unhappy with the emotional trauma that often comes with love. I do not mean this to be demeaning—to accuse many people of being "incapable" or "unwilling" to love; many people really want a comfortable, edifying relationship, and move from desire to domesticity with little of the experience of love (though often enjoying much satisfaction and even excitement). They do not want the self-transformation and trauma that love requires, and they may have no interest either in the self-reflective brooding that romance sometimes demands. On the other hand, there are people who passionately look for love but couldn't care less about a relationship; indeed, they may go out of their way (perhaps unconsciously) to avoid one. In other words, the desire for a relationship may be something quite different from love, and the exhilaration and drama of love sometimes makes a stable, long-lasting relationship all but impossible. Ideally, perhaps, most of us want the drama and the stability together, but there is always a compromise, always a choice. The most inspiring love may be the impossible love—which Denis de Rougemont mistakenly generalized to define romantic love itself in his classic, *Love in the Western World.*

This is, perhaps, the place to bring up the familiar, mildly tragic phenomenon of "unrequited love." It is often said that unrequited love cannot be love, for by its nature there is no relationship in which love spurned or unreturned can manifest itself. Actually, one might take our earlier insistence on the reciprocity of love as evidence that, because it is unreciprocated, unrequited love cannot be love. But reciprocation of love is a demand *of* love, not a criterion for whether it is love, and one can, obviously, make this demand without its being fulfilled. ("Going fishing" is defined as "trying to catch a fish," but this doesn't mean that the fish are cooperative.) The requirement is only that love as such desires its return, that any attitude of admiration, respect or even worship that does not include this desire cannot be counted as love. But unrequited love deserves recognition as full-blown if not fully developed love. The emotional process will be truncated, of course, for much of the process involves give and take of mutual emotional expression, with all of its misunderstandings, understatements and hypersensitivities as well as comforts and joys. But then again, Stendhal often argued for the virtues of unrequited love just on the basis of the fact that such love could remain pure and unadulterated by the messy business of daily life, and the imagination—which after all is the organ of love—could flow full-time, invent its own trials and tribulations, create its own dialogue with one's lover, even make love—with endless variation, without a single blemish or embarrassment—without the letdown that sometimes follows satisfaction or the absurd altercations that follow from intimacy. Unrequited love, while not our ideal of love, nevertheless stands as a case to be coped with for any theory of love.

Perhaps this is also the place to say something about the familiar query, whether it is better to love or be loved. My answer, very quickly, is that to be loved is not an emotion or an experience at all. Without loving, it is at best a compliment or a convenience, often an unwanted obligation, and at worst a burden or curse. It is loving that counts, and then being loved is the most important thing in the world.

There is an important sense in which a relationship is always public. It is not just two people but, as its boundary conditions, their connection to the whole of society. In a clandestine affair, for instance, secrecy quickly becomes the dominant feature of the relationship itself. Marriage has the function of formalizing this public relationship, which is why marriage is always something more than love and never "just a piece of paper." We often talk about love as commitment, but compared to marriage, all other romantic commitments seem abstract indeed, no matter how galant or loyal the lovers, no matter how often they say to each other—or to themselves—that they will always be together. Love can continue without commitment. Relationships, because they involve coordinated actions and mutual dependency (even if no more than arranging and showing up on dates), always involve some commitments and obligations. Love can continue (wisely or unwisely) in the face of all obstacles, including the utter incompatibility of two lovers.

Relationships are practical. They work or do not work, make us happy or fail to do so. Love is, to put it mildly, not practical. Love, too, might make us happy or miserable, but happiness is not the aim of love, and misery does not constitute its failure. No one wants to be miserable, of course, and obviously a workable relationship is essential to the satisfying fulfillment of love, but these are not the same. One works out a relationship, but one cultivates love.

Relationships, accordingly, tend to get managerial, and this is why they often interfere with love rather than provide the medium for love. Their purpose is to "work," to coordinate two busy lives with the rest of the world. Relationships employ devices and techniques, everything from lists on the refrigerator and dual-control electric blankets to counseling and joint vacations every June. Of course there is no difference here between loving relationships and those that are more matter-of-fact; lovers, like roommates and office colleagues, have to organize their lives together. But love necessarily involves a kind of tension, a deep but often invisible conflict between romantic and practical sensibilities. This is, perhaps, why those whom we call "romantics" tend to be so unworldly. On the other hand, it is too easy, too tempting to turn domestic arrangements into the very basis of love, the structure that love is forced to follow. This is why the Facilitators can do so much damage, and it is no surprise that the books on managing corporations and those on facilitating relationships often coincide on the best-seller list, sometimes written by the same authors. There can be no such treatment of love, for love—unlike domestic tranquility—cannot be negotiated. It employs strategies, to be sure, even shared strategies (moonlit dinners together, a bottle of wine and soft classical music to elevate spirits and ease tension). But there are no techniques in love, no devices. If a Don Juan is so skilled at getting women to fall in love with him, that is further proof that he does not love them. One rightly objects to such tactics as "manipulation." We trust love most when it is spontaneous and irrepressible, not engineered. The discovery of a "plan" can retrospectively wreck a successful romance, for love as an emotion can be cultivated but it cannot and should not be managed.

The confusion of love and relationships is of immense practical importance. There are so many people who want relationships but feel that they *ought* to insist that what they want is love. And so they go desperately looking for passionate love when what they really desire is the contentment of a marriage, a satisfactory sex life and domestic companionship. Until very recently this would be the most that almost anyone would hope for; most people were happy with a good marriage. But now romantic love has become almost mandatory, no matter how inconvenient, no matter how implausible. Clearly there is nothing "inferior" about a good marriage, even though it may have much less drama than romance. But we are taught not even to think about sex and marriage without romance and, indeed, a "meaningful relationship" means "a relationship based on love." The fact, however, is that one can have a perfectly happy life in a relationship—not necessarily "a relationship based on love"— complete with respect, mutual admiration, amusement, companionship, good and even great sex and conversation, trust, honesty and intimacy.

It is, one might argue, a delicate distinction, but I would insist that it is also an essential one. Love and relationships would seem to be inextricably linked, insofar as a "meaningful" relationship means one that is held together by love and in that love, in order to be fully developed, requires the reciprocity of a relationship. And yet not only the phenomenon of unrequited love but the fact that love typically precedes the relationship—if only by a twinkle of the eye—means that the two must be distinguished. Love is a state of mind, an emotional process, and to understand it is to understand the very special way in which a lover views the world. By conflating love with the relationships in which it develops and expresses itself we lose that sense of the private, subjective self, that sense of the phenomenology of experience which is quite different from the social psychology of relationships. It is in that sense of private subjectivity that the exhilaration of love develops, even in the best and closest relationships, for the truth about love—as opposed to relationships —is that ultimately one's love is one's own.

ALL OR NOTHING: THE IDEALIZATION OF LOVE

Idealization lies right at the heart of love; indeed, it is idealization that made possible the concept of love in the first place. Without it, sex might still be a mere appetite, surrounded by prohibitions and rituals, to be sure, but hardly anything like love. Idealization of one's beloved (and one's own idealization in return) is largely what makes love such a desirable emotion. Idealizations are sometimes dismissed as "illusions," but these can be more fairly characterized as glorification and an unusual insistence on accentuating the positive. There is nothing "wrong" with seeing your lover as "the most wonderful person in the world" or being of the opinion that he or she has "the perfect nose." Rarely does one feel so unreservedly good about another person, and rarely does one feel so ecstatically good about oneself. To love is to see the other as ideal, oneself as potentially ideal, and to love is to idealize love as well.

The idealization of love, however, is not an unmitigated good. Idealization can lead to falsification, obfuscation and, worst of all, to an evasion of love altogether in favor of some more mysterious and less accessible passion. In the *Symposium*, Socrates elevated eros—then a minor domestic deity—to the status of a divinity. To confuse matters more, he equates it with philosophy —the highest human endeavor for folks like Plato and Aristotle, perhaps, but hardly the stuff of most human relationships. Eros became the love of Beauty and then the love of Truth, Goodness and Wisdom as well. This may seem impressive but it is also excessive, and while it has elevated love it has helped very little in our understanding of the power and complexities of sexual love and its consequences. The overidealization of love thus begins with Plato, and in subsequent centuries love is lifted out of its human context to become the glue that holds the cosmos and even God Himself together. By the time these excesses began to be corrected in the twelfth century, the habit of speaking about (and listening to) love in incomprehensible terms of unqualified moral praise had become well-entrenched. Current-day Foggers are just the most recent version of that centuries-old testimony to public sentimentality and lack of critical sophistication in matters of the heart.

The idealization of love inevitably led to the demeaning of ordinary sexual relationships. For Plato, eros was the desire to "grasp" the form of Beauty, but in the interpretations that followed him all "grasping" was either eclipsed or denied, especially the grasping of particular human bodies. Plato never denied the lusty origins of love; he only urged us to aim them at a better, "higher" object. Love at its roots has always been passionate and this passion has always been, in part, sexual. The Christian version of "Platonic love" denied this. A good part of the excessive idealization of love thus manifested itself as a denial of the bodily, a rejection of the significance of interpersonal passion and a neglect of the dynamics of interaction between two people. This became apparent, for example, in the distinction between two very different concepts of love in early Christianity. (The several Greek distinctions, by contrast, overlapped, flowed together and reinforced one another.) Plato had idealized eros, but with the introduction of the contrasting term "agape," eros was degraded to mere "sexual love" and shorn of its idealistic overtones. Agape, in its turn, took on the honorable role of a relatively selfless and certainly sexless love of humanity. The distinction became drawn more and more crudely, so that eros became mere eroticism and agape was elevated to the point of such spirituality and selflessness that it was clear that it was an attitude ultimately possible only by God. We could only approximate agape in a small way, by giving and sacrifice and abstention from lusty attitudes toward others (including one's spouse). Eros by contrast came to be viewed as selfish and grasping, without even a hint of spirituality.

We have given up the exotic terms but we find ourselves still torn by the conflicting ideas. On the one hand, love is a secular, interpersonal, desire-defined if not lusty emotion; at the same time, however, we have convinced ourselves that "true" love is wholly selfless, ready to sacrifice all, indifferent to one's own interests and entirely concerned with the well-being of one's lover. Sexual desire, even where love is not in question, can still call up feelings of guilt, as if this is not the way to express one's love. The cost to some couples is the intolerable humiliation of finding themselves desperately lusty and mutually ashamed at

the same time, blaming what they take to be their profane feelings instead of the schizoid conceptions they have inherited from
the distant past. They "ought" to feel something pure and spiritual; instead what they feel is desire. They "ought" to be trans-
ported in a divine ecstasy together; instead they find themselves
facing divisive misunderstandings. The expectations are so high
and so conflicting that the reality cannot compete, even when it
is, undoubtedly, love.

The concept of a loving God, and the ethics that accompany
this concept, may be one of the more glorious ideas of Western
culture, but let us be very clear about the fact that—even for
very religious people—questions about the nature of romantic
love *must* be separated from these traditional religious doctrines.
Romantic love is not selfless, nor should it be. It is not sacrifice
but sharing. It is not sexless. Against the unflattering contrast
between eros and agape, sexual love is not unspiritual and sexual
desire is no mere grasping. It is (or can be) the desire to share,
and it is this sharing—as opposed to selflessness and selfishness,
sacrifice and lusty "grasping"—that is the key to romantic love.
Romantic love is not religious and it must not be turned into a
religion. This is not to say that in some marriages, religious faith
and interpersonal sensibilities may not go hand in hand, but the
degradation of sexual, self-interested love and the overidealization of an impossibly selfless love cannot possibly contribute to a
coherent understanding of this important *human* emotion. To
be in love is not to aspire to sainthood.

Idealization turns love into something more than just sexual
desire and companionship. It involves the glorification of a single
other person in his or her individuality and, by reflection, the
glorification of oneself and the relationship too. But we take
idealization to its extremes and turn love into an all-or-nothing
affair. We look for someone to love us totally, without prior
entanglements, without "hang-ups" and leftover passions from
former loves and things unsaid or undone—the supposed attrac-

tion of virgins and the alleged innocence of children. But try to find a partner who has a clean slate, an emotional *tabula rasa*, a life without the baggage of loves failed and lost, of dreams unrealized and fantasies unfulfilled. At twenty, perhaps, life seems all ahead of us, but by forty the wise person knows that the core of his or her identity is in the past—whether or not one has radical resolutions for the future. The freedom of adolescents is that they are so far without much of a self and their future, because it has so little basis in the past, is so malleable, so open. But not even a sixteen-year-old is without emotional baggage, and the fresh face many people seem to be seeking can only be infantile, inexperienced, pathologically lacking in historical affect, amnesiac or psychotic.

The problem with idealization in love arises when an excessive demand for perfection in one's lover outstrips the reality of the other person. This results in either (occasionally both) of two disastrous alternatives: the person is burdened with impossible demands and expectations and put "on a pedestal," capable of toppling any moment, or the person is viewed as falling far short of his or her "potential" and, even without losing the love, is nevertheless the constant source of disappointment and perhaps resentment. Needless to say, either of these alternatives (or the two of them in sequence) may well be the projection of the lover's own insecurities and shortcomings. Idealization can also become excessive when love itself is expected to answer all doubts, solve all problems, soothe over all disputes. Contrary to expectations, love is not "the answer." It presents as many problems as it does answers, and to love is not to enter a world in which there are no harsh words, no disagreements, no incompatibilities, no disappointments. Love can be spiritual and uplifting, it can even be the most perfect experience in life, but it cannot be "pure." We are only human, and an emotion that aims to last a lifetime cannot expect to evade the problems that life itself proposes.

The idealization of love has a cost. It is not true that "all you need is love." One also needs the mortgage money, some separate space, faithful friends and a good deal of understanding and patience. In so focusing on love, there is an inevitable neglect of other passions, very probably a neglect of larger social issues, possibly the neglect of parents, friends, a career. The idealization of love may be desirable, but it can also be used as a weapon, to intimidate those who ignore or deny it, to shame and humiliate those who quite rightly claim that there may be something more important to do.

Excessive idealization about love would make us believe that love is of exclusive importance—a ploy that has been used against women in the past several centuries to discourage them from education and careers. Such ideas make us think of love as an end, a guarantee instead of a challenge, a process. It confuses the desire of love with its fulfillment, like Freud's infantile "primary process," mistaking the idealized goal of total oneness and lifelong happiness with the long series of psychological efforts and compromises that love requires. But worst of all, such ideas make us intransigent and not just a bit stupid, insisting on what may be impossible while missing out on love even when it is right there in front of us. We demand that our love be either *this* or nothing, and since "*this*" is so often captured in extravagant terms ("swept away," "perfect happiness") we are bound to be disappointed. To make matters worse, as Jean-Paul Sartre points out, any strong emotion—he discusses sadness—gets accompanied by that peculiar nagging voice that tells us that it is not enough, never enough. We expect to feel more than we do, and so we suspect ourselves.

The idealization of love also leads to the self-righteous idea that love is a singular phenomenon, which one either "finds" or does not. But love is a spectrum of emotions, at one end perhaps the totally devoted obsession that the poets celebrate, of which few people are capable (or willing), at the other the quiet, caring familiarity that does not distinguish itself from friendship and uses the word "love" not as a desperate expression of passion but because, in such relationships, one is expected to. Love varies in its intensities, like any other emotion. We have no hesitation in describing ourselves as "a little angry" or "a little sad," but in love alone, it seems, we are unwilling to admit gradations. And since most of us are not capable of maintaining feverish delirium for very long (there is that job we have to get back to, the baby needs to see the pediatrician and the garage needs fixing) there soon come those nagging doubts about "Is this really love?" and "Do I still love him?" It is as if love is assuredly real only when it is explosive and obsessive, when it incapacitates and totally absorbs. But love manifests itself in many ways in many different lives. Like everything else, love has to fit into life, and often our lives are full to overflowing—whether or not satisfying—long before love appears. When our choice is "all or nothing," life will usually see to it that we wind up with nothing.

Why do we refuse to recognize that love can and usually must be part-time, that love, like sadness or joy, must sometimes wait in the wings? Love at its best is a convergence—a synergism—of many desires, some of them sexual, others ethical, many of them straightforwardly practical, more than a few of them romantic and fantastic. In love we want not only sex and security but also happiness, companionship, fun, someone on hand to travel with, go out with, get advice from, be proud of and be associated with who is a social asset and ally, who will share the housework and add to the income, who will be dependable in times of trouble and nurturing in times of distress, and so on. In other words, we would like "everything," both thrills and constancy, excitement and absolute convenience and security, and we would like it all together, in a single package, a package supposedly guaranteed by love. But love is in fact just one ingredient in this package. However undesirable, one can have love without companionship, love without sex, love without emotional support or encouragement, love without excitement, love without stability.

We want it all, but sometimes we must choose. What many people consider the breakdown of love is in fact the loss of one of these desirable accompaniments to love: the sex gets less exciting, two people are too busy to spend much time together. But this need not be loss of love, only loss of "the package." And then one must choose: is love really worth what else one has lost? But it is not as if love (or another love) will guarantee the package either. We realize that desires conflict—for instance the desire for novelty and excitement and the desire for convenience and security—and we realize that reality intervenes inconveniently to deny us the fulfillment of our cosmic gluttony. But this does not mean that life is absurd, or that our lot is bound to be unhappiness and frustration; it only means, quite simply, that we can't have it all. This reality principle seems painless enough—Freudian trauma to the contrary—except, that is, when it comes to love. In love we seem incapable of accepting what we get and enjoying what we can reasonably expect. In love alone we seem incapable of distinguishing passion from all of the good things that we hope will go with it—friendship, fantastic sex, constant companionship, encouragement and support in our work, a good housekeeper and provider, etc.—and acknowledging that love might eclipse many of these other desires. Our ideal, nonetheless, remains "the package"—everything together in a single parcel. And in a world so fragmented and frustrating, who can deny its charm?

It is too often assumed that any "critical" treatment of love must be negative, cynical, "against" love. But to adequately endorse any virtue it is also necessary to recognize its proprieties and its limitations. Love, like virtually everything else in life, has its place and its proper proportions. It can be wrong, it can be inappropriate, it can be disastrous, it can be fatal. This is just what the Foggers never mention, and it is there that they are guilty of fraud. One does not sell a potent miracle drug across the counter to all comers without mentioning its side effects or lethal dosage. Love is a particularly powerful emotional stimulant, which may often seem miraculous. But love destroys lives as well as saves them, presents us with terrible problems as well as answers, shuts off parts of the world to us even as it opens up others. Love is a very specific phenomenon that fits a specified niche in our lives; it is not that heavenly glow advertised by the Foggers that fits anywhere anytime, all for the good and for no cost at all.

In the same "critical" vein, it is necessary to insist that love is always alloyed with other emotions and their potential, including not only love's polar opposite, hatred, but also anger, envy, jealousy, self-doubt, pride, resentment, anxiety, frustration, etc. There may be moments of pure love, but this is more a matter of temporary focus than of metaphysics. To enjoy the emotion of love means also to make oneself "vulnerable" and readily prone to an entire network of passions whose logical structure ties into love. As love essentially involves a kind of trust, for example, it also embodies the possibility of betrayal. As love involves a sense of belonging, it embodies the possibility of loss, as in jealousy, and as love includes a kind of powerful interpersonal confrontation, it embodies the possibility of a twisting of that confrontation to hate. So, too, love fits into a matrix of needs, desires, hopes, fears and expectations. Contrary to such Foggers as Erich Fromm, there is no such thing as "unconditional" love—not even in parenthood—and certainly not in the willful, always contingent affections of romantic love.

LOVE STORIES

At the root of "romantic" love is the romance—a story. Love is not just a momentary passion but an emotional development, a structured *narrative* that is so familiar and seemingly "natural" to us that we rarely think of it as a story, a scenario that we are taught to follow, with all of its predictable progressions and conflicts and resolutions. When we hear the folk tales of other cultures, it is often easy to find them quaint or peculiar, but it is essential that we recognize our own romantic heritage as itself an anthropological oddity, a conflict-ridden and sometimes destructive set of scenarios. For example, our romantic love stories often center on the very young, though the fact is that love is just as inspiring and important to those of us who have made it past the watershed age of thirty. Our romantic protagonists are often rich, spoiled and exotic, though love since the last century or so has become thoroughly domesticated, middle-class and democratic. Indeed, our favorite protagonists are typically ill suited for long-term love, and it is not unusual for them to be killed off while still in their prime. The paradigm of romance is often forbidden or impossible love, from Lancelot's illicit love for Guinevere to the consumptive love of *La Bohème*. Or else the story is cut off with a happy ending, with an embrace and a suspicious "happily ever after." But whether the story is a tragedy or a "happily ever after," it excludes the rich development of love over time.

I once asked a group of graduate literature students what made *Romeo and Juliet*—supposedly our paradigmatic love story—

romantic. They listed, in order of elicitation, the fact that the two lovers:

die
don't get to know each other
face serious opposition to their love
face danger
live in an exotic setting
have to meet secretly
confide in each other
are young and beautiful
make speeches proclaiming their love
are impatient, full of longing and passion
have confidence in themselves
are obstinate
have no concern for pragmatics or practicability
can't think of anyone else
have a strong sexual urge for each other

One doesn't have to be a romantic scholar to be struck by this list, which quite innocently dismisses couples over twenty, not beautiful, living in Lake Wobegon, Minnesota, who enjoy the approval of parents and friends, date in the open and don't have to die at the end of the fifth act. The fact is that our favorite love story gives a very misleading impression of the nature of love and its narrative, and yet it and stories like it have defined the genre of romance since at least the twelfth century, with the first popular stories of Lancelot and Guinevere, whose love was adulterous and destroyed a kingdom.

But even without the illicitness, secrecy and fatality, it is not hard to pinpoint our paradigm love story: "Boy meets girl. Boy loses girl. Boy gets girl." (Why not vice versa?) They live "happily ever after." Our first question should be why we use "girl" and "boy" when love is or ought to be the main concern of adulthood, not just adolescence. It is also worth noting how unthinkingly we assume that two lovers have to *meet* one another. That is, they didn't grow up together. They encounter each other essentially *as* lovers, and all other attributes are pretty much beside the point. Presumably they are strangers, meeting most likely by chance. And what is worse is the ending. We cut off the real story line before it even begins with the disingenuous phrase "happily ever after." Marriage signifies the culmination of love rather than its vehicle. (Of course, weddings aren't often included. They're not usually dramatic events.)

Of course the heart of the love story, what makes it romantic, is the "problem," the conflict, the suspense. This is where romance writers get to ply their skill, rend our hearts, purple our language. Love is a challenge, an enormous and often pathologically stubborn effort to overcome misunderstandings, tragedies and apparent betrayals. "Why doesn't she just get herself another fellow?" is not one of the options. Love is perseverance and agony, even to the point of personal destruction. Of necessity the love story ends when the "problem" is solved and done away with. "Boy gets girl"—or vice versa. That is when we get the quasi-literary cop-out ("and they lived happily ever after") or the death of one or preferably both of the lovers (*Love Story, Romeo and Juliet, Tristan and Isolde, Sophie's Choice*). Occasionally the love abruptly ends *(Gone with the Wind)* or suffers a heroic parting *(Casablanca)*, but all of these options are, on reflection, utterly remarkable: our paradigm story of love leaves out the heart of love. It includes the initial melodrama but excludes the countless continuing details of real-life love. The story of love, in other words, leaves out love. It does not deny that love demands a protracted and possibly lifelong time together ("happily ever after" and premature death both point to that), but it totally ignores this. How, then, are we supposed to live our lives according to it? Surely we should not emulate those brief periods in history, for example the time of the publication of Goethe's unhappy romantic novel *The Sorrows of Young Werther* in 1774, when literary fashion dictated a rash of suicides among the young and lovelorn.

But here is another love story, one that, you can be sure, would not make it into a Harlequin romance. That elderly couple walk into breakfast at a Wisconsin Holiday Inn. They are sharing the morning paper and he offers dutifully to see to the acquisition of coffee and Danish. Their story is one of lifelong companionship. One can dimly imagine a brief but clumsy courtship, but this possibly forgettable or even (in their own minds) laughable experience is of little importance to this love story. They may remember some little misunderstanding, some early rival for affection, but probably not. They may remember the wedding, but most likely they were both too dazed and confused at the time. There may have been passion. There may have been some doubts at the beginning, but those were on page twenty of a 1,600-page novel. It is not hard to imagine that there have been days, weeks or even years of anger, resentment, contempt, even violence, but these passions, too, disperse into the mist of the years together. One can be sure that they rarely talk of love, perhaps an occasional "I love you" (on anniversaries), but certainly no philosophical discussions of love, no metaphysical skepticism about whether or not it's "the real thing," no agonizing personal reflections about "Is this what I really want?" and whether love is actually narcissism or an unjustifiable need for dependency. No question about its going on (the word "forever" would be superfluous). Their love just *is*. It is as real and as solid a foundation as the Midwestern granite they walk on. It does not even need a name.

It is tragic and absurd that our idealized storybook romance should be so different and so detached from the real story of love and our conception of love should, consequently, be so divided into two wholly separate parts, one romantic and exciting but unrealistic and the other a dull tale of domesticity and endurance, devoid of the excitement that many of us now insist upon to make life worthwhile. The two parts of this unfortunate conception of love complement each other in a thoroughly disappointing way. The romantic story is all about the thrill of newfound love, but it is so filled with suspense and excitement or pathos that it cannot bear the weight of the future. "Forever" is thus an evasion of time rather than a celebration of it. The infinitely less romantic part of the story is about the formation and working out of a partnership, legally defined as such by marriage. It is a topic fit for accountants, advisers and counselors, in which the market virtues of honesty and fair exchange and the business skills of negotiation and compromise are of great value. Or, for the less affluent, there is a lifetime of "seeing it through," raising children, waiting for grandchildren, earning the mortgage, coping with life. In other words, first there is the thrill, then there is the coping. In the beginning there are two independent people engaged in a melodrama; then they have to "work it out." One reason why love fades, it is not unreasonable to hypothesize, is because we define it in such a hopelessly schizoid and ultimately dreary way. By definition the suspense and excitement of romance cannot continue, the partners become compatible and confident in their love for each other, and, besides, there are simply too many other things to do.

The flaws in the two-part story of love are as conducive to unhappiness as they are unliterary. A good novel doesn't climax in the second chapter, five hundred pages from the end. Romantic love is not just the story of the initial melodrama, nor is what follows anything so dreary as a mere partnership. Love is not initial conquest followed by a relationship, much less by "happily ever after." It is the continuing story of self-definition, in which plots, themes, characters, beginnings, middles and ends are very much up to the authorship of the indeterminate selves engaged in love. Indeed, another problem with our love stories is that they sound as if they give us a complete outline and a detailed recipe for love, when in fact every romance just gives us one possible version of it. Even at the beginning, every story is different, and once one gets to the reality hidden beneath the "happily ever after" cop-out, it is every couple for themselves. We get disappointed when we don't have a storybook romance, but the truth is that all of us have to create our own story, our own romance.

Not all love stories get told; some of them we are forced to live, and at least some of the love stories with which we are most familiar are not all romantic. Emotions are learned in standard behavioral situations, in what philosopher Ronald De Sousa calls paradigm scenarios. Anger, for example, is learned in a situation where one is frustrated and learns to blame other people. And so we should ask "What is the paradigm scenario of love?" It is embarrassing to say that, for most of us, it was the *dating* situation. How should we describe this? It is an extremely artificially contrived circumstance in which two people are wrenched away from familiar contexts and the support of friends and forced to seek a complete stranger's approval, admiration and more. In other words, the story of love begins for most of us, not with a blank page, but with a character who has been imposed upon us, no background or history to appeal to and no real sense of who or what we are supposed to be or do. No wonder we need the comfort of the more sentimental love stories to soothe us through such an ordeal. And no wonder our current conception of love is so much at odds with our more general notions of comfort and sociability, so private and exclusive and so walled off from all other sources of support and appeal. We learn love in these conditions of total isolation, and we learn it as a cruel game of acceptance and rejection. And so of course finding love strikes us as both a necessity and a great relief. As one recent book puts it, an overwhelming reason for falling in love and living with someone is that one doesn't have to date anymore.

Life is notoriously sloppy, from a literary point of view. It begins before we know how to narrate and we never know how it will end. Philosophers such as Nietzsche may insist that we should "live life as a work of art," but the truth is that no work of art could be so complex, could fill up such a vast amount of time or deal with such a bewildering array of details. But in love, more than anywhere else, we recognize our urge for living life as a simple story, following a narrative with a beginning, a plot, a development and a climax. Of course it is not always clear where the climax is to be found (first kiss, making love, saying "I love you," marriage, first child, death?), but *closure* is what every story must have. It is its resolution. A novel might end just after the climax, but our story must go on. We try to live our lives as narrative, but we always find ourselves in the middle. And so when we try to find closure in any particular culmination of love —whether first kiss or marriage—we are haunted by the literary phrase "happily ever after." For us there is no phrase, just more life to live, more to work out. And so we try to start the story again, keeping conflict and frustrating plot twists to a minimum, or we invent sequels, which, as in the movies, too often seem imitative and inferior to the originals. We want to close it off and seal it with a definitive word or phrase—like all of those familiar romances. But we go on. And, paradoxically though not surprisingly, we periodically try to create closure, by provoking a crisis, by walking out, for "no" creates closure where "yes" only means that the story must go on. And there is nothing worse than a boring story, even if—especially if—it is one's own.

BEAUTY AS THE BASIS OF LOVE

> . . . this passion, whose very genuine manifestation is character-
> ized by beauty.

> —STENDHAL, *On Love*

This month (any month, any year) a popular movie ends with the suggested union of its lovely, pampered heroine and its rugged handsome hero. She grew up in a New York (Paris, Chicago) penthouse; he feels comfortable only in the jungle (in the desert, at sea, at war). The only thing they seem to have in common is physical attractiveness. Throughout the movie they have been adventuring together, he saving her and (once) her saving him. The movie ends as they get together; she breaks off her engagement to an urbane, lifelong suitor, he postpones his trip back to the wilderness. We do not hesitate to predict a divorce within weeks—utter incompatibility. The True Romantic will certainly object "Well, it *might* work," but think about building a whole romantic mythology on the slimness of that "might." The fact that two people find each other beautiful is not sufficient for love, and it is shocking that we are so often led to believe that it is.

This is not just a problem concerning the truncated structure of our love stories. It is also a problem in our very conception of love and lovability. We might admire success and respect intelligence but we are supposed to love and be loved for beauty. Whatever else he or she may be, the beloved must be beautiful. This feature, which is so often presented as essential to love, has little to do with character, accomplishment or personality—and little to do with the possible success of a relationship. The virtues that *attract* us as a lover seem to be very different from the virtues that make love warranted or workable, and, in any case, "attraction" presupposes a distance, a distance which the intimacy of love denies. This is the main point about beauty, not that it is undesirable but rather that it points in precisely the wrong direction for love—toward admiration and worship rather than sharing, toward arousal instead of wisdom, toward superficial attraction rather than deep intimacy and knowledge.

Not only Stendhal but Plato and hundreds of lesser (male) theorists on love have singled out that single human feature as the basis of love. One might complain that physical beauty has little to do with love, that it reveals very little of character, that its charms are in fact quite misleading or "superficial," that it has nothing to do with goodness or, more to the point, the probable success of a relationship. The reply will surely be that no serious theorist has in mind purely physical beauty, the sort of beauty that might just as well be found in a painting or a sculptured nude. Beauty includes charm, intelligence and at least the promise of personality as well as exquisite features and figure. Ultimately, Plato and the others insist that what one really seeks in love is a "beautiful soul," not just a beautiful face and body. But Plato only augments—he does not question—the obsession with beauty, and it is the attraction of beauty, rather than a personality or the possibility of a relationship, that carries us into love.

But are they—and we—convinced? Socrates himself was quite happy to entertain and be entertained by the most beautiful young men in Athens. Alcibiades, one of those young men, finds himself quite perplexed by the fact that he is in love with a perverse old man who has "a face like a satyr." The fear of the femme fatale is as old as love itself, the woman who supposedly entices and entraps with her beauty but is incapable of or unconcerned with love. There are all of those stories: how Samson was undone by the beautiful but treacherous Delilah, Antony by the seductive Cleopatra, all of Troy by fair Helen. In courtly love it was the woman's beauty that got mentioned first; it was perhaps the only feature visible from the distance of the tower. Chivalrous tales from the period inevitably emphasize the "fairness" of the maiden but are too often silent on her virtue. Romantic novels from the eighteenth and nineteenth centuries make it amply clear that it is beauty—if not *just* beauty—that brings men to love, whether happily or fatally, and women too. It was essential to the plausibility of the fairy tale that the frog or the beast turned out to be a handsome prince and it still appears, however enlightened we may be, that physical beauty plays a bizarre and central role in our conception of love.

The problem with beauty is that it seems to undermine everything we want to believe about love. It emphasizes the shallow instead of the profound, the advantages of nature and the concoctions of cosmetics instead of the talents and achievements of a lifetime. It emphasizes youth instead of experience, visual "looks" instead of personality; it is inegalitarian on the most arbitrary basis and it has nothing to do with virtue, goodness, caring, compassion, companionship and all the other good things that love is supposed to offer. What is worse, many of the specific features that we find attractive indicate the very opposite of what Plato called a "beautiful soul." Look at advertisements: men and women who appear sadistic, self-centered or just plain silly. The fear is commonly expressed by men that, if a woman were sufficiently beautiful, nothing else would get in the way of love. It is as if beauty, physical beauty, *alone* is enough reason for love, even in the face of a flawed personality, dubious character, a serious lack of sophistication or intelligence. For the sake of beauty one stands up to contempt or resentment of one's best friends and even the screaming dissent of one's own "better" judgment. Flaws are not only tolerated, they are excused or ignored—at least until the impossibility of a serious relationship and continued humiliation force their way into even the most beauty-struck lover.

There is no good reason why beauty should have such trump status in love. True, the history of romantic love begins with beauty as a particularly desirable trait, but courtly love emphasized character and poetic talent as well as beauty, and part of the democratization of love in modern times has been precisely the extension of romance to everyone, regardless of wealth or class, and regardless of physical attractiveness too. It is one of our dearly held beliefs that "there is someone for everyone," that beauty is "in the eye of the beholder"—and so anyone can be beautiful when they are loved. We will all say, indeed insist, that beauty should not be an important consideration in love, that beauty, unlike character, "fades" with age, that personality and intelligence and being "a good person" are far more important than being beautiful. And yet beauty seems to hold on to its status. Love is still typically portrayed as one young and beautiful person falling in love with another, the odd case of love between two ugly or elderly persons appearing only as a sentimental but eccentric exception, usually with more than a hint of comedy.

It used to be the case that this obsession with beauty was a predominantly male obsession. It is male theorists like Plato and Stendhal who define the aesthetic tradition of love; women, being (in their forced nonpublic status) more dependent upon the outcome of love, have taken the trouble to be beautiful but have never been taken in by its romantic dominance. They have seen, as they had to see, the factors of trustworthiness, intelligence, gentility, conscientiousness, honesty and integrity as the more lovable features of a man—granted that he should not be repulsive. In other words, they recognized the importance of those virtues that would make love and marriage work rather than those which are simply attractive. It is one of the odder ironies of the contemporary state of romantic love that this feature is rapidly changing. As more and more women become economically, socially and emotionally self-sufficient, they, too, are becoming free to emphasize the more frivolous, merely aesthetic and sometimes self-destructive attributes of love. We now find women going after men for the same inadequate reasons that men have so long gone after women—unfeeling, unloving concepts of sexual attractiveness and performance, the challenge, the conquest and getting away without "complications" (Erica Jong's "zipless fuck"). Many women have joined their male counterparts in their embarrassment about talking about simple affection and dependency, and men in turn are encouraged in their irresponsibility. It used to be that sex was the "consummation" of love; now it is too often its raison d'être. The result, not surprisingly, is an ever-increasing number of disastrous romances.

This bizarre emphasis on attractiveness is not restricted to questions of love and sexuality. Being attractive, research has shown, leads to better jobs, grades and advancement, quite apart from questions of sex or sexism. It also crosses over ethnic boundaries. Attractive children find themselves liked more; they are perceived as being smarter and thought to be more friendly and less mean. The lesson evidently starts very early. And so it is hard for us even to imagine, much less tolerate, lovers who are not attractive, no matter what their other virtues, their wit or charm or intelligence. It does not matter that they could make us very happy, and we them. We feel that we all *deserve* beauty, that love without beauty is a sign of misfortune or bad taste. Yes, we often rebel against this; we reiterate Plato's insistence on a "beautiful soul." But when it comes right down to it, we are drawn in by the looks, and hope that good character will follow. For all the talk about "inner beauty," usually by movie stars and other very attractive people, the fact is that inner beauty can be seen by most people only through a frame that is itself equally beautiful.

I'm not suggesting that one should love a person because he or she is unattractive or that Quasimodo should become our romantic hero. Beauty does indicate health, vitality and, to some extent, self-confidence and physical security. But the weight of this emphasis on physical beauty has become so burdensome, so obsessive, that men as well as women now indulge themselves in desperate and mindless (not to mention tasteless) vanities that would have been considered an embarrassment—if not a sin— just a few decades ago. It now becomes a self-fulfilling prophecy: to be lovable is to be beautiful, and to be beautiful is to be lovable. There is nothing wrong with being attractive, of course, and it is easy to understand as well as feel the connection between beauty and desire. Biologically, it makes good sense to suppose that good looks in some sense are tied to health, and thus to fitness and the ability to have and protect children. But it is quite obvious that much of what we find beautiful has little or nothing to do with survival in the wild or survival in the cities, either. Indeed, much of what we find beautiful points the other way—looks that indicate being pampered, being utterly self-concerned, being incompetent or incapable (a significant ingredient in what we call "cute"). What sort of "health" is indicated by the emaciated figures of our most glamorous models? What sort of biological advantage has been enjoyed by women with large breasts or high cheekbones or by men with straight noses or strong chins? Imaginative biologists might have a field day: Desmond Morris, for example, suggests in *The Naked Ape* that large breasts are attractive because they resemble—geometrically at least—the dorsal view of a woman ready for coitus. This is entertaining, perhaps, but also absurd. Beauty, too, is a cultural contraption, not a mere product of nature. What is beautiful in one group or culture may well be repulsive in another.

Why do we find some people attractive and not others? The features we find attractive are learned, not instinctual. Male breast fetishism has far less to do with residual desire for mother or any other infantile or instinctual appetites than it does with the American film and magazine industries, traditional male locker-room gossip and, consequently, female fashions in sweaters and the ever-changing architecture of the well-dressed bosom. There may be some sense to the attractiveness of a man who is strong and physically protective (given that, only 50,000 years ago, we were all running around naked), but the obvious truth is that physical strength in most urban settings today serves little function other than vanity and in any case it is success in this world rather than vestigial ability to cope in the jungle that tends to define attractiveness. But we are not surprised that Woody Allen or Albert Einstein should become romantic ideals, and though it is a slower change than we would like, the success and achievements of women, too, are beginning to replace the narrow focus on physical features as the basis for romantic and sexual attraction. We are not so stupid as to allow our residual modern preference for "V-shaped" male and "hourglass" female bodies to blind us to the fact that these have little to do with love or lovability. But tastes change painfully slowly, and meanwhile we will continue to find ourselves occasionally attracted to the point of distraction by someone entirely unworthy and find ourselves struggling to feel passion for that "inner beauty" in someone whom we know to be a much more worthy and desirable partner.

The peculiarities of physical attractiveness become especially evident in the context of biology. Vanity is one of the many kinks in Darwinian survival-of-the-fittest theory. There are several male birds—the peacock is the most celebrated—whose attractiveness to the female has utterly nothing to do with survival; in fact, it is hard to imagine any trait more disadvantageous to a bird whose flesh is notoriously tasty than bright heavy plumage that makes it unable to fly or even run effectively, and one can imagine any number of traits that would make a peacock more "fit" for some role in life other than sidewalk entertainer in zoos and plantations. Neither is the attraction of the male peacock aesthetic—if one could talk of aesthetics in birds. It is, pure and simple, sexual attraction, what we call fetishism. Biologists who have tampered with bird bodies to make tails even lusher and more ridiculous find that every female in the vicinity will quickly forsake all others for this parody of male attractiveness. They mate and, presumably, hatch a brood of ever more attractive, and useless, males—and females who are attracted to them.

It is sometimes supposed, without evidence, that the features we find beautiful are those that are *sexually* attractive, but this only relocates the problem. A person's features are certainly not attractive because of their sexual function. The face is a focus of beauty, and it has no sexual function as such. Beautiful bodies have a more plausible claim to sexual function. But it is worth noting that the organs most directly involved in sex and its satisfaction are not particularly known for their beauty, and virtually all other features become sexually attractive only because they are deemed beautiful; they are not beautiful because they are sexually attractive. Furthermore, there is nothing intrinsically sexual about most of the traits we find attractive. The hips and thighs of a woman may remind one of sex, but there is little evidence that the differences in proportions and distribution that are always so much a matter of concern make any difference whatever in sexual performance or function. Male paunches in this society represent "being out of shape," but during William Howard Taft's presidency, for example, and in many other countries, the paunch was considered a sign of prosperity. Trying to understand beauty and its attractions in functional terms, I would suggest, is a waste of time, however amusing. We will get much farther in an investigation of beauty and its role in love if we ask what certain features *represent*, and why, then, we are so attracted to them.

The most obvious answer to this line of inquiry is that we find beautiful and attractive just those features that we have been taught to appreciate as beautiful and attractive. We are inundated with such images every minute, and it would be hard to deny that those filter deep into our taste and consciousness. But this, too, just pushes the question back a step: why do we (as a culture) find such traits attractive? There is no single answer, of course; what is considered beautiful in one culture is considered grotesque in another. American men find hypertrophic breasts desirable, but the eighteenth-century French decadents who were titillated by François Boucher's plumpish nudes found large breasts uninteresting if not repulsive. There will be a different rationale for the features men find attractive in women in contrast to the features women find attractive in men, and this again will be different from those that women find attractive in women and men in men. Subcultures will vary markedly, and the parental paradigms that Freud insisted upon will certainly have their influence—though nothing like the power that Freud himself suggested.

If we go back to the crux of the mystery—that the features we find most attractive in love are those which seem to serve no function—we can see that this lack of function may itself be a determinant of beauty. In societies that are all work and survival, function is all-important—and there is no time or room for romantic love. But in leisure societies, the sort in which romance tends to flourish, it is precisely the evidence of leisure that is considered most beautiful—long fingernails, time-consuming makeup, uncomfortable but expensive gowns, neckwear, shoes. In women it is not muscle but well-positioned fat that has most often been found beautiful, representing, as it does, the absence of any need for physical work. Today's emphasis on a sleek, athletic body is not surprising in a culture where most work is done sitting at a desk all day and exercise requires leisure time and a surprising amount of money. Some of the argument is circular; we find ourselves sexually attracted to those features that we find seductive—where seductiveness itself requires time and leisure. So understood, it is not surprising that alabaster skin should have been especially prized by the colonial English aristocracy, for only a young woman who had never had to toil in the fields—as opposed to the dark-skinned natives—could be expected to be untainted by the telltale signs of work in the hot sun. Nor is it just culturally curious that we tend to think that a suntan is attractive and sexy because it represents (in most parts of the United States and Europe) the leisure time and money to lounge aimlessly and travel to luxurious parts of the hemisphere. The traits that we tend to find beautiful are those which we tend to associate with status—whether or not they have any plausible functional explanation in terms of the life of a culture (indeed, their role as aristocratic traits explains why they are so often antifunctional). A man or woman from a poor family who is blessed with the right features finds it easier to climb up in society, not because he or she is good-looking but because, by good fortune, these are precisely those features that connote success and class. Attractive people do not so much succeed in our society because they are beautiful as because it seems to us that they "belong" there. Beauty lies in the status of the holder.

Some traits deemed beautiful are degrading. We all know enough stories about how Chinese women were required to bind their feet and how South Pacific or African tribes painfully mutilate themselves to achieve some standard of beauty, but how many of our own efforts to be beautiful are equally mutilating—not always in terms of physiological distortion but often in terms of time spent and attention misdirected and self-respect abused (pierced ears, dyed hair, toupees, plucked eyebrows, tanning-salon suntans, breast implants, nose jobs and tummy tucks). Jean-Paul Sartre pointed out how many of the features associated with sexual attractiveness are merely *passive*, "reducing the other to an object" as he put it. Large breasts, for example, may remind some cultures of motherhood, but in our culture we would be closer to the mark to suggest that they represent passivity, a kind of awkwardness, a burden that lucky women are forced to carry around. Like those birds whose plumage makes them easy game for predators, many of our attraction virtues seem to be liabilities. For women, as for the male aristocracy of other ages, what is deemed beautiful seems to be those features which make them seem least capable of functioning on their own.

At the same time, however, these liabilities and dysfunctions are revered as marks of *status*, and here we get some underlying sense of why we are attracted as we are, even though the fashions may change and fat may be in one year, scrawniness the next. What remains constant—and in our society is amplified a thousand times over through the intrusive power of the media—is the current look of status, coupled with the desire to acquire some of that status. There is nothing intrinsically more beautiful about a delicate nose than a pug nose (though one might hypothesize that pug noses once represented lost fights). And one does not have to be very old to remember any number of cases in which facial features once considered ugly (i.e., no status) came to be considered beautiful because of some new celebrity in the world.

So what is wrong with our emphasis on beauty in love, granted that the features we consider beautiful are rarely functional and would seem to have more to do with vanity than romance? The first objection is that the features we too often treat as beautiful are precisely those that represent character traits that we otherwise object to—elitist, spoiled, helpless, arrogant, slothful, self-absorbed vanity. We should be suspicious of the *kind* of beauty that we find so attractive—"out-going" personalities who effectively ward off intimacy, narcissistic models obsessed with their looks. One would not be wrong in suggesting that what attracts us most is not seductiveness but rather deep unavailability.

Second, it would seem that the features that today seem so attractive to us (as evidenced by current trends in advertising and movie marginalia) are those which seem most inappropriate for any successful relationship—the cool, indifferent, detached and impersonal look, the rush-for-success and who-has-time-for-a-relationship image of the hard-driving businessman or woman, the I-can-do-without-you and I-don't-give-a-damn attitude (famously expressed by Rhett Butler after several years of aggravation with Scarlett), which now seems to be an attractive come-on instead of a good-bye. We might also hypothesize that our culture—the primordial media society—has canonized a type of cinematic and photogenic beauty that is virtually guaranteed to have little to do with real life. And then we are taught from childhood that the ideal beauty and perfect lover is one that looks just like *that*, the perfect figure, face and smile, with all lines written out and the familiar love scenes orchestrated in advance. A beautiful face or figure may well attract us to another person and hold our interest, but it is hard to see what plausible connection such charms might have to the bonding of love. In fact, the very notion of "attraction" already implies a distance to be crossed, and though there must be some initiating factor bringing two people together, it is clear that physical attraction cannot continue to be the key connection between them. Moreover, it is not at all clear that physical attraction is the most appropriate invitation to the intimacy of love.

Finally, the emphasis on beauty and being beautiful shifts our attention, as Erich Fromm wrote in *The Art of Loving*, from loving to *being* loved. Today, he might say, we are so keen on looking good and seeming successful (especially to ourselves) that we all but ignore not only loving but being lovable too. "Coming on" with the latest fashionable look is not the same as inviting love: in fact, it often seems to invite precisely the opposite. And then one complains, "I'm attractive and successful. Why can't I ever meet a decent lover?" Our sense of beauty is such that it tends to celebrate not the features that most of us share but rather those that we do not. We try to make ourselves seem exotic and even inhuman instead of simply accessible. We lionize rare specimens of humanity who are not like the rest of us, who are more desirable not only in degree but in kind. It is as if we discovered a culture that found men or women quite different from themselves, perhaps of other races, to be more beautiful than their own. It is not only degrading; it makes satisfaction in a relationship all but impossible, for not only is the person one wants to love not up to standards, it is as if he or she isn't even of the right species.

It is essential that we redefine beauty along with love. The problem is that we have shifted from a perfectly "natural" sense of beauty as health and vitality to a contrived and artificial sense that conveys more about leisure time, money and status than it does about personality or love. Against this it should be argued that there is one important sense of beauty in love and that is the sense in which beauty reveals personality and character. It is not just "skin-deep" at all, but discloses a great deal of what we call "the inner person." A person's "looks" refer not just to physical appearance but also to what one is, how one lives, how one sees the world (the cast of the eyes). And it is simply not true that physical appearance is just physical, natural and beyond a person's doing. People *work* at their appearance and what it expresses. We reinforce our own chosen stereotypes—*trying* to look tough, or cool, or sensitive, or innocent. It has been said that after a certain age, a person has the face he or she deserves. It is also said that there are no ugly people, only lazy individuals. Both comments are no doubt unfair, but they make an important point: how we look is never just a matter of appearance. It is always also a matter of *expression*, and for the great majority of us who are not actors or charlatans this expression of who we are is at least as striking as the more impersonal notion of beauty as such.

Once we have gotten past our overly visual and cinematic concept of beauty and get to appreciate the importance of beauty as expression rather than appearance, the notion of "a beautiful soul" becomes much more plausible. For Plato, at least, it is not a question of rejecting the physical for the purely spiritual but of seeing the one *through* the other. More recently, Wittgenstein wrote that "the best picture of the human soul is the human body," and so, too, we make the easy inference from beauty to virtue. (It is easy to understand the perverse horror of Oscar Wilde's *The Picture of Dorian Gray*, where vice holds on to beauty and expresses its putrescence only in a hidden painting.) Beauty, if it means anything, must be the personal expression of virtue, not that stylized conceit of vanity called "glamour." At its best, Stendhal argued, beauty should follow from love rather than precede it. In other words, we should not love someone just because he or she is beautiful but rather find them beautiful because we love them. That is the kind of beauty that does not "fade" and in fact increases, and it is a kind of beauty too that presupposes rather than eclipses everything that is important about a person in love.

BEYOND *ROMEO AND JULIET:* LOVE AMONG THE ELDERLY

... there is a hidden proviso. Sex is for the young. Few if any advertisements show older couples in loving embrace—unless those ads are for life insurance or prepaid funeral arrangements! Small wonder, then, that older people soon have the idea that sex, like childbearing, has its season. ... The thoughts of sexual relations between persons in their fifties or sixties or beyond seem ludicrous or repulsive in this youth-bound culture.

—BERT KRUGER SMITH, *Aging in America*

Contrary to popular advertising (laxative and iron-tonic ads excepted), love is not essentially for the young or even "the young at heart." Our paradigm of love—two beautiful youngsters bounding over with joy and hormones—is part and parcel of our generalized "youth culture" and fraught with the same fatalities. In Los Angeles, where "successful aging" is understood as looking less than thirty, in a culture where "getting old" is feared more than death itself, it is not surprising that love is geared to the young. Many psychologists who analyze love, buying into the same image (since the most available subjects for observation, interview and experiment are eighteen-year-old college students), take initial "arousal" as an essential indicator of love, if not as the essence of love itself. The idea is not new or uniquely American, of course; Goethe (as a young man) also held that "there is no love like first love"—to which many of us would add "Thank goodness!" But then there is also that bit of wisdom from Frank Sinatra that tells us that "love is lovelier, the second time around." And, we might add, the third and the fourth, for love like wine, when cared for, improves with age.

Age is rarely discussed as a factor in love. Articles on elderly

couples who still have a sex life are as often intended to shock as
to encourage us, and the idea that old people might newly "fall
in love"—rather than drag it along from earlier, more energetic
years—is at least surprising to most people. But that is because
we have an idea of health and selfhood which, in almost every
other society and age, has been considered the antithesis of wisdom. We celebrate youth instead of sagacity and experience, and
we celebrate the initial stages of love instead of the love itself.
We deny that love has anything to do with death (the phrase "till
death do us part" is considered a strictly idiomatic expression)
and we do not even think—despite some fine phrases to the
contrary—that the beauty of love can coexist with wrinkled skin
and failing organs. But in a society in which mobility not only
continues but increases until one's seventies, in which a near
majority of the "romantic" population is approaching if not leaving behind middle age, in which every successfully married couple is of necessity no longer young and in which the list of eligible
singles fairly construed includes a large number of the elderly,
this obsession with young love is intolerable and inhuman.

Two friends of mine in Texas just celebrated their golden anniversary—their fiftieth. I've known them for only sixteen years
of that epic span, but it would be hard to describe their love for
each other as anything other than romantic. Not romantic by
resemblance, or by some poor comparison with their grandchildren or the youthful love they occasionally tell me about with
more humor than nostalgia. They still look at each other with
moistened eyes and display an unmistakable joy at the bare physical fact of being together. They giggle (not merely laugh) at each
other's jokes and listen intently as one of them tells a third party
some story that the other has heard at least fifty times before. I
haven't inquired into their sex life but I simply assume that it is
happy, and I don't have to ask whether they've ever fought; on
rare occasions I see the last remnants of an argument being
washed away with caring tenderness rather than refueled by
clandestine comments.

Other friends are embarrassed in their presence, even critical. The caresses seem quite inappropriate, and their constant mutual attention and romantic self-reference seem almost unethical. But by what standard? The media appears to be selling little but health-spa first encounters, perfect teeth and suntanned muscular limbs and bellies, cardboard figures devoid of knowledge or care or any romance worthy of the name. And sticking with commercial video, what do we find when we see a middle-age married couple?—a couple of wimps, worried more about the stains in their laundry or the price of their auto insurance than the amorous electricity that might exist between them. We are being deprived of *exemplars*. We see another *Romeo and Juliet* every half hour, but we are starving for examples of true long-term love. Indeed, when one tries to think of the few elderly heroes and heroines in American arts and pop culture, it turns out that almost all of them are *alone*. The occasional example of a feisty and accomplished sixty-year-old may appear, but the idea of two sixty-year-olds deeply in love? That is not fit for the children of the *Rambo* generation to see.

We ought to distinguish between two separate questions here, which I have so far run together. There are two sorts of situations at stake here: long-term marriages between now-elderly couples, and more or less new love between two senior citizens (and a spectrum of ages and anniversaries in between). Given what most of us still believe about love and successful marriage, the former ought to be an ideal, but our fear of aging and our celebration of youth and novelty make this impossible. The latter should be just as acceptable as youthful encounters—and even more welcome—but, tragically, it is not. We would rather think of old people as "beyond" such passions—except, of course, when we ourselves are old.

The idea that "arousal" is the basis of love is remarkably ill suited to almost any romantic experience—including even the passionate throes of the first few days. It may capture the physiology, but it surely misses the phenomenon, and when our concern is (as it must be) not a five-day fling but the hoped-for possibility of a lifetime together, arousal is much too momentary and existentially insignificant to serve any function at all. What we need—and what we will get only by looking at love that has been around for decades—is an understanding of how love "grows" or, to use another enticing metaphor, how it "deepens." (Curious how these two metaphors seem to come together as "entrenching"—the way roots do when they grow deeper down into the soil, anchoring and nourishing the aging but ever sturdier plant.) It is often said that the growth or deepening of love is mainly a matter of mutual knowledge, but, while knowledge is important and inevitable, I think that it plays only a supporting role to intimacy and an ever-increasing sense of shared identity. (Again, it is essential to distinguish between intimacy itself—which can last a lifetime—and the initial thrill of intimacy.) It is far more essential to the life of a couple that they have "been through so much together"—even if much of this "much" is negative, and even if, as in extreme family crises, it eventually blows them apart. It is sharing experiences and creating hopes and fantasies together that broaden the base of love, until at last two people have shared so much together—indeed a lifetime—that any other identity is all but unimaginable. Desire may continue and caring will no doubt do so, but what characterizes the success of love is that sense of identity that makes separation painful and indifference impossible. It is not a structure that can be realized all at once; it is a structure that can be created together only over a lifetime. Couples who have spent that lifetime together are not enjoying the residuum of love but the real thing. The fact that they might no longer feel the hormonal arousal that seems to excite (rather than amuse) us so in teenagers is quite beside the point.

It should be evident, however, that durability—while perhaps a mark of success in relationships—is not in itself the mark of successful love. A couple can stay together and make adequate "arrangements" for a hundred different reasons, none of which have anything to do with love. They may stay together "because of the children," or the grandchildren, or because it is a matter of shame or failure to get divorced, or because it would be impossible to find another apartment, or because life is at least less painful than it could possibly be apart, or because one is afraid of being alone, or just because "we've spent so much of our lives together"—not a sufficient reason for love, perhaps, but often, from an investment as well as a nostalgic point of view, a good enough reason to stay together. (The dubious claim to "maturity" too often accompanies such passionless compromises, giving long-term love itself a bad name.) While a lifelong relationship may be the ideal medium for love to grow, it does not follow that where there is duration (or endurance) there will also, always, be love.

Old people as well as young meet, fall in love, start what just might be a substantial life together. They just don't make so many movies about it, and so (the media being the stamp of cultural approval) they don't feel so comfortable or "natural" about it either. There are differences, of course. Two twenty-year-olds can fantasize a lifetime together—even if the statistics for their socioeconomic Yuppie group give them a one-in-five chance of making it. A newly met couple in their sixties will hope for perhaps a dozen years—and in fact have a better chance— and much more perseverance. ("Forever" means something quite different at sixty than it does at sixteen.) One might speculate that it is when two older people meet that Aristophanes's fantasy most comes alive. Two young people are only partially formed, quite flexible, unsure of who they are or what they want or how they can or should fit together. Two mature adults, on the other hand, already have a lifetime of experience and self-hood behind them. They know (more or less) who they are and what they want, and if they fit together at all, it is not because two soft and malleable hemispheres can be pressed and modeled together but because two already hardened halves find themselves miraculously well fit and suited to each other. Of course there is no such thing as a perfect fit, and it will always be fortuitous that two lives already so rich in experience can come together harmoniously. But richness improves love as well as character, and incongruities enrich a relationship as well as complicate it. Our ideal of love should be the late movies of the solid and immutable Spencer Tracy and Katharine Hepburn, not the short, innocent tragedy of *Romeo and Juliet*.

So, too, lifelong love would seem to provide an ideal example of the convergence of love and friendship. Love may be no less possessive but one's sense of possession should now be secure, without the doubts that plague new love and without the resistance that the long dialectic of love and individuality require. This is emphatically not to say that love can be taken for granted, but only that it seems settled and doesn't have to be fought for, as identity is solidified and no longer only hoped for and projected. Nor is it to say that possessiveness ceases to be a possible problem, for as long as love has its claims there will always be the threat to the individual will, and an elderly lover, as well as a rebellious young one, will (and should) insist on his or her rights. But as sexual jealousy diminishes there is more not less room for attention to the love itself. Here is the time when love can reflect on itself and, as Hegel supposed of the world spirit, consolidate and realize itself as epic history. This, not "childhood's careless days," is the time for romantic dinners, vacations, flowers and tender conversation. It is ironic that when love has its most opportune time for fruition so many people let it wither, falsely assuming that there is nothing left to be done, or fritter it away with idle conversation and bickering, sadly ignoring what might have been the towering accomplishment of their lives.

3

. . . .

"FALLING IN LOVE"

I am lodged in my body, like an ice cube in a furnace.

—REBECCA GOLDSTEIN,
The Mind-Body Problem

What is "falling in love"? The very phrase suggests something sudden, involuntary, unnerving, disruptive, physically disturbing, probably dangerous. Metaphors distort as well as illuminate experience, and the "falling" metaphor is too easily exaggerated. What gets ignored is the extent to which love turns on a decision (or several decisions) rather than a misstep or a lucky accident; love is a leap rather than a fall. It is a choice—or a series of choices—which makes something significant out of the excitement we experience with another person (rather than, for example, deciding just to be annoyed by the discomfort). It is a decision to pursue an essentially evasive and abstract goal of shared selfhood and mutual concern, a decision to pay attention —whole-hearted attention—to a person whom one may never even have met before. What also gets ignored in the "falling" metaphor is the extensive preparation for this sudden experience: years of fantasizing, listening to and watching stories, thinking about possibilities and carving out a space—perhaps a face—that will serve as the stimulus when one finally gets the opportunity to "fall." The meeting, the circumstances may be sudden and unexpected, but love itself—even the most spontaneous, unexpected love—requires a lifetime of emotional cultivation and readiness.

Falling in love is the initial phase of love. This obvious point is quickly lost from view, however, and many respected theorists insist on divorcing this first phase from love and insisting, in some cases, that it has nothing to do with love at all. Thus M. Scott Peck suggests that falling in love is a kind of "infantile regression," and one popular author, Dorothy Tannov, has invented a particularly ugly name for the initial, disruptive phase of love, "limerance," which connotes that usually obscene poem, the limerick. On the other hand, there are those who exaggerate the importance of this stage—its excitement and novelty, the sense of discovery and the often overwhelming sense of mutual sexuality and see the rest of love as a downhill slide, a slow fade to the dull comforts of domesticity. Both views are absurd and dangerous; love is an emotional process and processes need beginnings and development. Love cannot appear from nowhere, and love cannot simply be cut off at its earliest stage and still be considered love—though of course love is often interrupted or rebuffed by rejection, by circumstances, by misunderstandings, by an unworkable relationship, by death. Falling in love is an essential part of love; it cannot be dismissed, but neither should it be confused for love as such. Love is a process, and love takes time. Falling in love, accordingly, is for the most part anticipation, exploration and fantasy, but it is no less love for that.

Falling in love is first of all a new way of looking at the world, scuttling the mundane and routine and focusing (at first) on a remarkably simple set of desires, stimulated and egged on by a smile or a look—or even the possibility of a smile or a look. Love goes on, or rather we keep love going, because like all emotional processes it has a logic of its own, an obsessive, intransigent quality and a cultural narrative that we tend to follow even if it seems that we are simply following our "heart" (or some other dumb part of the anatomy). It is true that love is and seems "bigger than both of us," but what is "bigger" in fact is the culture of love, the established story line and the forces of influence and internalized demands, hopes and expectations that make it seem as if love is so beyond our control. But love is not always sudden, nor is it such that, once started, it cannot be stopped. One does not usually want to stop it, of course, for the initial experience of love is typically so exciting, so promising, so energizing, so clearly focused and inspiring, so filled with hopes, fears and expectations that curiosity if not passion demands at least a glimpse of "how this might work out." "Falling in love" can be slow and deliberate as well as sudden and surprising. It can happen gradually between two people who have known one another a long time, with no experience of a "falling" stage as such, without the usual period of confusion and disorientation. It can be simple and matter-of-fact, with a quiet joy but no melodramatics or "boy loses girl" story line. The "falling" stage can even be a period of mutual hostility and confrontation—no stars or flowers or rainbows to start, but instead harsh words and angry accusations. What is essential is that two people (or each alone) engage in a process of extraordinary receptivity with each other, putting the other at the center of attention, fantasizing as well as noticing the other to an unusual degree. Sexual attraction, desire, fantasy and fulfillment serve this purpose to a remarkable degree, but so might any number of other less erotic shared interests if only they were sufficiently intense to temporarily wed two people together, get them fascinated with each other and make them mutually dependent, allowing them to begin weaving the fabric of shared self-identity through a process of single-minded mutual self-discovery.

Love at first sight, intense physical attraction coupled with protracted anxiety and frustration, days or weeks of alternating hope and desperation, offer us a familiar example of the "falling" phenomenon, but there are many others, and, anyway, it is an all-too-common mistake to confuse these unpleasant symptoms of incipient love with the "falling" itself. And in any case, again whatever the circumstances, whether the beginning of love is traumatic or quietly exhilarating, sudden or the gradual realization of two friends or roommates who have known each other for years, falling in love is a decision. Sometimes it is a gradual series of decisions—the decision to stick around till the end of the party, the decision to stay in town for another six months, the decision to "give it a try" for a year or two. Sometimes, at its most spectacular, falling in love is a mutual, explicit decision. Two people having been "seeing each other," as the euphemism goes, for several months. Perhaps they met in an evening class or on a bus, but they quickly discovered that they shared similar ambitions and a number of personal tastes, in particular an intense and perhaps obvious mutual erotic interest in each other. An erotic interest, of course, need not be fully sexual, and it certainly need not involve any conscious aim or fantasy concerning sexual intercourse. But to make the case more explicit, and to remove frustrated sexual desire from the list of factors that can so easily be confused with love, let us imagine that this couple consummated their mutual desire by the end of their first week together, on a Thursday afternoon, after a particularly embarrassing set of tennis. They continued to "see" each other two or three times a week, reveling in their bodies, cooking dinners and talking late into the night, sharing problems as well as pleasures but always being a bit cautious, never saying too much or revealing too much or crossing those unspoken boundaries that separate sex and friendship from love. But then, on another Thursday afternoon, after a particularly delightful walk and roll in the park, they "fell" in love. They may have felt a bit more exhilarated than usual; they may have felt the contrast with their rather pointless fight the night before. They may have felt especially sentimental, or they both may have looked particularly adorable. What happened, what distinguished this set of "feelings" from any other tender or rapturous feelings they may have felt at other times, was that they made a decision. It may well have manifested itself in the ritualistic formula "I love you"; "I love you too" perhaps said between them for the first time. Or if not the first time, with some special even urgent notation, such as "No, I mean, I *really* love you." The feelings had been there before, but of course the feelings as such weren't really essential. It may have been that the circumstances were not ever so conducive, or that the coincidence of their mutual affection had never before been so well timed. But what happened, what initiated love, was the decision—in this happy case the mutual decision—to interpret their feelings and their relationship in that special way, to see it in terms of an endless future instead of for the time being, to see each other as mutually dependent and intertwined instead of as two sexually compatible friends. It may have been that they never felt so sensitive to each other at the exact same time before, and here is the seeming suddenness (in retrospect) of their "fall." It may have been that they occasionally thought or felt such things before but never announced them or otherwise made them explicit to each other. But it is with that decision, made explicit by the usual announcement in its prescribed form, that love begins.

LOVE AND ITS VICISSITUDES: ''THE REAL THING''

I don't believe in love at all—that is, any more than I believe in hate, or in grief. Love is one of the emotions like all the others—and so it is alright when you feel it. But I can't see how it becomes an absolute. It is just part of human relationships, no more.

—D . H . LAWRENCE, *Women in Love*

At the beginning of a process we are usually not in a position to tell how it will turn out. We can't even know whether the whole plan or project is absurd, corrupt or inadequate. One begins a hitchhiking tour of Eastern Europe with enthusiasm and full of hopes; in retrospect these may prove to have been the appropriate anticipations of a wonderful adventure or they may turn out to have been the foolish, self-deceptive excitement that so often disguises an ill-conceived, irresponsible plan. But the initial experience, the initial conception of the adventure, may be just the same in both cases. So too in love. At the outset, during the "falling" stage, there may be no telling whether love is wise or foolish, truly promising or based on illusions and self-deception. In retrospective wisdom we have a variety of ways of judging the prognosis of love, but only in retrospect. It is in this light that we can understand such love-related vicissitudes as infatuation, vanity love and being "swept away," which are often contrasted with "the real thing."

Infatuation, vanity love and being "swept away" are often

treated as fraudulent emotions, mimicking love but inevitably disappointing and occasionally quite self-destructive. But let us say, first of all, that each of these emotions may have its proper place (which is not to say that they are thereby healthy or a "good thing") and, second, that there may be no difference whatever between these emotions and "the real thing." The exhilaration of infatuation and the exhilaration of love may be not dissimilar in either kind or intensity. The fantasizing that dominates early love need be no more "realistic" than the idealization that characterizes infatuation, and the sexual frenzy that often explains infatuation may be no less obsessive and single-minded in love. In retrospect, when nascent love doesn't work out, we console ourselves (or criticize ourselves) by noting that it was "just infatuation." But the truth may be that it was, or could have been, love at an early stage.

Conflicting circumstances, blameless ignorance about the character of the other person, too much sex and not enough conversation, overly zealous hopes about what might be possible —all of these might undermine a developing relationship and make love impossible without thereby denying that it was, in fact, love. So, too, the popular current dichotomy between true love and being "swept away" tries to force a distinction between really being in love and being so obsessed with sexual needs and pleasure that one feels forced to rationalize what one feels as "love" in order to give it legitimacy. But here again the beginning of love may well consist of just such sexual obsession, and it is only in retrospect—when sex has begun to become disappointing or when other aspects of the relationship begin to be intolerable—that one judges that "it was just the sex; I didn't love him at all." The judgment may not be true, however; it may indeed have been the beginning of love, but love built on an insufficient foundation, love that could not continue when other needs and aspects of one's personality came into play, as they must. Being "swept away" in the name of love and falling in love in the fullness of sexual enthusiasm are not in themselves distinguishable.

What some recent authors call fraudulent or "counterfeit" emotions are more often than not just love projected on an insufficient basis, of too little knowledge, too little experience, too much of one kind of excitement to the exclusion of others. It need be no less love for that, even if it cannot last. It is the beginning of a process, miscast, ill-aimed or ill-conceived, like a pot-to-be thrown at the center of the potter's wheel. It is the same lump of clay, the same wheel and the same caressing hands that produce the perfect vase in one case and an unwieldy mess in another. It is the same cauldron of passions, desire and romantic mythology that cook up satisfying love in one case and an unworkable mess of a relationship in another.

Vanity love is perhaps the most interesting case of supposedly fraudulent love. Vanity love (the name comes from Stendhal) is love that, in retrospect, turns out to have been based far more on self-interest and self-image than on any concern or affection for the other person. Unlike infatuation and being swept away, which are often self-ascribed, vanity love is usually an accusation aimed at someone else. As so often in disappointed love, the accusation is frequently overstated, so that one complains that one's ex-lover was *only* self-interested and not at all in love. (It is sometimes added that he or she is also "incapable of love.") But the distinction between self-interest and altruism is far more complicated than our usual contrasts between selfishness and sainthood would indicate. Uplifting one's opinions of oneself through association with another person requires a positive view of that other person, and even an associative (as distinguished from intimate) relationship with another requires some degree of interchange, coordination and mutual support.

A man feels good about himself because he is "with" a beautiful woman, or a woman feels good about herself because she is with a wealthy man, but one is not renting such a person for the evening, and it is not just the accompaniment but the association that one enjoys, even if this is overly defined by appearances rather than interaction. In other words, even the most obvious cases of "using" another person to serve one's own vanity involves some complex mixture of self-interest and requisite interest in the qualities, attitudes and interests of the other. Purely selfish actions are as rare as truly altruistic ones, not because altruism is so unusual or superhuman but because purity in action is. Our motives are always "mixed," and while we would all rather be loved "for ourselves" instead of for our utility to someone else, these two are always intertwined. "Vanity love," too, is a retroactive judgment, a kind of denouncement to the effect that "you didn't care about *me* as much as I thought you did." But the expression betrays the source of the complaint as well as its nature; it registers disappointment rather than a description of a certain kind of pseudo-love.

All love is a mixture of self-interest and self-image and care and concern for the other; there may be no such emotion as wholly "selfless love." The proportion of self-concern and other-concern is by no means fixed, of course, and it will inevitably vary enormously in different relationships, from the case in which two generous and compassionate people each take the interests and well-being of the other as their primary concern in life to the no less familiar case of two narcissists whose love of each other is almost entirely self-love enhanced by the reflection of self in the other. Many couples function quite well with one generous and one self-absorbed partner, and moralizing here, as elsewhere, is more likely to be vindictive than helpful. The charge of "vanity love" is not the description of a kind of love so much as it is the refusal to tolerate (or to continue to tolerate) a certain proportion of self-involvement in a relationship.

Why do we put a premium on such distinctions? What I would suggest is that our mania for quick decisions and instant answers has taken over love. We want to know right away—even on the first meeting—whether this is in fact "the real thing." (One doesn't, after all, want to waste any time.) And so we too easily confuse the beginning of the process with the process itself, too readily look to the features of initial attraction as proof of love instead of waiting for love to prove itself. But what brings two people together may be very different from what keeps them together, and the basis for mutual attraction may be very different from the foundation that supports love. The beginning of the emotional process of love may in fact be based on some mutual interest or form of admiration that is quite frivolous. It may well be based upon sexual attraction or unusually exciting sexual activity that will not survive the honeymoon. All that is essential to the "falling" part of the process is that there be some basis for getting together and motivation for spending time together, providing the chance to get to know each other and to establish the web of mutual feelings and thoughts and activities that make two people into "one." Whether or not this basis becomes the foundation of love, or whether that motivation continues into the relationship as such, is of very little importance.

This is not at all to deny the value and importance of what we call "falling in love"; it is only to say that what makes love "work" may have very little to do with its initial attractions. Conversely, what makes love so exciting at the beginning need not be the same as what makes it so successful later on. Accordingly, we can understand without condemning those who prefer the "peak experience" of early exhilaration with another person to the whole process of developing love, knowledge and intimacy. The early process of discovery and mutual conquest has its own virtues and rewards, even if love fails to progress and doesn't work out. But the early part of the process doesn't disclose the fate of the process itself, and the problem arises only when one confuses the two, mistakes the early "peak experience" for the fulfillment of love rather than its initial boost and substitutes the motives that move us to love with the short-term motives that provide inspiration and excitement but leave the self relatively unchanged. It may be enough for some people (and not necessarily to the disadvantage of their lovers) to be satisfied with serial infatuation or the periodic joy of allowing themselves to be "swept away"—as long as these are not confused with love. Vanity love may be, in our acquisitive and self-oriented society, a perfectly legitimate form of self-aggrandizement, as long as it is perfectly clear, or as clear as possible, that this is what is going on. But much of this can be known only in retrospect or—better —through experience.

The beginning of love can be a spur to creativity, a temporary boost in self-esteem or an awakening of one's sexual powers, and these may be legitimate goals quite apart from love. But love is something else, even though it may begin in exactly the same way. It is only time that will tell, along with the hard emotional work that must go into any self-involved, passionate process and the patience, attention and caring that nourish the relationship in which love matures. It is not a matter of "commitment" but rather one of devotion, an early decision to stick with it and see it through. There may be no evident difference between the feelings of love and infatuation but there is all the difference in the world between love's patient intentions and the mere excitement that cannot see beyond its own satisfaction.

THE JOYS OF SEX

Sex isn't something you've got to play with; sex is *you*. It's the flow of your life, it's your moving self and you are due to be true to the nature of it. . . .

—D. H. LAWRENCE

Falling in love is often, but by no means always, tied up with sexual excitement. In more chaste and cautious epochs than our own, such excitement had to be entirely anticipatory—though by no means any less exciting for that. The actual sexual experience might be completely unknown, even dreaded or feared, so that its very possibility was overwhelming. Today, by contrast, sexual experience is so familiar, so devoid of that mystery that accompanies wholesale ignorance, so much the *right* of every man and woman that the sexual basis for love is rarely just anticipatory, whether or not a couple decides to wait until later in the relationship or even marriage before "going all the way."

Our conception of love is such that it not only includes but is often based on the notion of sexual satisfaction (a concept that would have been unintelligible for women, at least, in certain romantic ages, given the misinformation, the threat of pregnancy and even the condemnation of female sexual desire and enjoyment). We readily conclude that there is something seriously lacking in love if strong sexual desire and adequate performance are not readily available, and we too readily conclude that obsessive sexual desire and perfect performance together are virtually tantamount to love. What has changed is that, whereas sexual intercourse used to be considered the "consummation" of love and came rather late in the emotional process, it is now frequently the foundation and the starting point of love. This is not to say that it will or should continue to play that role; it is a very rare relationship indeed (Stanley and Stella Kowalski aside) that can sustain itself on sexual desire and its fulfillment alone. But in an extremely impatient society that no longer has tolerance for protracted courtships, sexual satisfaction and temporary obsession are a most efficient means of getting two people together, forcing them to pay attention to one another and very quickly establishing an intricate interplay between their lives that might well—but of course may not—lead to love.

It is perhaps surprising that one still has to insist, at the end of the twentieth century, that sexual excitement is a good thing, not just as biological preparation for reproduction or as a necessary preliminary to performing one's conjugal duties. Sexual excitement is in itself exhilarating, inspiring, engendering a keen sense of one's embodiment and our essential interconnectedness —especially in love. Such vitality can easily be frustrated, but it is not, as the whole history of the subject from Saint Augustine to Freud might suggest, an essentially degrading, frustrating experience that at best is legitimated in marriage bearing fruit in reproduction and (though this in itself is a claim worth pondering) can be turned into an expression of love. (How can something intrinsically shameful and degrading be employed as an expression of what is "highest" and most spiritual in us?) Sexual desire and activity do not represent the emergence of the bestial in us but, as Roger Scruton has recently argued at length (in *Sexual Desire*), the manifestation of what is most human about us. As a basis for love it is unmatched in its ability to bring two people (who may hardly know one another) together with tremendous force, establishing within minutes a mutual desire which is by no means "just sexual" and has prefigured in it (sometimes mistakenly) an entire future, not just a passing desire.

But it is possible to overplay the importance of sexual excitement, too, and for some couples the intensity of sexual frenzy may be inversely proportional to the solidity and intimacy of love. The sex is compensation for communication that is otherwise lacking, or the sensuous grasping for connections that are otherwise not there. Sex may be the only situation where two such people have anything to "say" to one another (and it is then usually not a message of love that gets expressed). The excitement of sex may be a function of the distance and not the intimacy between two people, like the exhilaration one enjoys while flying at great speed over enormous distance. It may be the product of the novelty or the difficulty of two people who otherwise do not know one another getting together in what can be the most intimate of all circumstances (thus the thrill and anxiety of first sexual encounters and the addictiveness of sex for two people who never otherwise get close).

Sex and friendship, by way of contrast, mix with tenderness and quiet joy, not explosiveness. The fact that sex can be so comfortable does not preclude its also being exciting and exhilarating, even an ecstatic religious experience, but it never leaves the solidity of love and does not provide that reckless, thoroughly intoxicating experience of being "swept away." The excitement of some sexual relationships may be more a product of anxiety and the fear of being abandoned than affection, and what is "missing" in some established love affairs may be nothing more than that sense of danger.

Sexuality provides the initiating motive for love in a great many cases, but it should not be thought that it thereby must decrease with time or that love cannot be motivated by anything else. It is much too easy, if not glib, to explain "falling in love" in terms of sexual attraction and fulfillment. It is obvious that there can be sexual attraction and satiation without love and that there can be love without the possibility of sexual fulfillment. But, on a much deeper level, love cannot be just sexual desire because what Aristophanes called the "infinite yearning" of love is never satisfied by sex, no matter how passionate or satisfying or often repeated. To understand falling in love is to understand the powerful dynamic of a set of underlying ideas, particularly those ideas concerning the desirability of a "fusion" of identities, the reformulation of one's personal self-identity so that it is indistinguishable, both in one's own eyes and in the eyes of the world, from the identity of that special other person. Sexual desire, so understood, need not diminish in substance or intensity but only in novelty, which in the eyes of "infinite yearning" is no great loss.

In Chapter 1 we insisted that what distinguishes romantic love from other kinds of love is in part its intimate tie to sexuality. Again, this is not to say that love must be consummated, nor even that sexual desire must be a self-evident and explicit aspect of love. Just as love may be unrequited, so, too, it may be sexually unfulfilled or prohibited. A nun who once took one of my courses admitted to me that she was in love with the priest whom she worked for, and he with her. They maintained their chastity, and quite obviously emphasized the spiritual and personal aspects of their love. "But why," she asked with a kind of despair, "does it seem that the only adequate expression of our love has to be physical?" So, too, we sometimes feel, when we are experiencing love most deeply, that sex just isn't enough, that, as Aristophanes predicted, we have this "infinite longing" that can't be satisfied by anything less than a total and permanent union. But nevertheless we experience sex as the closest that we can come to that union, at least for a while. It is a powerful desire that expresses itself both through love and as love, not only in the desire for sexual intercourse, but in the many small desires to touch, to caress, to gently kiss or stroke a cheek. It would be wrong to say that romantic love is sex, and it would be dishonest to insist that love requires sex, but nevertheless the tie between love and sex is powerful and undeniable. It is not just that sex expresses love (for sex can express many other emotions as well), but that sexual desire is what fuels as well as defines romantic love.

It should be obvious that what we mean by sex and sexual desire here cannot be restricted to, nor even focused upon, the sexual "act." We need not knock the genitalia to point out that they are overemphasized in sex (though sometimes underemphasized in overly pious conceptions of love). A tender caress or even a touch can be profoundly sexual, while sexual intercourse can sometimes signal a break instead of a culmination of intimacy. We sometimes think of sex as essentially exciting (where "excitement" is then too readily understood as preparatory for and leading toward intercourse) but sex can also be soothing, calming, tender, not just in the heat of genital excitement, but also in the quiet embodiment of a fingernail softly trailing up and over the shoulders. There can be no doubt that there is, somewhere in that labyrinth of instincts and basic learning that con-

stitute the "lower" parts of our brain, some primal urge to intercourse, more subtle perhaps and in any case more complex, but
nevertheless much like the instincts so evident in the courting
patterns of certain wild animals. But though the end may be the
same, this instinct plays only a minor role in sexual desire and
even less in love. Sexual desire in love is bound up with the
entire body, a delight in the other *person* rather than an impulse
to *do* anything in particular. Sex in love is about contact, not a
biological achievement, and that contact can be just as well (or
better) expressed through the touch of two fingertips or the protracted exchange of a look or a glance.

It is often said (and reconfirmed daily) that sex is much better
in love. This happy claim must be distinguished from the moralistic insistence that sex is permissible only in love (or in marriage), though it must be admitted that the sense of guilt-free
openness that makes sex enjoyable may be possible for many
people only in love. Some of this is easy to explain. Sex in love
carries with it the expectation of continuity and trust. Sex in love
has something delightful to express—namely love—while sex
outside of love is often an expression of much less delightful
passions and impulses—conquest, vanity, revenge, fear or
hatred of the opposite sex, domination (or submission), proving
oneself or overcoming timidity or insecurity. It has been argued
(for example by Russell Vannoy in *Sex Without Love*) that sex
can be even better without the familiarity of love, but this thesis
invites the celebration of untender passions and dangerously
confuses sex in love with sex in a no longer passionate long-term
relationship. The latter may dull, but the former, at least as
expression, does not. Sex with a stranger may be exciting, but it
can also be humiliating, foolish, guilt-ridden and filled with anxiety—which may ironically serve to momentarily bolster the
thrill of the experience. Sex in love is very special sex, whether
or not one wants to insist that it is the only proper or desirable
context for sex. Sex in love is not only the desire for and enjoy-

ment of another person's body, it is the reflection of and acceptance of one's own body, of oneself *as* a body. One of the most
delightful virtues of love is the sexual expression and fulfillment
of the self. But most of all, what makes sex *meaningful* is the
sense that it ties into one's essential self as a bodily shared self,
that it is not just for the moment but looks far into the future.
Falling in love is so sexually exciting not because sex itself is
somehow more exciting but because it is pregnant with promises
and possibilities. Falling in love is exhilaration about the future.
Sex in love is the ecstasy of the moment made possible by the
promise of unending ecstasy to come.

LOVE AT FIRST SIGHT

Whoever loves, loves at first sight.

—SHAKESPEARE, *Twelfth Night*

Love takes time, and it is with this in mind that we should
broach the delightful mysteries surrounding the dramatic phenomenon of "love at first sight." Love as such may not be a
mystery, but love at first sight certainly ought to be. We are
regaled with stories about the sailor who walked into the bar or
the woman who walked into her sister's wedding and, on first
seeing some complete stranger sitting there "across a crowded
room," declared then and there that she or he would be one's
spouse—and indeed they are happily married still. Of course
some of the paranormal implications of this can be explained
away as retrodiction: the many many instances in which one
similarly suddenly falls in love but nothing happens, or love is
rebuffed, or the relationship doesn't work out are simply forgotten while we remember and celebrate that rare minority of instances where the passionate prediction actually came true.

Moreover, what one "remembers" of that fateful first meeting is richly invested and embellished with passions in hindsight, filled with meanings in memory that may not have been evident in fact.

This kill-joy explanation does not, however, explain the phenomenon itself. Why should a perfect (or not so perfect) stranger inspire love, long-term ambitions and trust? Lust is easy to understand, but lust at first sight isn't the issue. We want to know how it is that the initial mutual attraction is so strong, and how such a "superficial" and spontaneous, merely visual basis for love can provide a confidence in, and foundation for, long-lasting "true" love. In love at first sight, one *knows* (or thinks that one knows) that one wants to spend the rest of his or her life with this person, an enormous leap of faith to say the least. Here is a couple with no shared experiences or memories, who have not even had a conversation together, who have no knowledge of each other's public personalities, much less the other's secret and perhaps convoluted private intimacies. And yet, with a single look, they fall in love. It is a phenomenon that would be incomprehensible in most societies, but it is the image on which much of our conception of romantic love is constructed.

Given the virtually total absence of knowledge, information and emotional background, the phenomenon of love at first sight suggests two fairly plausible explanations: first, that the stranger we find so attractive is in fact a "stand-in" for some other love from the past, and, second, that what we call "love" is really just lust, plus an extravagant rationalization to make it personally and morally meaningful. The first theory owes much to Freud and his theory of the "Oedipus complex," which explains why it is that so many people fall in love with men or women who closely resemble their parents. But while the Freudian hypothesis as such has limited plausibility, the general theory of "stand-ins" has application to millions of cases. The most common illustration of this phenomenon are those instances of "love on the rebound" in which one quickly finds a new lover who remarkably resembles the old and loves with a passion that is inappropriate for a new and presumably unknown partner. The theory suggests, in somewhat "hydraulic" terms, that the old love has been displaced or sublimated toward the new one, which would explain both the resemblance and the unusual passion. So, too, the theory would help explain why it is that so many of us keep choosing lovers who resemble one another and seem to be all of a type, perhaps even a type that has proven disastrous or destructive several times in the past. Such theories are compelling because we can find no rational basis for such deep personal involvement with someone we do not even know—no matter how good-looking, charming, intelligent and seemingly trustworthy he or she might be. And yet the attraction is so powerful, so obsessive, that we are certain that there must be some explanation, something not evident in the experience itself.

The idea that love at first sight is in fact a return to an earlier love is a plausible theory if one doesn't take it to its extreme and assume that this earlier love can only have been the first—an infant's love for its parents. Freudians seem so embarrassingly preoccupied with this paradigm, which fully explains romantic preference in only a small number of instances, perhaps limited to only and oldest children and presupposing an overly simple model of nuclear family relationships even then. In fact, there are many alternative prototypes: older siblings, peers and friends (recent as well as in childhood), characters from novels and movies and, most plausible of all in many cases, one's first *romantic* love—a childhood sweetheart, a high school flame, the darling of the neighborhood whom one always admired in adolescence, characters from novels, idols whom one never had the nerve to approach. The prototype in question might be as recent as one's last lover, an ex-wife or husband or "the one that got away." What is clear—the force of this retrospective prototype theory— is that such powerful attraction cannot come out of nowhere.

Powerful emotional attraction presupposes a powerful emotional basis.

The Freudian prototype theory often dwells on frustrated love, but just as plausible is the happy alternative that, having once found near-total satisfaction in love, one has reasonable confidence that it can happen again and quite naturally looks for another partner who in relevant ways resembles the last. The emphasis, in other words, is not on the pain or frustration of the final days, the breakup or its aftermath, but on the relationship and its success. As opposed to the entrenched pessimism of some psychoanalytic theory stressing the pain of one's losses, this view explains the confidence, not the hopeful foolishness, of new love. The question is whether the limited evidence of "first sight" is sufficient to justify that confidence, for it takes no great wisdom to know that two lovers who look alike or even act alike—especially in the semiformalities of the "dating" situation—might indeed be very different. The resemblance may be just superficially close enough to be deceptive. The unhappy possibility, however, is that having once (or more) been frustrated in a certain kind of relationship, one stubbornly seeks, "this time," to make it work. We may praise love and happiness above all other affections, but pride, vanity and stubbornness sometimes prove to be more demanding. Love at first sight may thus represent more of a challenge than an invitation, the promise of old troubles repeating themselves as well as the repetition of old delights and satisfactions. On the other hand, what initiates love at first sight does not usually determine the development of love, and we should always beware of that "genetic fallacy" that would have us confuse the origins of love with its ultimate nature.

The second theory, that what seems like love is really lust plus rationalization, certainly accounts for the well-known psychological finding and common wisdom that men typically conflate sexual attraction and satisfying sexual activity with love, but it also captures the experience of a significant number of modern women. Sexual attraction, unlike love, presupposes no prior experience together, requires no mutual interests (save one) and can be oblivious to questions of personality and character. Sexual attraction, unlike love, does not look far into the future, need not care about compatibility as a couple and makes very limited plans together. Sexual attraction, unlike love, tends to focus on stereotypes rather than individuals, and the object of intense, spontaneous lust at first sight is much more likely the product of atavistic biological instinct and all-permeating media hype than any affection or interest in an individual person. The glamorous individual that inspires such lust quite likely resembles the latest Hollywood heart throb or, more locally, the darling of the college or the country club. Of course questions of status and acquisitiveness enter in here as well as questions about the cultivation of sexual tastes and preferences, but the only point that needs making here is that such stereotyped sexual attraction should not be confused with love, not even love at first sight.

In a sense, of course, love at first sight is typically sexual. "At first sight" what else does one have to go on besides "looks," a certain demeanor, and the obvious fact that the person in question is a male or a female with, presumably, the appropriate sexual orientation? And, in the same sense, love at first sight also makes use of stereotypes and resemblance, for, again, what else does one know about this individual other than his or her seeming similarity to someone else whom one has known and perhaps loved before? But falling in love with someone on the basis of sexual attraction and resemblance is not the same as simply being attracted to a stereotype, and the main difference is the *meaning* one gives to that attraction and to the *individual* whom one is just beginning to love. It is not just sex that one wants but a life together, and it is not the type that one desires but that particular person. Love is different from mere lust in its exclusive concern for the individual, in its long-range planning, in its essential development of a scheme of mutual identity and dependency. Of course we can explain love at first sight in terms of sudden sexual desire, but it must be understood that this is only part of the explanation. What must be added is the fact that this desire is immediately embellished with fantasies and long-range projections, a sense of the personal that may be lacking in sexual desire alone, even if sexual desire alone is sometimes sufficient to get the whole process going.

Part of the problem and the puzzle about love at first sight is the fact that it is so often misleading and downright dysfunctional even when it is not a pathological echo of a frustrated Oedipal or Electra complex or the short-sighted excitement of lust. If love at first sight were always or even usually right on target and a good predictor of romantic success, we would treat it simply as a kind of benign foreknowledge, an intuitive sense about what is good for us rather than a troublesome obsession that (we might even know) could be very bad for us. And it is not simply a matter of making a series of bad guesses; what is so infuriating about romantic attraction is that we often make the same mistakes again and again—though we rarely are capable of recognizing, much less admitting, that we are doing so at the time. We are attracted by certain faces and features rather than others and, with time, we may note that we seem to be attracted over and over again by the same type of person, not for Freudian or sexual reasons but because of something else that, to our consternation and misfortune, escapes us. A woman finds herself attracted to weak-willed, bitter, older men, and only with time and therapy starts to understand that the role she plays right from the start of such a relationship allows her to cast herself as a flighty, beautiful, young optimist—though inevitably she finds herself getting dragged down in bitterness and cynicism too. A man finds himself attracted to young, spoiled, demanding women, and only slowly he begins to see the connection between this series of disastrous relationships and a serious deficit in self-esteem, which he tries to fix by proving himself to someone who will not approve of anyone but herself. Such stereotypical cases illuminate the nature of falling in love much better than the usual Freudian and sexual examples, for they illuminate the dark side of both love and romantic attraction, even in love at first sight.

Love at first sight is a glimmer of the possibility of joining that person to play out the roles through which we seek to define ourselves. Some of these roles are sexual and some may involve physical attractiveness and glamour, but romantic roles dig far deeper into the personality and one's passions. Where love at first sight succeeds, that is where the sense of shared identity really "clicks," and where love at first sight ends in disaster, that is where the elements of attraction have little or nothing to do with the real possibility of shared roles and identity. It should be evident that Freudian prototype theory can therefore explain successful love as well as clinical pathology, for with whom can one feel more at ease than the very people and in the very kind of relationships that one has enjoyed all of one's life. So, too, it is obvious why sexual attraction can be such a misleading as well as persuasive guide to love at first sight. There is no force more effective in getting people together and getting them to fantasize about one another, but also there is no realm of human behavior where our personal needs are so out of touch with our cultivated tastes.

Love is ultimately a matter of personal identity, and falling in love, including love at first sight, is a kind of profound projection, a kind of reaching or (in Plato's terms) "grasping" for one's future and better self. Love at first sight is in fact only a small part "sight" and a much larger part fantasy, the first, immediate grasp of those possibilities, so quick that one cannot even explain, so certain that one never feels the need to do so. But of course this reaching and attempting to transcend oneself continues as long as life and love continue. Love is always in process, from first sight to the final days, but we can appreciate the drastic difference between our experience of initial love and love well under way as a function of the difference between reaching after something—which for all we know may be inaccessible or impossible or ill-conceived to begin with—and experiencing love as a dynamic identity that has already been tested and proven any number of times. Falling in love is the growth of hope prior to any real mutual identity; love at first sight, when it is on target, is the magnificent, immediate insight that makes even falling in love unnecessary. One *is* in love right from the start, and with a lot of luck and attention, it might well remain so for the rest of one's life.

THE PERILS AND PLEASURES OF ROMANTIC ATTRACTION: WHY WE FALL IN LOVE

He knew how she was, didn't he?
Sure, he knew how she was.

—KATHERINE ANNE PORTER

Falling in love is exhilarating, but it is worth asking where that exhilaration comes from. Is it sexual excitement, perhaps sublimated? Again, one can experience sexual excitement without love, and love certainly involves excitement about much more than sex. Novelty? That would bode ill for the possibility of lasting love, but in any case novelty is not always so exciting or rewarding or even so pleasant. Falling in love involves exciting fantasies, but it is what those fantasies are *about*—not the fantasizing as such—that is so exciting and inspiring. What makes falling in love so dramatic and thrilling, I want to suggest, is a rapid conceptual transformation of the self, in which sex and novelty and fantasy all have their place. Enthusiasm about the other is essential, but it is not in itself the source of the unusual frenzy and mental activity that characterize the experience of "falling." The source of that exhilaration is rapid conceptual movement, a sense of enormous mental speed, not only closing the distance between oneself and another but closing in on oneself, desiring, hoping and fearing but also changing to meet and fit the other. Romantic attraction is not only getting excited about a new lover. It is, even more, getting excited about the transformation of oneself.

We fall in love with a person who complements us, perhaps by exemplifying ideals that we share, perhaps by encouraging ideals we strive after, perhaps just by encouraging and complementing what is best in us. Understanding love as a projection (*not* just a reflection) of self helps us to see how, in one sense, falling in love (and especially love at first sight) can be hopelessly "superficial." It cannot possibly know the more profound aspects of a person's personality and may have to base its important decisions on such frail romantic observations as a few awkward looks across the room, one or two casual conversations or—in the case of love at first sight—appearance alone, hardly a sound foundation for love. Love would seem to require knowledge and a solid sense of shared self-identity, but falling in love may not yet have either knowledge of the other or a shared identity. So much of what it employs in its own propagation is fantasy, wishful thinking and hope. Thus it is often suggested by cynics that falling in love is a combination of "deprivation and ignorance" (Kingsley Amis, *Lucky Jim*), and it is similarly suggested that romantics most often go wrong here because their extravagant imaginations substitute their own projected images for the realities of the situation. But the truth seems to be that it is those of *too little* imagination who are most likely to confuse the attractions of the present with the foundations of love. Love is, in large part, imagination—fantasies about a future together, visions of a kiss, a conversation, a lifelong adventure. Moreover, one's alleged ignorance regarding the other person must be balanced with the often neglected knowledge one has of oneself. What we *say* about our needs and desires is typically more fanciful than our tastes and actions betray; what we do and whom we choose is a much better indicator. But here again we have to distinguish between those virtues that attract us to another person and those which in fact can function for love. What one finds so delectable in anticipation and delicious on the first taste may not be palatable much less nutritious over the long haul. A sensual curve or a muscular back may be thrilling at first sight and a source of continuing aesthetic and erotic enjoyment, but it is little compensation for a lack of sympathy or sense of humor. What makes love such a "deep" experience does not depend upon our knowledge of the other (which may be minimal) but rather what we dig up from the depth of ourselves. The exhilaration that accompanies falling in love is only half the discovery of one's lover; the other half is a (re-)discovery of oneself.

Why do we fall in love? How is it that, especially in love at first sight, we are so willing to stake so much on the basis of so little? For one thing, the basis for romantic attraction doesn't ultimately matter. Couples interviewed early and late in their marriages typically report that the basis of the initial attraction (looks, charm, popularity) plays a relatively small role in love later on. But though the reasons change, the love constitutes a process which in one sense remains the same: it begins as a dramatic form of self-transformation and, as it continues, the basis for the mutual self-transformation becomes more and more evident, more and more established, and less and less founded on such initially superficial features as those that one can so easily ascertain upon a first meeting. Initial attraction depends upon such vague but informative data as "good vibrations" (a remarkable if dated phrase, capturing that sense of mutual compatibility without moral judgment of any kind). The mutual sense of attraction increases first, as the distance between two people decreases, then diminishes, as intimacy eliminates that distance altogether. That part of our excitement that is based solely on novelty and the overcoming of distance thus diminishes too, but it is an impoverished relationship or a poor understanding that thereby suffers from any diminution of love.

Plato asked whether we love someone because they are attractive or find them attractive just because we love them. Attraction certainly fits into love in the sense that the person loved quite naturally tends to grow more beautiful and endearing with time, but loving someone *because* he or she is attractive strikes us as risky and frivolous business. Again, why is it that attraction is so important to us, and why is it so often the basis of love?

In our discussion of "beauty" in the preceding chapter, we rejected the notion that physical features were nothing but "superficial," and we distinguished between "looks," cultivated by the media and the presentation of self so that one displays a great deal of one's character and personality. A person's "looks" already include a picture of a form of life, and the way one might envision a life together. A person looks dull or sadistic; a man tries to look brutal or tough or contemptuous; a woman tries to look pampered, disdainful or vulnerable. In each case it is hard to avoid the appropriate images of what life with such a person would be—and what we in turn would ourselves become. Finding the other attractive, therefore, has much to do with the way we envision—or would like to envision—ourselves.

We are attracted to others whose attitudes and behavior reinforce our own, and our own presentations of self are, essentially, invitations (or warnings). The "stand-in" phenomenon is not about resemblance but rather concerned with role-playing. There is nothing very tantalizing about the vulgar version of the Oedipal complex that delights in pointing out that both Marvin's mother and his wife are short and blond, or the self-reflective

curiosity that notices that one always ends up with men who are
bald. Attraction is rarely just a preference for the physically attractive. It is also an impulse, possibly a compulsion, toward
certain behavioral characteristics that match up with or complement patterns of one's own. A person who is socially gregarious
may well seek only another who shares that trait, or he or she
may seek just the opposite, a comparatively shy companion who
will offer the intimacy that society does not provide. But in either
case these are traits that display themselves openly in one's self-
presentation, and to betray them (in order to attract someone
else) is ultimately to betray oneself. So, too, a person who is
particularly somber and (in his or her own eyes) overly serious
may very well look for and choose a person who is fanciful,
cheerful and a bit flighty. One may not be attracted to weakness
as such, but given a desire for control and a strong tendency to
avoid confrontations, one will very likely seek out traits—even
physical traits—that suggest obedience and timidity, flatteringly
redescribed as "sensitive" or (in a woman) as "demure." But
again there can be no fast generalizations. We often choose partners on the basis of roles that we can play together (two timid
people, two brash and vulgar socialites). And complementary
roles can sometimes be confusing. She chooses a nonconformist
with maniacal tendencies because, inhibited herself, he encourages her and makes her feel wild. But then, by contrast, he also
makes her feel even more inhibited. Indeed, much of love can
be analyzed according to this particular dialectic—sometimes
summarized in the observation that "the reasons you fell in love
with a person are the very things that later drive you crazy." The
problem with attraction is that it is still only perception and
expectation, not experience, and what excites us in its promise
may turn out to be disastrous in practice. One might fall in love
and marry for safety and security, only to find life dreary and
uninteresting when one has it. One might fall in love and marry
out of rebellion, but rebellion tends to find little enthusiasm once

the point is made. One might fall in love and marry for sexual "chemistry," only to find after a year or so that sexuality was a cover-up for aggression or compensation for the inability to express oneself. Attraction tends to be short-term, whereas love is for the long haul. What attracts us to a person may very well be the trap that later kills love.

Of course romantic attraction can be self-destructive by design. It is not at all uncommon for us to be attracted to precisely those people who are all but guaranteed of being unsuccessful lovers: successful women who fall in love with married men, older men who fall in love with frivolous younger women. Sometimes the prophecies are self-fulfilling, as for those men who, insisting against all evidence that women are incompetent, go out of their way to choose an incompetent woman or create a context for the woman they love in which she cannot possibly be anything but incompetent. Or for those women who, embittered from past experience or ideology, expect men to be bastards and, not surprisingly, choose men who are contemptible or create a context in which any man would become so. Men who respect women will find that most women are both competent and attractive. A woman who likes men will likely find most men neither unattractive nor diabolical.

Our celebration of romantic attraction and attractiveness tends to eclipse the purpose of romance, which is to build a shared self and provide a foundation for love. Attraction initiates romance, and there can be no love without it. But to elevate attraction from the impetus to the ongoing essence of love will too easily confuse the virtues of attractiveness with the virtues of love itself. Love is exciting, but excitement is not necessarily love. Finding one's mate continuously attractive is certainly desirable, but it may be so because of love rather than vice versa. And ultimately attraction always indicates a distance—inevitable at the beginning, but excessive later on. Love is ultimately a being with and not an attraction toward. Those who think too much of the virtues of attraction, or who insist too much on the dramatic virtues of physical attractiveness rather than the quiet and less visible virtues of humor, tenderness, toughness and sensitivity, may just be locking themselves out of love.

REASONS FOR LOVE

It does not appear to me that my hand is unworthy of your acceptance, or that the establishment I can offer would be any other than highly desirable. My situation in life, my connections with the family of deBourgh, and my relationship to your own, are circumstances highly in my favor; and you should take it into further consideration, that in spite of your manifold attractions, it is by no means certain that another offer of marriage may ever be made you.

—MR. COLLINS,
proposing to Elizabeth,
in Jane Austen's *Pride and Prejudice*

"How do I love thee? Let me count the ways . . ." begins the most famous poem by Elizabeth Barrett Browning. But the "how" turns out to be a "why?" and the ways turn out to be *reasons*. We usually don't think of love as "for reasons"; indeed, it often seems as if loving for a reason is not loving at all but rather a sham, a strategy, a bit of hypocrisy. This picture is supported by all of those infamous examples of the *wrong* reasons —loving someone for his or her money, or for status, position or opportunities. But then, of course, it usually turns out that one doesn't *love* the other person at all; one just loves the money or the status or the opportunities and puts up with the person. Such cases do not refute the claim that one always loves for reasons.

Then again it is often said that, in love, one necessarily loves "the whole human being" and that love is "unconditional." But if love has its reasons, then it is not the whole person that one loves but certain aspects of that person—though the rest of the person comes along too, of course. And if love is for reasons, then love is never "unconditional," though those reasons may be extremely tolerant and may change over time. True love does not diminish because the lover is crippled in an accident or fails in a career, but as trust and mutual caring are reasons for love, betrayal and cruelty are perfectly good reasons for the rejection of love. There are always "conditions" to love, no matter how basic, even if these are sometimes foolishly waived.

Love is for reasons, but there are good kinds of reasons for love, and there are bad reasons. It is usually assumed that good reasons have to do with the qualities of the other person, but the central argument that I would like to put forward here is that the best reasons for love are those that are not (just) qualities of one's lover but reciprocal and mutual qualities that one shares (or would like to share). A good reason encompasses one's own integrity and well-being, for there may be good impersonal reasons for loving someone, that is, he or she is "lovable," but it would, nevertheless, be a disastrous mistake for some particular person to love him or her. That a person is particularly gregarious may be a perfectly good reason for love or admiration, but it is no reason for love if one wants and needs a companion who will share one's hut in the mountains and enjoy the solitude of nature. To accept as good reasons for love those reasons which are publicly promoted (for example cinematic beauty, popularity or that form of plasticity that we call "charm") can be a recipe for disaster. And, of course, there are all sorts of negative reasons for staying in a relationship—the hassle of the divorce, not neglecting the children, one's fear of living alone, the complexities of dividing up the record collection—but these should not be confused with reasons for love. We love someone for reasons of respect and admiration, for reasons of history and obligation, for reasons of sentimentality and personal need, for reasons of entertainment and inspiration, for reasons of straightforward self-interest. Which of these are acceptable, which not—and why? Which indicate true love, and which betray mere self-interest or foolishness or worse—deceit and "using someone" in the guise of love?

Ultimately, there is only one reason for love. That one grand reason, which was seen so clearly by the ancients but has gotten lost in the modern stress on individual autonomy, is "because we bring out the best in each other." What counts as "the best," of course, is subject to much individual variation. For some people "the best" in them might be an opportunity to show their compassion and sensitivity; for others it might be the inspiration to write great poetry, stand up to great odds, take enormous risks. For many people "the best" represents just that heightened feeling of "being alive" and a renewed energy for daily life that is so easily lost in routines and responsibilities. "Bringing out the best" is an ancient formula. One finds it repeated throughout the speeches in Plato's *Symposium* and in Aristotle's long discussion of friendship as well as in various religious formulations throughout the history of Christianity. It was the underlying theme of courtly love—that love endows the beloved one with perfection and, in return, encourages the lover to strive for perfection too. Eighteenth-century Romantic philosophy spoke about the "higher" versus the "lower" self, insisting that love would elevate us "higher," and modern writers still insist—though without any explanation—that love alone will make us better people and the world a better world. But most important of all, the experience of love tells us so unambiguously that we ought to and can be "better"—better for her or for him, worthy of her or his love, the best that we can be. There is no room for sloth in love, and the generous supply of energy one enjoys in love is not mere excitement, it is fuel for living well. One can be "comfortable" in love but one should not confuse that comfort with static contentment; love is dynamic and always improving itself. When the self-improvement stops or becomes a matter of indifference, love has become a mere habit, full of affection perhaps, but hardly love at all.

Whatever our reasons for love, they are not often stated, and rarely even thought or articulated to ourselves. "The heart has its reasons," Pascal tells us, but we tend to deny the reasons of the heart or reduce them to reasons of only the most general sort. The problem is that reasons seem to make love too rational, too self-interested. But of course love *is* in that sense rational—i.e., the reasons and usually good reasons—and it *is* self-interested. After all, it is ourself that is ultimately at stake. But because we can't or don't say or even articulate most reasons, we conclude too quickly that we don't love for reasons at all, or we retreat to such self-deceptive formulas as "love is about the whole person," which makes all distinctions between good and bad reasons and all self-scrutiny unnecessary. It is as if one either loves *everything* about a person or one does not love at all, when the truth is obviously that we do not love everything about a person. There is much that we merely tolerate or ignore—traits that we euphemize ("looking on the bright side") without thereby making them reasons for love. And also there are many things that we really do appreciate without their being reasons for love—kindness and skills, for example. To love is to have an identity with one's lover; it is not, contrary to much traditional wisdom, to accept one's lover—any more than one accepts one-self—"unconditionally." Some reasons for love may be unspoken, but there is always a limit to love, and because a lover doesn't complain about your bad habit (he or she may even pretend to be amused) doesn't mean that it is also a reason for love.

The worst reasons for love may be those that go unacknowledged. For example, it is not unknown for a young woman to fall in love, not once but in an unmistakable pattern, with married men who will not abandon their wives and families. One (certainly not the only) reason for love in such cases, it eventually becomes evident, is the safety of such a relationship, the fact that it has built-in limits in terms of time and commitment. An extremely experienced and insightful person might recognize this in herself as an operative reason for love, but this would be rare indeed. So, too, the recognition that a lover satisfies one's more neurotic needs—the need to be punished or martyred, the desire to take care of a truly pathetic human being, the need to play God with someone. These are reasons for love that might be quite effective without ever being acknowledged. Of course one might well insist that these are not *good* reasons, but the point is that even a sick relationship is not without its reasons. Indeed, it may have stronger (not the same as "better") reasons than the rest.

Many unacknowledged reasons are not sick but are, nevertheless, far less than altruistic or heroic and not at all a question of admiring the other person. Loving because of one's insecurities includes hundreds of such reasons, but even thinking "I love her because I'm afraid to be without her" sounds like a strike against love rather than an explanation for it. Loving for money is sufficiently unacceptable as a reason for love so that it, too, is usually suppressed and covered up with some more acceptable if vague reason ("He has a great personality"). This has historically created a real double bind for women, who until recently found that all practical considerations forced them to marry for material security while at the same time expected them to marry for love. Indeed, it has often been said that one reason for the existence of romance is the fact that it allows them to rationalize this contradiction. (A more recent but equally degrading theory is that love allows women to rationalize sex, which would otherwise repulse or degrade them.)

The idea of unacknowledged reasons for love opens up a vast territory of mysteries and accusations. Once it is allowed that one might not be aware of and even deny the reasons for loving someone, the way is cleared for all sorts of anxiety-inspiring theories about loving for revenge, loving because of infantile neuroses and unresolved Oedipal problems, loving out of perversity and self-destructiveness. The theory of female "masochism" continues to enjoy dangerous currency, suggesting that women "really want" to be hurt and put down, which ignores reasons why many women's romantic situations are untenable or their images of love self-destructive in consequence rather than design. And too often we dismiss the obvious in favor of the kinky, the mysterious or the degrading. A man or woman who is completely enamored with a young and beautiful face is diagnosed in the most dreadful clinical and moral terms. But sometimes, Freud himself insisted, a cigar is just a cigar, and so, too, the reasons for love may be just what they seem to be. Nevertheless, the most significant reasons may be the hardest to identify or to acknowledge—even when "the heart knows."

The reasons for love are the motives, the moving force as well as the focus of the thinking and feeling that constitute love. When this focus is very limited it is what we call *fetishism*— loving someone because of his or her possessions, wit or ability to do modal logic as well as the more celebrated sexual cases of foot fetishism, breast fetishism and penis envy. The problem with fetishism is not that such narrow focus cannot provide a good reason for love but rather that there is a problem making the leap from the specificity of the reasons to the person as such. We have already insisted that one never loves "the whole person" in the holistic sense, but nevertheless it is an ontological fact that in order to enjoy the wit or intelligence or feet or breasts or penis one must spend time with, possibly live the rest of one's life with, a person who must have many attributes other than the fetish in question. It is for this reason that one might suggest that a good reason for love is not, as we tend to think, one that will stand completely alone but rather one that fits in with as many other reasons as possible, enough reasons to provide at least an outline of the person. Loving someone because he or she is "a terrific person" manages to build all of this into a single phrase, but the truth is that most of us love people who provide us with only selected reasons for love, and the trick is to fill out the picture without self-deception.

Because the best reasons for love involve both lovers, some of the reasons for love (and most of the reasons for first falling in love) refer to the future rather than to the past or present. They involve the other person's *potential* and what one can, as part of one's own identity, *make* of the other. Pygmalion is the classical allusion here, but everyday examples are not hard to find. (The love of children consists very largely in this, by the nature of the case.) One can also love because of what we expect will be made *of us* in love, and we might say that at least *some* of the reasons in love ought to be of this kind. (Perhaps one more way of characterizing infatuation is in terms of the temporality of its reasons: love always involves some reasons that point forward. When all reasons are limited to the present, one can suspect that there will not be much of a future.)

Because the most important and effective reasons for love are those which are actually shared in the relationship itself, falling in love is necessarily deficient in reasons compared to a mature and established relationship. A sense of history, for example "what we've been through together," is perhaps one of the most important reasons for love, although it is all but absent in the initial enthusiasm of love. We too often pay attention to only those reasons that are relevant to a person just falling in love or to defending or explaining a new love, but two people who have been in love and together for a substantial period of time also have their reasons for love, and their time together is one of them. (In any less than ideal relationship, of course, that time together may also provide reasons for several less celebrated emotions, including anger, resentment and even contempt.) Time together is one of those reasons in which sharing is built into the account itself, not just as mutual need, desire or enjoyment but as *accomplishment*. And what's more, historical reasons alone escape that dangerous question that always haunts all discussions of reasons in love: wouldn't one—shouldn't one—equally love another person who satisfied all of those same reasons? Where the reasons are historical, however, this question doesn't even make sense. It may not be the case that each of us is, as we like to think, unique in any significant way. But the odds of one repeating the history of any substantial relationship are virtually zero, and though one might well create a new substantial history in a second or third love, there are obvious limits —in a way that there are not when we think only of such reasons as virtue, beauty, wit and interests and intelligence—to how many people in the world might share these same attributes and provide us with the same reasons for love.

LOVE AND FANTASY

But love . . . it's only a story one makes up in one's mind about another person, and one knows all the time it isn't true. Of course one knows; why, one's always taking care not to destroy the illusion.

—VIRGINIA WOOLF, *Night and Day*

Falling in love is almost entirely a matter of looking forward, of envisioning the future, of becoming rather than being. The two primary ingredients in falling in love, accordingly, are fantasy and desire. Both look forward, and both involve the lavish use of the imagination. First we fantasize about love, about the (sort of) person we would like to meet; we imagine possibilities and encounters, perhaps using the striking face of some most casual acquaintance as a stand-in but in fact leaving the matter entirely open. Later on, after we've "fallen" or started to fall, we imagine a more concrete but still unrealized future, and abstract possibilities now get replaced with quite specific desires. But desire too —if it is worthy of the name—is a product of the imagination. Sexual desire in particular is as much a matter of fantasy as it is the longings of the body. Indeed, it is hard for us to even imagine the latter without the former.

Sex and fantasy dominate the experience of falling in love, though sex requires fantasy and not all fantasies are sexual. Fantasy is the employment of the unrestrained imagination, and its content is limited only by the power of the imagination itself. The most imaginative people love the best, though no doubt those without imagination can be affectionate and devoted. (Cats and dogs do not and cannot love us, sorry to say, not because they are not affectionate and loyal, but because they can't imagine; they can't tell stories, and they can't formulate fantasies about the future.) It is too often said that love should be "realistic" and tied down to the facts of life, but the fact is that it is the transcendence of dull factual reality that distinguishes love from just another domestic relationship and the elevation of one's lover above the democratic anonymity of real other people that separates passionate devotion from mere respect and objective appreciation. This doesn't mean, of course, that one must fantasize one's lover as a god or goddess or that an ideal fantasy must envision a relationship that is literally in a galaxy of its own. But such simple but elegant fantasies as a hoped-for vacation alone on some Nassau beach or a daydream at the office about the beloved's beautiful eyes are already a trascendence and an enrichment of mundane reality, and it is with such enrichment that love begins—and continues.

Love has an established narrative structure, which makes most of our romantic fantasies quite predictable, at least in outline. The fantasy of future marriage is virtually built into our concept of romantic love, so much so that the absence of any such fantasy (which might well, however, be accompanied by a dozen reservations) is often taken as clear proof that "you don't love me after all." The fantasy of a quiet dinner in a romantic setting, the fantasy of a sex-filled week alone, the fantasy of a supreme test of self-sacrifice and devotion—these are all part and parcel of the fantasy structure we have inherited along with the concept of love itself. But there are always individual variations, due to circumstances and, more romantically, subject to the shared whims and cleverness of lovers. It is fantasy that places two lovers in a "world of their own," and fantasy that adds the magic that distinguishes romance from mere companionship. In fact, whim and individual eccentricity are also part of our romantic heritage, and the ideal lover can be expected to do the unexpected. If the virtue of "realism" is that it prevents disappointment, the virtue of fantasy is that it is unpredictable.

To say that fantasy is the product of the imagination is not to say that it must remain in the imagination. We *live* our fantasies; we express them in action. Sexual desire, for example, is as much a function of the imagination as of the libido, and sexual activity is the imagination as well as the body in action. No matter how "turned on" we may be, we are "enamored" only when we start to imagine, to picture ourselves together, fondling and undressing on the private stage of the imagination. It is impossible to imagine sexual desire without imagination, not just as an immediate consequence but as the content of desire. Fantasy permeates all romantic sexuality and is in many ways more its focus than sex itself.

The role of fantasies in love has been greatly degraded and demeaned through the equation of fantasies with illusions—fantasies opposed to any possible reality or truth—rather than recognizing fantasies as plans, predilections, hopes and desires. Fantasy is contrasted with reality, so that the prognosis for love is not very promising. Roger Scruton recently writes, for example, that "fantasy replaces the real, resistant objective world with a pliant substitute—and that indeed is its purpose. Life in the actual world is difficult and embarrassing. . . . The fantasy blocks the passage to reality, which becomes inaccessible to the will." His conclusion is that fantasy is degrading and necessarily illusory. Indeed, his central example of a sexual fantasy is that of a lover making love and imagining himself making love to *someone else!* But this represents an extremely impoverished notion of romantic fantasy and excludes almost all of what turns sexual desire into something more than mere desire. And what's worse, the literature on fantasy has been invaded and virtually taken over by some appallingly bad imaginative writing on *sexual* fantasies exclusively, in which various authors have competed to see which of them could dream up the most aesthetically or athletically challenging, most perverse, most paradigmatically Freudian or Jungian sexual possibilities. But the truth is that most of our sexual fantasies are romantic fantasies, and few of these require quite the breadth of outrageousness that is required to sell magazines or supermarket-rack books. Fantasy is an extension, an embellishment, an enrichment of reality, not an alternative to it. Fantasy should be opposed only to that dull, practical planning that is too often rationalized as "realism." Love, like music, lives in the imagination, but it is no less real for that.

Our fantasies typically amount to doing the usual sort of thing in the usual way and (usually) with the usual person, and the highlight of the fantasy is probably a look or a gesture that would make a wonderful evening but poor reading. A romantic fantasy may be nothing more than the conjuring up of that one wonderful face, imagining that he or she will, finally, look at me, warmly and invitingly, perhaps say my name, tenderly, or touch my wrist with a gentle significance. A romantic fantasy might be the rehearsal of a simple speech that one would like to deliver, or anticipation of a romantic dinner at a famous restaurant, or simply remembering a dinner last year and imagining another one. And indeed most sexual fantasies are not much more than playing out in one's mind a scene that we've experienced several times before, perhaps with someone new, perhaps with some slight new twist. This is not intended to be kill-joy, but if we are going to stress the importance of fantasies in love, let's not think that this requires anything like imagining a ménage à trois with two strangers on the Lexington Avenue IRT at rush hour. We should note, however, that fantasies can be dangerous, gross and lethal as well as pleasurable. Indeed, it is the danger of some fantasies that produce their pleasure. At least some of the pleasure of falling in love involves facing the danger of rejection and humiliation—and not being rejected or humiliated. Many romantic fantasies fill out the picture but never get put into practice. One might fantasize Leander diving into the Hellespont to prove his love, or Mark Antony falling on his sword for Cleopatra, or Erich von Lichtenstein, who cut off his finger and sent it to his beloved to prove his devotion. In jealousy one might fantasize about Odysseus slaying all of his wife's suitors. Some fantasies are just plain gross: Charlemagne had a woman he loved embalmed and placed her in his bed. And some fantasies are extravagant and require genius: Richard Wagner awakened his wife on her birthday with a full orchestra playing a new piece he had just composed for her.

The fantasies of falling in love reach into the future, and therefore, in one sense, they are never true. Fantasies might be reasonable or not, but reasonability is not a particularly important virtue for romance. The shared fantasy about "someday" living in a castle may be much more effective in tying two people together than the fantasy of redoing the kitchen next year. And *shared* fantasies are almost always more important than individual fantasies, even those that are about the other person. A shared sexual fantasy, whether or not it is workable, can be a wonderful impetus to sexual stimulation and enjoyment, while one person's unrequited fantasy concerning another—even a generally willing other—can be a real turn-off. And whether shared or not, only a fool would suggest that all of our best sexual fantasies *ought* to be played out. Often the fantasy is better than the reality, and certainly much safer. The function of fantasy is to weave two futures together and thereby form a union of two selves. The question of whether the fantasy is realistic or reasonable is not nearly so important as this.

Does this mean that reality has no place in romance? Of course not. But because all fantasies are in some sense false— they portray events that haven't happened yet—they should be viewed not so much in the managerial context of schedules and policies but in the romantic context of imaginative possibilities. Of course if all plans and fantasies come to nothing, it is not just one's sense of reality but one's love that might well come into question. But the point and purpose of fantasy is to enrich and solidify an imaginative life together. Early in love, fantasies project the possibilities of exciting lives together, lives that may share very little in the past. Later in love, fantasies are what we refer to when we say that love is still alive, that it is not just routine, that it still provokes the imagination and inspires hope. Plans are less important than the planning, the life we dream of together no more important than a life of dreaming together.

What are romantic fantasies? The usual view is that fantasies are primarily imagined *events*, singular possibilities in the future, a kiss, an unusual sexual experience, a trip to somewhere exotic. But the most significant romantic fantasies are not isolated incidents but continuing stories, roles in which one casts oneself and would in fact cast oneself in "reality" if only the opportunity presented itself. The fantasy concerns not something happening but a state of being, a new way of life, a transformation rather than a mere occurrence. A woman reports her fantasy of being "swept away," not a single event but a suddenly initiated long sequence of events and, more important, feelings. The very metaphor "swept away" points to the fantasy nature of this image and helps to explain the suspicion with which most people tend to treat it, on the one hand as the epitome of love, on the other as dangerous and degrading. Any fantasy worth more than a daydream or a paragraph is going to be something more than a single imagined encounter. It is substantial fantasy, fantasies about roles and new ways of feeling and existence that guide us through love and live, not the kinky little stories that get made up as examples of "fantasy life."

Fantasies, as an essential part of love, form the glue that holds loving relationships together. Accordingly, the fantasies that count are not the daydreams of a hopeful lover-to-be but the *shared* fantasies of two people in love. But again this is not the usual view of the matter. Popular discussions of fantasy typically focus on the fantasies of people not yet in a relationship or, if they are in a relationship, fantasies about some sexual or romantic encounter outside of the relationship. The fantasies are rarely shared or based on shared experience. This explains why it is that fantasies are so often considered *substitutes* for romance instead of an essential part of it, and it also explains why it is that so many people complain that love never seems to come up to their best fantasies or, to put it more accurately, that their fantasies are such that they seem to be doomed to disappointment in love. But the importance of fantasies, let us repeat it again and again, is that they tie two people together in love. Fantasies that are only thinly veiled self-congratulation, or fantasies that are clearly *impositions* on the other person, are diametrically opposed to this. So, too, the a priori fantasies that go into "Personal" advertisements, and less explicitly into the demands and expectations of those not yet coupled, are often obstacles and barriers against love rather than invitations to love. Their function is to weed out the ineligibles rather than to attract a lover.

Fantasies shared bring two people together. Fantasies merely imposed on the other person tend to drive two people apart. Thus Plato's criticism of Hypothales in *Lysis*, often repeated since, that love is not love of a *real* person but rather of some idealized or fantasized substitute. Freud, too, argued that love is ultimately love of a "phantasm," a fantasized prototype of a parent or other loved one and not at all about the actual person supposedly loved. But this is to confuse some fantasies with fantasy as such. Reality does not live up to fantasy when fantasies are developed in isolation, out of frustration, often with belligerence rather than romance. Fantasies are not opposed to but congruent with reality when their function is not to superimpose unreasonable expectations upon an already bleak romantic social scene but rather to visualize and set up a reasonable framework within which love can develop and grow.

In the absence of a partner, such fantasies can only be imagined alone, and the danger is that their specificity will get in the way of opportunity. ("I couldn't go out with a man who doesn't like Mozart.") With a partner, however, shared fantasies can be as specific and as detailed as one likes, for the function of weaving a sense of the future together is already being fulfilled by the act of fantasizing itself. Fantasy is also congruent with reality in the very special and important sense of "idealization," including what Stendhal famously entitled "crystallization." It is one thing to want or expect that a lover will have certain features—which one's actual lover may not have ("I adore blondes. It's a shame that you're bald"). It is quite another, more positive thing, however, to celebrate the features of an actual lover ("I just adore your nose"). Fantasizing a type always raises the danger of disappointment, but idealizing a particular person is virtually a guarantee against it. Of course one can always change one's mind (the process André Gide calls "decrystallization"), but fantasies can set limits as well as explore possibilities. When one is just "falling in love," fantasy may be all that one has to go on, and while there is a real danger that excessive and unrestricted fantasy can lead to impossible expectations, there is also the less-heralded danger that the inhibition of fantasy—in the name of being "realistic"—may suffocate love and make its development impossible. Later on in a relationship we utilize fantasy to expand and solidify love. But in the beginning it is fantasy that sets the foundation for love.

FROM FALLING TO BEING IN LOVE: THE COORDINATION PROBLEM

In every union there is a mystery.

—AMIEL

One of the great advantages of the initial phase of admiration, attraction and fantasy—in unrequited love too—is that one need not in any way compromise one's opinions by way of "working it out" with the other person. But it is one of the rude shocks of that first date with someone you have admired from afar, or that first night together with one you have long desired, that things do not usually go as planned. Reality doesn't match the fantasies, her fantasies don't conform to his or his to hers. She expected him to be courteous and gentle; he thinks of himself as a man at war with the world. He expected her to be compliant and respectful; she is self-assertive and calls a spade a spade. She opens the door for him, and he is humiliated. He insists on paying the bill for dinner, and she feels patronized. And when two people survive the first date and start to form a relationship, there are even more surprises and compromises ahead of them. Falling in love has the luxury of unrestrained fantasy, but being in love, developing love through the medium of a relationship, faces throughout "the coordination problem."

When love has fully developed, much of what has happened is the meshing of two lives. Emotions have been fitted and complemented—a morally indignant person has learned not to impose on his or her laissez-faire lover; two mild-mannered private people have learned how to express themselves to one another. The emotional coordination may have been there from the start by virtue of similar or reciprocal temperaments, or by virtue of natural selection (anyone who couldn't take it didn't stick around), or, most likely, as the practiced product of many misunderstandings, unintended offenses and misreadings. Schedules have now grown together and habits have intertwined, through years of accommodation or compromise. But, in the beginning, love is always a coordination problem, a matter of two quite different people who do not know one another trying to fit their lives and fantasies together. Living together, of course, involves a thousand adjustments and confrontations, including such cosmic questions as who sleeps on which side of the bed, who does the dishes and which nightly news program to watch. But even a casual dating relationship has more than its share of coordination questions, ranging from a mutual understanding of time (does "Be there at eight o'clock" really mean eight o'clock?) to the recognition of topics better not discussed ("Well, I happen to like George Bush!"). In times of trouble, love may seem like little more than a series of coordination problems, lubricated and made tolerable by ample amounts of sexual affection. But then even sex—especially sex—is itself a coordination problem, and solving that problem (when to touch, when not to, who's on top, when and how to kiss and when not to) is often the first and sometimes a fatal coordination challenge to a budding romantic relationship. It certainly was no easier, however, in those traumatic days when sexual coordination was necessary only after the romance—and perhaps the marriage—were well under way.

Love is often said to be a miracle, but the real mystery of love is how two people from entirely different backgrounds and very different habits and expectations manage to get along so well together. With casual acquaintances or colleagues the rules of courtesy usually suffice to keep us at an acceptable distance and off of each other's toes. But in the intimacy of love—especially new love—the rules of courtesy are stilted and, for the most part, too crude and formalized. There are cultures in which marriage requires formal courtesy—in eighteenth-century England or latter-day Japan for example—and while it is easy to imagine how such formality reduces awkwardness and uncertainty in an arranged marriage or a "marriage of convenience," it also all but eliminates intimacy. We remember how awkward it was simply sharing a room with someone at college. It seems almost impossible to maintain close quarters and coordination when there is no romantic motivation to move us to do so, and romance in many ways makes it harder rather than easier—by increasing closeness several-fold, by raising expectations and vulnerability even more. In nonromantic difficulties, two people either create all the distance that they can between them or resign themselves to a kind of silent truce, doing as little as possible that might interfere with the other. In love, however, two people insist on being as close as possible and, quite the contrary of restraining themselves, feel quite free and even feel the necessity of expressing their needs as explicitly as possible. That, in turn, makes the coordination problem all the more difficult—and more necessary.

All human interactions require coordination, and when one thinks of it, it is remarkable that we are in general so good at it. Imagine, for instance, walking quickly along the street of a big city. Another person is walking directly toward you at an equally fast clip. There are other people walking and running at different rates beside both of you, and there is a curb, a storefront, a light post, a trash receptacle in the way. Neither of you slow down but you walk past without even brushing shoulders—not even a flinch, a wince, or a movement of the eyes. How did you do it? It is clear that you didn't just go on ahead or you would have crashed into each other. It is not evident that either of you made a dramatic move or shift to the side. Unlike the road or the waterway, there are no clear conventions that made both of your reactions automatic. Indeed, the dozen or so calculations made by each of you, on the basis of the very slightest information from the other—a tiny almost invisible shift to the left, perhaps —allowed you both to coordinate the pass. There was not a single decision, no declaration, no demand or orders, just a series of mutual adjustments, with split-second timing.

By way of contrast, we remember "Stooges" Moe and Larry walking toward the narrow doorway. Moe steps back courteously just as Larry does too. Larry steps forward with a smile of gratitude, and Moe does too. They get wedged in the doorjamb. Frustrated and indignant, they push each other away. Moe gestures defiantly to Larry and steps boldly forward. Larry takes a step out of spite, and they are wedged again. Both furious, they stand with arms folded, refusing to move. Disgusted, they both lurch forward, jammed again. Then they both back up, run forward together and literally ram their way through the door, destroying half of the entryway as they do so. This is not unlike many a romantic and marital squabble. It begins with a simple mutual desire aided by courtesy and turns into a furious, frustrating and mutually destructive battle of wills.

A couple making love, especially for the first time, endures a gamut of coordination problems whose frustration is only partially excused or compensated by excitement. Issuing directives —one solution to any coordination problem—just isn't (or shouldn't be) done. That would reduce intimacy to an engineering project ("Now you move up a little, and I'll slide over") and breaks the spontaneous equality that such a situation demands. While we rarely take the time to observe, every caress and movement is the result of countless small gestures, felt rather than seen and perhaps not even noticed. "Good" lovemaking is far more a matter of attention and coordination than it is of strength or stamina, and we can all remember with that quaint mixture of amusement and humiliation our "first time," when we didn't know the signals and, despite the best of intentions, had to depend on the ineluctable directions of nature to complete what was certainly an awkward set of circumstances.

Coordination problems are, for the most part, not matters of confrontation or compromise but the no-less-difficult attempts to satisfy mutual desires. Indeed, confrontations and compromises are often more easily satisfied just because they can be made explicit and solved by negotiation. But the sorts of little kindnesses and courtesies that make love work are best left unspoken and unplanned, and negotiation—as any couple that has faced the politics of the kitchen (much less the bedroom) knows all too well—can too easily reduce romance to a business partnership. Also, it has been argued by many sociologists that love is essentially an arrangement for mutual approval and admiration, but we can readily appreciate that such an arrangement can hardly be made explicit. "I want you to say that I'm attractive, but without my asking you to do it, and in return I'll tell you again how wonderful you are, but don't you dare ask me to do so."

Falling in love is particularly prone to such quandaries of coordination. One is not quite sure what to say or when to say it, but at the same time one can imagine later hearing the lament "Why didn't you tell me that before?" Coordinating time schedules is routine compared with coordinating emotional schedules; how often is too often, and when is it not enough? One cannot simply ask, but both people recognize the importance of getting —guessing—it right. The coordination of gestures is particularly difficult. A man gives his love a little pat on the buttocks; she isn't sure whether he has just expressed adoration, dominance, sexual desire, disrespect or anger. Or perhaps he is just "being cute." Maybe he's trying to make her mad. Perhaps he's still stupid enough to think that such gestures are flattering, or worse, exciting. But she cannot ask, and in all likelihood he knows no more than she does. Earlier that evening she had mentioned out loud among friends that he had driven the car up the sidewalk and had missed the driveway. They laughed. He slightly sulked, for he did not know whether he had been attacked or teased, abused as a joke or treated with endearment as an absentminded but lovable lout. Ambiguity is a major part of the romantic coordination problem; multiply the above example by a few thousand evenings or so, and you have a partial portrait of a marriage.

The coordination problem is nowhere more evident than in our use of language. We like to think that the meaning of what we say is already evident and unmistakably embodied in the words themselves, that the words mean just what we mean and what we mean is what we say. But even the simplest greeting, "How are you?" is bound by context and prone to abuse—a forty-minute reply describing the details of a recent gall bladder operation, for example. Every utterance involves a whole series of reflected intentions, even a "hello." But just think of the myriad requirements that surround the use of "I love you." Learning what to say and when to say it—and when not to say anything at all—is an essential part of the coordination problem. We sometimes think of intimacy and "openness" as the ability to say anything that we feel exactly when we feel it. But the truth is that the difference between being in love and seeing a therapist consists mainly in our concern for the effects of what we say on a lover and a relationship rather than a concern for the catharsis that may be enjoyed in the saying of it. In the days of courtly love it was sometimes said that love is largely language, and though this may be exaggerated, it does capture a distinctive element of romance that is often ignored in our emphasis on inner feelings. Love is the articulation and verbal formation of feelings, not the feelings themselves, and the reciprocity of love is not so much the simultaneous beating of two hearts (and other anatomical synchronisms) as it is the mutual coordination of expression. The beating of hearts may be "natural," but the co-ordination of language is an art.

The coordination problem involves the matching of desires, emotions, habits, moods, a sense of time, a sense of space, the use of language, the use of sex, and, indeed, almost every one of the details of a life and an identity together. But perhaps one illustration will bring into focus the centrality and subtlety of the coordination problem in an area that is rarely even noticed in love but, at the same time, is obviously one of its dominant features. I call it the problem of "sleeping together," but I do not here have sex in mind.

SLEEPING TOGETHER: SNUGGLERS AND SOLIPSISTS

There are two kinds of women: those who move to make room when you sit on the bed and those who remain where they are even when you have only a narrow edge.

—EDMUND WILSON, *Diary*, 1955

Isn't it odd that one of the most common acceptable euphe-misms for having sex is "sleeping together"—when there is prob-ably no activity so antithetical (though it may be eventually conducive) to sleep. And yet where it is love and intimacy that concern us, how a couple sleeps together may have more to do with the success of a relationship than the joy of sex, for sexual enthusiasm may wane but the need for a good night's sleep goes on forever. Sleeping together, as most of us know, can be some-thing of a challenge—or an accomplishment. A sensuous evening of sex can be more than undone by the too familiar incompatibility when sleep is the concern. One cuddles; the other won't. One rolls over; the other complains, or grunts (same thing) or leaves for the safety of the sofa. One wakes up early, ready to leap into action. The other prefers to sleep late, taking full advantage of the already warmed bed and blanket. Indeed, modern couples who are unintimidated and undaunted by sex fearfully avoid the dangers and humiliations threatened by a night together. One arranges to leave, complaining that he or she has to get up very early the next morning—to go to work, to catch a plane, to catch up on work, to—it doesn't much matter. On the other hand, one might even suggest that sleeping together, not sex together, is the natural medium for intimacy. And sleeping together—or rather, not sleeping together—is the more prominent source of antagonism and disaster.

Sleeping together, like love itself, says a lot about one's identity and how one "fits"—quite literally here—with another. Experience seems to show that there are two basic types—although perhaps the more imaginative or more experienced could uncover a half dozen more. There are *snugglers* and there are *solipsists*. Snugglers relish the presence of another warm body. There are passive snugglers—who crave to be held, and active snugglers—who enjoy holding but resist being held, but most snugglers are both active and passive, or indifferent to the distinction. It is enough for them that the other is present, warm and cuddly. Snugglers can tolerate or adjust to a remarkable amount of rolling, stretching, jerking, groaning, squeezing and even smacking. Even in their sleep, they recognize this as a small price to pay for love, warmth and comfort. *Solipsists*, on the other hand, can stay awake all night because of a fly in the room. The dog on the rug is okay, so long as he doesn't snort, wag or move. The cat who tries to leap on the bed is soon thrown out of the room—or the house. Solipsists may love sex, and during the sexual act they may hug hard, throw themselves into it and allow themselves to be "swept away." They may be sociable. But, deep down, they want to be alone. They may even describe themselves as loners. One should never be surprised, after a short affair with a passionate lover who nevertheless has great trouble sleeping, to hear that he or she "needs space." (We have developed all sorts of fancy ideologies and metaphysics to explain this phrase.) Some people want the chance to sleep around, others the opportunity to explore new talents and try out new activities. The truth may be that solipsists just want to sleep and wake up alone.

Both snugglers and solipsists will complain rather quickly that their sleeping habits do not betray their real personalities. Solipsists will point out that one might like to sleep alone but nevertheless love intimacy and snuggling. Snugglers will insist that they are in fact quite independent and do not need to hold on to or be held on to in order to feel perfectly at home with themselves. I don't believe it. One is never more at home than in sleep, never more oneself, never more free—as the philosopher Jean-Jacques Rousseau used to fantasize—from the artifices, expectations and conventions of society. In sleep we are free, not free to do anything that is productive, perhaps, but free if also compelled to insist on the basics of independence and dependency. These are the basic ingredients of the self—as G. W. F. Hegel pointed out years ago, as Freudians (in different terms) have argued too. In sleep we betray our fundamentals—the need to be alone, the need to be held. We should not be surprised or offended here when a Freudian tells us that we carry these attitudes from infancy, and much has to do with how and how much we were held or not held in that crucial first year of life. This is flimsy evidence for the Oedipus complex, but in sleep there can be no question.

Whatever the multitude of bad arguments about love and sex and regression to childhood, the obvious truth is that if we ever regress it is when we sleep, and sleeping together, like sleeping alone, is primal. One might well need sex for any number of reasons—because it is socially expected, for encouragement, for the challenge, because it is maximal hedonism, or power, or a way of killing time. But we all need sleep, and how one sleeps is not an expression of that need but an insistence on the conditions that foster sleep—the security of another hugging body or the isolated safety of sleeping alone.

Two snugglers together is the very portrait of bliss, the sort of mawkish scene that became a standard for nineteenth-century academic romantic painting. This is true even of two uncompromising active snugglers, whose competition for mutual holding may be as active and as satisfying as their sexual snuggling some hours before. (There may be a temporary problem with two passive snugglers, but they quickly realize that their need to be in an embrace is much more pressing than their preference for being embraced.) Two solipsists can well survive, but preferably in a king-size bed. There may be nagging doubts at first, for instance, about when it is permissible to break away from the embrace and set out across the bed on one's own, and there is always the danger that whoever does so first may offend the other —even though he or she is also a solipsist. Feeling neglected is always the ironic bane of the solipsist—even if, in a sense, he or she prefers it.

The real tragedy or farce begins when a snuggler and a solipsist come together. The embrace during sex does not betray the secret nor give any evidence of the deep incompatibility between them, and the warm comforts of sex do little to give it away. There is no moment of truth, but rather a slow unraveling of illusion, starting perhaps in the exhaustion that follows, but more likely remaining dormant (so to speak) during an initial and most misleading round of sleep, that fifteen minutes to an hour that is the most sound and satisfying sleep of all. It begins when one—the snuggler—reaches around and embraces the other and is rebuffed, at first gently perhaps, but soon with sleepy resentment. Or it begins when one—the solipsist—rolls over and turns away, leaving the snuggler caressing the air and feeling rejected, worrying about being found repulsive. Needless to say, the one thing leads to another, but rarely to sleep. The snuggler tries another embrace; the solipsist mutters and pulls away. The snuggler, confused, wonders what has gone wrong. The solipsist, now beyond the realm of rest and relaxation, may get up and go to the next room—"to think," to drink, but really just to be alone and conclude, angrily, that this person is just too possessive to consider. A self-confident snuggler will then go to sleep, having chalked off the relationship as "too weird" to be followed through. A less secure snuggler may well lie awake, plagued with self-doubts, hugging the pillow (or both pillows), to sleep. And since we rarely think of sleep as a romantic issue, the idea of an honest confrontation doesn't even arise. We have all become artfully articulate about sex as an issue, but we have little practice or even vocabulary to talk about the intimacies of sleep. As a consequence, more couples hit the skids their first night together because of sleeplessness than sexual mal-performance. One can excuse and talk about clumsiness or lack of coordination; there is no apology appropriate for in-compatible sleep.

To make matters all the more complicated, however, one and the same person can be both a solipsist and a snuggler—at different times, with different partners. This is why sleeping together is so relevant to love. A confirmed solipsist may become a wanton snuggler when he or she is sufficiently in love, and there is no more magnificent transformation in the world (as long as the partner is a snuggler or a fellow solipsist-turned-snuggler). The many metaphors of lights and fireworks that have been employed to dramatize and poeticize love are nothing compared to the quiet, warm comfort of a converted solipsist. And when two former solipsists find themselves snoring joyfully in each other's arms through the night, that is indicative of love indeed.

LOVING AND IN LOVE

That expression of "violently in love" is so hackneyed, so doubtful, so indefinite, that it gives me very little idea. It is as often applied to feelings which arise from a half-hour's acquaintance, as to a real, strong, attachment.

—MRS. GARDINER, in Jane Austen's
Pride and Prejudice

Our language of love is sufficiently impoverished that we are often at a loss to describe the difference between kinds of affection and, in particular, between those forms of falling in love that are indeed the beginnings of love and those which are mere imitations, similar in intensity, perhaps, but hardly even candidates for serious, ongoing passion. Among the clumsy distinctions that we make concerning love, none is more crucial than that between "loving someone" and "being in love." It is a distinction that is too often used to mark the division between affection and infatuation, between really loving and just falling in love. The distinction is also used to separate friendship and passion, respectively, but it is too often used to demean one or the other. A standard way of softly rejecting a declaration of love is "Yes, I do love you, but I'm not 'in love' with you." "Loving" gets regarded as a limp or lukewarm passion, more desirable than nothing but hardly sufficient to motivate sex or a relationship. Or being "in love" is treated as a temporary aberration, a form of transient insanity, and therapists tell their patients how to get rid of it. Plato talked about the pathology of being "in love" in his dialogue *Lysis*, in which the noble statesman Hypothales becomes hopelessly enamored with the beautiful but dull youth Lysis and makes quite a fool of himself. Being "in love" is often conflated with infatuation, and Plato's diagnosis, essentially, is that Hypothales fails to recognize anything about Lysis. What he loves is a phantom of his own creation, and so he does not in fact love Lysis at all, but rather himself. Freud developed a similar view of obsessive love as love that is essentially narcissistic, with little or no relation to the actual other person or to reality in general. Thus being "in love" gets reduced to pathology, while "loving" is rendered bland and uninteresting.

The first thing to say about loving and being in love, therefore, must be that they are both desirable and legitimate and not so easily distinguished as it would seem. They are different and serve different functions in life, but the difference between them is not blandness versus passion and neither is pathological as such. Of course either can become pathological—as can the extreme form of any legitimate emotion (grief or anger, for instance). And both are passionate—though passion can take many different forms, calm as well as violent. Neither pathology nor passion is the difference between loving and being in love, so what is the difference? One familiar way of making out the distinction is in terms of time. Being "in love" is described as transient and merely a matter of hormones, while loving is durable and "forever." But this makes it a mystery how a couple could still be "in love" even after decades, and it raises the unflattering possibility that loving survives only because it is already stale and does not change. It is sometimes said that being "in love" is an obsession, but loving can be as obsessive as being "in love" and being "in love" can be treated as something of a lark. And what is wrong with an obsession if it is sufficiently ennobling and magnificent, one of those grand passions that, on occasion, can make the whole of life worthwhile?

The truth is that the differences between loving and in love may be more of source, situation and expression than of emotional structure. They are differences that have nothing to do with durability or, for that matter, intensity, but it is easy to see how these differences can produce differences in durability and intensity. To begin with, we might note that "to love" is an active verb—it is something that one *does*, where the phrase "in love" rather points to a situation or a quandary in which we find ourselves. Loving straightforwardly requires the involvement of the other person, whereas being "in love" typically suggests a one-way activity that may take place even if the beloved in question is completely ignorant of the passion. (Thus Plato in *Lysis* points out that the beloved may even despise the lover who is "in love" with him.) Being "in love" can be painfully unrequited, but loving seems to be content with the other's happiness (as in the idealized love of a parent for a child) without excessive concern about reciprocity. In other words, "in love" is taken to refer to a state of passion, while loving refers to an established relationship. Accordingly, being "in love" is often characterized as a desperate reaching, whereas loving is calm and comfortable. Being "in love" is Stendhal's "passion-love"—the only love that he thinks counts for anything. "Loving," on the other hand, is too often presented as something bland, mere companionship plus regard and affection, or as selfless devotion, indifferent to reciprocity. In truth, it is loving that is the ultimate passion, not obsessed with but wrapped up in reciprocity.

Because the distinction between loving and being "in love" has too often been exaggerated and employed for polemical purposes, the dynamics of the difference have too often been neglected. The difference is first of all a difference in our experience of love; the two "feel" different (which is not just to say that the difference is one of divergent feelings). It is not that being in love is necessarily more intense or more passionate than loving, but it is an experience of being more passive, open, even helpless, while the experience of loving is much more of a feeling of being in control. But feelings are often misleading; what they represent may be very different from what they show. For example, while being in love typically feels like a passive experience, the truth is that in love one renders oneself passive. The function of this "softening" is not hard to discern. Especially in the initial stages of love, it is of vital importance to open oneself up to the other, to soften one's harder edges, to allow oneself to adjust to the needs and interests of the other and, of equal importance, to invite and allow the other to more easily complement our own perhaps eccentric contours. Much of the seemingly silly behavior that expresses or accompanies love— talking baby talk, assuming childlike postures and caresses—can be understood as tested techniques for reducing friction and resistance. The feelings that accompany these behaviors seem like passivity, but they are active and purposive nonetheless. But we can appreciate how it is that, although such behavior and feelings are particularly appropriate and necessary at the beginning of love, they are fully appropriate and may be necessary throughout the duration of a relationship. Two feisty, difficult, argumentative people manage to love and live together for a lifetime by softening their responses to each other, and they remain "in love" just on the basis of this behavior—with appropriately soft and seemingly passive feelings. Loving, on the other hand, may be more the assumption of control than its actuality. It may resemble something of a Stoic posture in love, an acceptance of "come what may." But this is hardly "control," and loving accordingly can become just as passionate, indeed, just as desperate, as being in love.

On the other hand, being in love is sometimes treated as the active emotion; loving is taken to be more of a spectator's emotion, love at a distance. But love as we are considering it is not a spectator or a philanthropic emotion; it is an emotion that hopes, expects and even demands something in return, an emotion that is part of or at least looks forward to a relationship, not a solipsistic fantasy. With that in mind, let us insist that loving should be understood as a function of a relationship and therefore inseparable from it. Being "in love" is more tentative; it may be new and enthusiastic love looking forward to a relationship. It may already be based in a relationship, but in either case it remains

unsure or, at least, well aware of the contingency of any relationship. It is this sense of contingency, even anxiety, that produces
the characteristic feelings of being in love, but it is the sense of
contingency, not the feelings as such, that is primary. Loving,
too, has its characteristic feelings (of warmth and affection, of
care and desire) but here the relationship is primary and the
emotion is secondary—which is emphatically not to say that it is
any less intense or devoted, even obsessive. Accordingly, friendship will be a key ingredient in loving, perhaps even its criterion.
Being "in love," on the other hand, is often contrasted with
friendship. It affirms passion as primary and sees a relationship
as its vehicle for realization and fulfillment. This is not to say
that the relationship is unimportant; indeed, a powerful passion
may come to see the success of the relationship as the most
important thing in life. But being "in love" is possible even "at
first sight," in a few moments after a brief meeting, before anything even vaguely resembling a relationship has had a chance
to develop. Loving, on the other hand, presupposes a relationship already in progress and is almost inseparable from it. After
some time—perhaps months or years, certainly decades—loving
and being "in love" are indistinguishable, except to make a point.
To say that two people are still "in love" with one another after
many years is just a way of saying that they still really love,
respect and desire one another. What gives the word a bad name,
unfortunately, is all of those couples who feel entitled to the
word "love" just because the relationship has endured—whatever the passion or lack of it.

Because being "in love"—unlike loving—does not presuppose
a relationship, or, for that matter, actual reciprocity, it is reasonable to suppose that it is more self-involved than loving. Even if
we do not think of that pure loving known as "agape"—which is
selfless concern only for the other—one's energy and attention
in loving must be aimed at awareness of the other and his or her
interests and concerns (including, of course, his or her interest

and concern in oneself). Being "in love" on the other hand often finds itself much more caught up in self-evaluation and fantasy —though, again, one should not leap from this to the false conclusion that loving is devoid of self-reflection and fantasy and consequently bland and unromantic whereas being "in love" alone is exciting and romantic. (This is a more reasonable version of the objection to Stendhal that the Spanish philosopher Ortega y Gasset pursued some years ago.) So, too, sexuality in being "in love" tends to be not more intense but more ambitious, for it becomes the medium for tying passion into a relationship, for fostering pleasure and dependency, for reaching into the deepest recesses of a person's selfhood and literally "grasping" them to oneself. Sexuality in loving may be just as thrilling and intense but it has less to prove. It is an expression of love. It does not have to be one of the instruments of its creation.

It is often said that one can love many people but can only be "in love" with one. This bit of dubious folk wisdom should be contrasted by the opposing (equally dubious) dictum, that one can be "in love" with quite a few people—serially within a short period if not exactly at the same time—but only truly love once (or at any rate rarely) in a lifetime. We can see how one might make sense of both of these with our theory. Because loving admits of so many degrees and variations, it is clear that one not only can but virtually must love several if not many people at once, good friends, cherished colleagues and family members as well as one's lover. One also loves old lovers—at least some of them—whose former intimacy has left and perhaps still leaves an indelible mark on one's life. And yet the romantic ideal is certainly that one *really* loves only one's lover, perhaps even for one's entire adult lifetime. There is no doubt that this is how we think of love and loving, but there is no logical reason why this should have to be so. It unifies life instead of dividing it into distinct chapters. It focuses love without distraction. And then there are the formidable obstacles of possessiveness and jealousy that are part of almost all love, which when threatened by multiplicity or the possibility of being replaced can be vicious indeed. So, love tends to exclusivity, "I love you" becomes something of a contract and "I have to tell you that I'm in love with Blake" is at the same time the implicit message "I don't love you anymore." Loving is a passion that, at the lower-frequency end of the spectrum, can be generously shared, but at its heights it is— like the most desperate being "in love"—reserved pretty much for one lover and one lover alone.

Being "in love," on the other hand, tends to be exclusive by default; its usual intensity and insistence on forming a relationship leaves little or no room for anyone else. But if this fails—or if one soon decides that he or she was wrong about the possibility or the desirability of developing a relationship—the doors are open to consider another candidate, and in periods of intense searching there may well be a new candidate—and a new experience of "falling in love"—virtually every week. There is nothing wrong or hypocritical about this (nor need we too quickly conclude that these are all only infatuations) as long as we remain convinced that the expected and hoped-for end of this peculiar emotional auditioning process is in fact a relationship. The duration of the process and precise number of "fallings" are not the critical question but rather the intent. If we come to suspect that the audition is everything and there is no intention to develop mutual interest into something more, then we can start talking about pathology, hypocrisy and worse. It is for this reason that seducers and "mashers" and other disreputable types (women as well as men) find the words "in love" so convenient; "I'm in love with you" suggests only the moment (or less), with not even a promissory note attached. The magic words "I love you," on the other hand, point boldly into the future, and consequently can be betrayed. "I'm in love" is at most a prognosis; it can turn out to be wrong, but it is not easily demonstrated to have been false. ("Well, I did feel it at the time.") What is more, being "in love" is never innocent, as loving may be, and it is quite clearly possessive—thus justifying some possibly vile manipulative behavior. In *Lysis*, Plato insists that love is not a state of mind but an acquisition. That is an image of being "in love" that is quite a good corrective to the overly romanticized version we get from Stendhal and some romantics.

There is a sense in which being "in love" is always desirable, even as a complement to the most secure and comfortable loving. Being "in love" is always a reaching, even when two people are already long together. This might sound as if being "in love" undesirably introduces a certain distance into a relationship, and a certain amount of insecurity. But in different and less ominous terms, being "in love" may just be not taking one another for granted, always recognizing the other as an independent person to be won over and not assumed. The introduction of a distance, and a modicum of insecurity, is thus in this sense a very positive thing; it keeps a relationship dynamic, always changing and growing. Being in love adds the delight of consciousness to the caring and affection of loving.

There are many other consequent differences, needless to say, in the fact that loving presupposes, while being "in love" only looks forward to, an established relationship. Loving, because it is established, tends to be practical, calm, unassuming—which is not to say tedious, dispassionate or indifferent. Loving presumes a stable, working, healthy relationship—a solid friendship —and so it builds confidence in the future and a sense of one's own health, stability and autonomy even as he or she devotes all time and energy to the other. Being "in love," on the other hand, tends to be anxious and preoccupied and, consequently, impractical, even foolish or self-destructive. Fantasy is its main ingredient, where loving has the much more solid basis in friendship. Being "in love" always seems momentary—filling the moment— even if it should in fact last a lifetime. Being "in love" typically involves the experience of desperation, of being "swept away."

In return it is more often exhilarating and thrilling than loving, which tends to be more content with happiness. But these are not alternatives; they are both an essential part of love. We tend to be "in love" at the beginning of love, and we may remain so indefinitely as long as love remains an ideal and a challenge as well as the loving comfort of an established relationship. In other words, we can have the security of loving and the excitement of being in love long after the "falling" phase has ended, but to see how this is so we must understand much more about the essential nature and dynamics of love.

4

· ·

THE SELF IN LOVE

O Romeo, Romeo! Wherefore art thou Romeo?
Deny thy father, and refuse thy name;
Or, if thou wilt not, be but sworn my love,
And I'll no longer be a Capulet.

—SHAKESPEARE, *Romeo and Juliet*

Romeo and Juliet Montague recently celebrated their fourteenth anniversary, a quiet dinner at home, no banquet, no family invited. The two children stayed the night at Benvolio's house. Romeo intends to take the next morning off. He is now an electrician specializing in computer repairs, working by and for himself. Juliet is working on a bachelor's degree in accounting with an eye on law school, having spent much of the past dozen years raising two rambunctious boys, teaching them Shakespearean English and depriving them of those dangerous rubber-tipped play swords. Romeo and Juliet, we are happy to report, are still very much in love.

According to an earlier version of their story, a series of tragic misunderstandings ended their teenage marriage. But thanks to the last-minute intervention of the Northern Italian Teenage Suicide Prevention Unit, they foiled the plot set out for them and, after an angry farewell to their families and a trip around the Mediterranean, settled down in a modest suburb of Verona, Wisconsin. She no longer thinks of herself as a Capulet, and he, despite his retention of the name, no longer thinks of himself as a Montague. Those strong kinship ties tended to be an obstacle to what they later learned to call "self-actualization," though neither of them knew at the time that they were part of a movement with its headquarters on the coast of California. What they did know was that their identities as members of feuding families was embarrassing and stultifying. They were tired of having their friendships circumscribed by neighborhood alliances.

Romeo and Juliet fell "madly" in love. That is to say, they used their love to break the bonds of socially acceptable and "rational" behavior and define themselves anew—in terms of and with the support of each other. An unromantic sociologist might call it "adolescent rebellion," but this would suggest that breaking social bonds is no more than a "phase," the sole province of the young and restless. This also completely leaves out the positive part of the process by which new bonds are forged and a new identity is created. By falling in love, Romeo and Juliet redefined their lives and themselves. They were no longer a Montague and Capulet for whom family obligations were primary. They were lovers who identified themselves and their obligations only with reference to one another. The old Romeo was no more; in his place was the lover and beloved of Juliet. The old Juliet was a memory in the convent; the new Juliet defined herself by Romeo's touch and gaze. Years ago they had proclaimed in their childish enthusiasm that their souls were inseparable; now that was literally true, for neither could imagine him or herself without the other.

Romeo *and* Juliet: can we even consider the names separated? They define each other. Neither exists without the other. Of course one might object that they are merely invented characters in a work of fiction and exist as nothing but the lines given to them as lovers. But the truth is that love provides a similar if less poetic script for all of us. The tragedy of Shakespeare's lovers is not that they did not exist but rather that they had a chance only to peek at love. Indeed, our own fear of understanding what really happens in love—once past that intoxicating enthusiasm that Romeo and Juliet only tasted—is such that we have elevated their truncated tragedy into a paradigm of romantic love itself, just so that we need to look no further.

What is intriguing about our Romeo and Juliet is the fact that they survived and their love survived too. It is no longer enough, however, to palpitate in the garden and address each other in plaintive pentameter. Neither, we should quickly insist, have they allowed their lives to be wholly taken up with domestic routines and duties. They know that—whatever else they may be in life—they are first of all Romeo *and* Juliet, and that is the essence of their love. They think of themselves first in terms of each other. They not only care about each other and desire one another; they share a life, a self together. They, too, can no longer think of a Romeo without a Juliet, or a Juliet without a Romeo, not because of Shakespeare but because of love.

Love is shared identity. And what this means is not just that Romeo and Juliet think of themselves primarily in terms of each other. At the same time, however, they each need some time alone, and their periodic fights attest not only to their lack of complete agreement but even more to their continuing need to establish boundaries, to mark off certain areas of privacy and concern, even from each other. But their overwhelming impulse is to push themselves closer together, to share each other's life and mind and body. They occasionally whisper to one another, in the act of love, that they can no longer tell where one flesh ends and the other begins, can no longer be sure whose gasp of pleasure belongs to whom, for all flesh and pleasures are shared. So, too, they can no longer remember—nor do they care—who it was who first conceived the idea that Juliet would be a fine lawyer, for that ambition is equally both of theirs, even if it is Juliet alone (more or less) who will have to struggle with torts and procedures. They do not doubt that their heavy time commitments will cause some added tension, and they have already talked about the problems that could arise when her income exceeds his. For as long as they have been together, neither Juliet nor Romeo has a conversation without wishing that the other were there, if only to listen, and there is no doubt that Romeo will learn as much law as he can, if only to understand what she is talking about. That is what shared identity means— not a loss of individual identity but a redefinition of personal identity in terms of the other person. Once the love of Romeo and Juliet had been desperation, hoping for even a moment together. Now, spending their lives together, there is no longer desperation but it is no less love for that.

THE IDENTITY THEORY OF LOVE

I *am* Heathcliff—he's always, always in my mind—not as a pleasure, any more than I am always a pleasure to myself—but as my own being.

—C A T H Y , in Emily Brontë's
Wuthering Heights

The key to lasting love is the concept of the self. Nothing else provides the solid bond that makes love endure, that allows love to weather calamity and crisis, that carries it through frustrating or infuriating periods of sexual disinterest, self-obsession, mutual anger or disappointment, distance and the wrenching pressures of separate, demanding careers. Nor will the much-touted emphasis on "commitment" provide such a bond; indeed, commitment enters in precisely when that bond will not hold, when some extra effort is needed to hold a relationship together and love is no longer sufficient. Love endures because love creates a conceptual bond that is something more steadfast than sexual exhilaration, mutual concern, companionship, admiration, intimacy and dreams. The durable core of love is a set of ideas, a very specific and well-focused way of conceiving of the world, oneself and one's lover. In love one views the world in terms of a single intimacy and sees one's self—no matter how successful and otherwise fulfilled—as something incomplete, in need of the lover who is similarly incomplete and needful. Love is, as Aristophanes tells us in the *Symposium*, an attempt to create for ourselves a sense of wholeness or completion through a union— of both body and soul—with another person. That whole, unlike the fragmented halves, has a solid integrity, and the love is so powerful because it promises that durable wholeness. We can forget about Aristophanes's whimsical tale about double androgynous creatures with two heads, four arms and four legs with twice our intelligence, arrogance and hubris. It is enough that we take his metaphor to heart and think about the idea that "ever since" we have been running around in this frenzy, trying to recapture our other halves. Love, in other words, is the attempt to find another person who will give us a sense of our "true" selves and make us feel complete, once and for all.

What is philosophically profound about Aristophanes's story is the idea that love is not just companionship or desire but the desperate effort to recapture something that is already ours but yet not ours, something that already defines the self but nevertheless seems elusive. As opposed to Socrates's classic view, also developed in the *Symposium,* which takes total self-sufficiency as the ideal and the love of abstract universals as the true meaning of love, Aristophanes recognizes that no one can be self-sufficient or complete alone and that love must be the concrete and detailed love of a particular individual who is in some sense literally one's other half. Thus where Socrates seems to believe that sexual desire drops out of the picture with true love, Aristophanes recognizes that sexual love is inescapable. No matter how ethereal and ideal the love, sexual union has its essential place just because we are physical beings and no sense of union —no matter how spiritual—can be intelligible without it. Our sexuality is not a specific desire so much as it is part of our basic bodily being—the way we comport ourselves, the way we move and the way we feel as well as the way we sense ourselves with others. Sexuality, like the self, is too often conceived as self-contained, something private and personal that a person *has* instead of a constant, pervasive bodily reaching out toward others, a sense of physical incompleteness. This is part of that "infinite yearning" of love that includes the desire for physical union but always goes beyond it too. It is a familiar part of our most beautiful sexual experiences—not just the brief sense of complete union but also that raging sense of not being close enough, not yet being truly merged as one. What we really want—as Aristophanes suggests we would ask of Hephaestus, the black-smith of the gods—is to be welded together forever, body and soul.

The "identity theory" of love insists that this is indeed the nature and the purpose of love: to seek and establish a shared identity with another person, which may involve a drastic revision of both one's sense of oneself and each other. Because our most basic concepts of ourselves are at issue, much of the expression and development of love takes place where we are most vulnerable, most naked, most self-concerned. Thus the tight and often dramatic linkage of romantic love with sex and self-esteem, not because love is nothing but sublimated sexual desire (as many have argued) and not because love makes us so vulnerable (it can also make one feel invulnerable) but because love essentially provides our most basic sense of self-identity. It is a sense that precedes and takes precedence over notions of public success and social status and all of those other grand goals that, at least occasionally, move us to ask whether or not "it is all worth the trouble." In moments of despair, such a question may be aimed at love, too, but the query never catches because we know that lasting love is clearly worth the trouble. It has come to define who we really are.

The images of "merging," "union" and "fusion" have been a part of the love literature ever since the *Symposium*. They played a central role in the descriptions of courtly love in the late Middle Ages and are still an important part of post-Freudian accounts of love, as in Erich Fromm and Willard Gaylin. The problem is that these images of unity remain metaphorical. They are perhaps an apt description of a certain vague experience we enjoy when in love, and they clearly point toward something that, if literally true, would be striking and important indeed. But as a metaphor, what does it mean to say that two people "merge"? Physical union, even if it were not transient, would

surely not be sufficient. Two minds can merge, at least temporarily, in the sense that they can get locked together in intense
conversation or, a very different interpretation, they can agree
about so much that they are, in a familiar sense, "of one mind."
But intense conversation as such is not love, nor is agreement.
And in our normal way of thinking about things, each of us has
his or her own mind and the idea of two minds being shared
makes no more sense than the idea of 1 plus 1 equalling 1. One
can talk metaphysically, perhaps, about the merging of two
souls, but this is to explain the metaphorical in terms of the
obscure, for it is by no means clear what constitutes a single soul
and even less clear what it would be for souls to mingle much
less merge. So what is it for two selves to merge that is something
more than physical intercourse, intense conversation, shared interests and opinions and some symbolic sense of two souls having
come together? The answer is that selves (and, perhaps, souls)
are not in fact so individual after all. Our selves are underdetermined by the facts about us—our appearance, our physical and
mental abilities, our past history of accomplishments—and they
are mutually rather than individually defined, defined with and
through others. So conceived, the idea of sharing selves is not so
implausible. To this we should add that our selves are constituted mainly out of emotions rather than of what we *think* of
ourselves, and that the roles we play are far more important to
the identity of our selves than any fixed "inner" truth about the
individual. It is a strange distortion of Western thinking that has
made the private, reflective self primary instead of the active,
passionate self, and the shared identity of love is often misunderstood just because of this overly rational, overly "inner" view of
the self. Love is the concentration and the intensive focus of
mutual definition on a single individual, subjecting virtually
every personal aspect of one's self to this process.

Every aspect of this merging of selves must be balanced by the
fact that we are, before we fall in love, different from one an-

other—different individuals with different backgrounds, our own eccentricities, a history of other romances, catastrophies, crushes and frustrations. We were not originally halves of some primordial creature. Our "edges" do not fit together so neatly as two torn halves of a stick of wood or a broken plate. The smoother the fit, in fact, the less the passion may be, while the most intense love affairs may well be those whose fit is most difficult, even impossible. Thus passion is often the enemy of lasting love, not because love and passion are antithetical as such but because passion often represents the degree of implausibility of love. And in virtually every case the fit is a matter of compromise and adjustment, always imperfect, and so it lacks the absolute integrity that Aristophanes promises us. In other words, the ideal of shared identity gives us only half of the story. Love desires nothing more passionately than union with one's lover, but the presupposition of this desire is precisely that concept of individual existence that makes such a complete union impossible. Thus Irving Singer, in his monumental three-volume study *The Nature of Love*, rejects the "idealistic" concept of merging that played such an enormous role in medieval theories and nineteenth-century conceptions of love. He argues, rightly I believe, that the notion is indeed idealistic and impossible and neglects the importance of individuality in the conceptualization of love. This dialectical tension between union and individuality is what we earlier (Chapter 1) called "the paradox of love," and it must be taken very seriously. Individuality is the presupposition of love, but love itself is the desire to overcome that same individuality. It is the merging of two selves that makes love last, but those two selves are always to a large extent preformed and consequently ill-fitting, and it is this individuality, the difficulty we have in fitting together, that threatens even the most passionate and devoted love. Love is the dialectical tension between individual independence and autonomy on the one hand and the ideal of shared identity on the other. But before we try to tackle this paradox we have to understand what is literally true about love as shared identity. "Merging" and "union" are not just metaphors but deep insights into the nature of the self and the transformation of the self in love.

THE INDETERMINACY
OF THE SELF

I am not what I am, and I am what I am not.

—JEAN-PAUL SARTRE,
Being and Nothingness

The late Ernest Becker argued, against Freud, that the passion that ultimately drives us is not sex but self-esteem. Love that lasts, ultimately, is love that mutually maximizes self-esteem. Love that fails, love that falls apart, is passion or companionship that leaves the self untouched or worse, that degrades the self and renders the shared self something less than it was before love came along.

Self-esteem is important to us precisely because the nature and status of the self in our society is so unsettled. It is one of the exemplary characteristics of contemporary thinking that the self is not a given, not an inheritance or a place in society but rather a creation, a combination of what we do and have done ourselves, what we think of and say about ourselves and what others think and say of us. The contemporary self, in other words, is notoriously *underdetermined* in the sense that who or what we are is always an open question. In a single day we may play a multiplicity of roles, each with its own self—parent, child, teacher, student, friend, nemesis, intruder or center of attention. Within this confusion and occasional conflict of roles we try to pick out our "true" selves, give priority to some over others, denying some ("I wasn't myself last night") entirely. But there is rarely a "right" choice in such matters; there is no "true" self that dominates all others and, even if one self, one set of roles were to dominate, that identity is still always a choice, always an option, always less than a self that is simply given, as one was given a self in feudal society. Of course the self can be determined only against a background of "givens" that are beyond dispute—from the time and place where we were born to the fate and circumstances of our bodies, our looks, our talents and opportunities. The self depends upon what we think of ourselves but we need some substance to think about as well as a mind to think with. And whatever life has made of us, we have to decide what to make of what has been made of us. No number of facts adds up to determinacy. No one, we may like to think, is a criminal as such, regardless of the criminal acts he or she has performed. No one is perfect, and no one simply is what he or she does—a lawyer, a gardener, a prostitute, a bum. The self is always more than the sum of its facts, and our self-esteem is defined not only by our place in the world but also by how we think of ourselves and decide to react to that world. We are never simply passive victims; we are always the coauthors of our own personalities. We make ourselves, and our primary aim in life does indeed seem to be the specification, the solidification if not the glorification of the self. We play our own stereotypes, even parody ourselves. We know all too well that the self is never assured, that it must be acted out—it is often overacted—for self-esteem consists of proving oneself to be what one is, once one has decided what that will be.

It has often been pointed out—in fact, it is the basis of the whole field of self-help pseudo-science—that people are successful because they see themselves as successful and people are failures because they see themselves as failures. Good lovers think of themselves as good lovers, for loving is first of all a way of thinking about oneself. There is obviously a great deal of truth in this. We are, in part, what we think of ourselves. We are also, of course, what we do and have done. But what we think of ourselves is not so autonomous as we would like to think, and even what we do and accomplish is not independent of what others think and the way we "fit" in the world. Even the most confident people experience that nagging self-doubt, that unbearable questioning of one's established accomplishments and seemingly "proven" good character. It is for this reason—and not just for the bland reasons of "compatibility" and "shared interests"—that we choose the friends and—especially—the lovers we do. What we are and the worth of our accomplishments depends a great deal upon their opinions, and it is not surprising that most of us prefer the constant company of those who make us feel virtuous and worthwhile. It is our selves that we choose in choosing our intimacies.

Jean-Paul Sartre, one of the most vehement defenders of this modern "existentialist" view of the self as our own responsibility, was well aware that any self-contained vision of the self is dangerously incomplete. If that view were true, each of us might well simply think ourselves—or fool ourselves—into thinking that we were anything we wanted to be—generous, heroic, the perfect lover, a terrific person. (Indeed, what would be the difference between thinking and fooling ourselves?) To take but one dramatic example, Jean-Jacques Rousseau, surely one of the most corrupt and despicable (if also brilliant) characters of modern philosophy, discovered in his lonely breast an "inner goodness" as he strolled alone through the forests of St. Germaine. If self-conception alone determined the self, we would have to agree, as if Rousseau's philandering and malevolence toward those closest to him could not possibly count against him. But the opinions of others can be influential, and it is all but impossible to think of oneself as generous if everyone thinks one a miser or as heroic if one's cowardice is renown. If we could assure our self-esteem just by thinking well of ourselves—as so many fraudulent "self-help" books tell us—we would all be self-satisfied and secure within the realm of Freud's "primary process," in which, before reality intrudes, thinking is being and there is no difference between wanting something and getting it. But reality always intrudes into the self; it is in and against reality that we create ourselves. And reality is, in almost every instance, *other people.* We are the persons we think ourselves to be and become through the eyes and opinions of the people around us, whom we choose for ourselves and determine in turn.

Our selves are formed in intercourse, in conversation, in touching, in acting together and separately. It will do no good to think of yourself as a good person if everyone, including your best friends, thinks of you as a bastard. Of course one can always think of oneself as a person "out of place" or "untimely," or as a misunderstood genius. But these alienated roles, too, require the backing of other people, perhaps at first only imaginary people but later on, one hopes, a real appreciative audience—the so-called vindication of history. But for every Nietzsche or Rousseau who proves himself in the eyes of future generations, there are hundreds of others who simply disappear, even in their own lives, without a trace forever after, people who refused to accept the overriding requirement of selfhood—that one is not a self alone.

It is sometimes objected that such definitions in terms of others deprive us of our individuality. The result is one of the most tragic conceptual disasters in American life—the false belief that to love someone is a weakness, a sign of loss of self, a loss of autonomy and independence. The truth is that such definitions make individuality possible. Without such connections with other people, individuality is just another abstraction, almost an existence without qualities. "I love, therefore I exist" may be a bit unimaginative, but it is not far from the truth. It is through love that we find and make our place in the world, through identity rather than conflict, expanding ourselves and our world by concentrating all of our energies and our attention on a single individual who is both other than, but a more important part of, ourselves. The self needs this other, not just for sex or companionship but for its own completion.

This, I want to argue, is what love is. It is the mutual creation of self-identity. Sex plays such a powerful and central role because no matter how cerebral and soulful we may sometimes pretend to be, we are ultimately sensual creatures for whom a touch and a gesture is often more meaningful than an eloquent soliloquy. Sex, solitude, intimacy and privacy play essential roles in love partly because it is when we are naked and alone together that the self comes to especially appreciate its incompleteness and the importance of shared identity. (Conversely, it is also alone with another that we come to appreciate how intolerable two ill-fitting selves can be.) Societies that deny their members privacy, cultures that shun solitude and discourage sexual intimacy, shut off the possibilities for romantic love (except, perhaps, for a few rebels). Societies that thoroughly define the self in social terms, cultures that consider identity wholly in terms of kinship relations, leave no room for the redefinition of self that is crucial to our notion of love. Fantasy plays such an important role in love because it, too, both presupposes and feeds the freedom to imagine and plan and choose one's future and determine one's self; a thoroughly determined self would neither need nor have any fantasies. Idealization of one's lover is important to love, not just because it is such a flattering way of viewing someone, but because it actually determines the self of the other; one truly does become "the most beautiful person in the world" if only one's lover thinks so. So, too, the idealization and determination of the other is an inspiration to oneself, for who else has the unmatchable advantage of being loved by the most beautiful person in the world? We can also understand, on this identity view of love, why love is so explosive and can end so badly in accusations of betrayal; in love we literally put our selves at risk, in the hands of someone whom we may not know as well as we think we do. Losing love is losing part of oneself, but, to put it more positively, to love is to gain a sense of ourselves reborn, beginning again anew, building a new and more durable identity through lasting love.

THE ROMANTIC CREATION OF THE SELF

We cannot understand love until we get over the idea that the self is, in each case, individually and inalienably our own. A strong and independent self is an incredible and rare achievement. But independence is an act of defiance and perversity, not a return to a natural state. We define ourselves in terms of other people and we are largely defined by other people, no matter how nobly individual we may be. The modern idea of the isolated self-defining self is a myth, but it is a myth that is at the basis of romantic love and at the core of the paradox of love as well.

The concept of a shared self—and the tensions it engenders—

can best be understood by contrast with our seemingly simple everyday notion of the individual self. It is perhaps an expression of cowardice, an unwillingness to fight for ourselves, that each of us thinks of ourselves as already a self—self-contained, self-defined, individual and independent. We might admit that much of what we have to work with was given to us or imposed upon us (by our parents, siblings, place of growing up, etc.) but, nevertheless, each of us is—or in each of us is—a true self, a soul, an ontological nugget of Being that is our very own. We may, for convenience, define ourselves in social categories—as a student, a housewife, as Mary's husband. But we pretend that, really, each of us is a unique human being, even if (out of weakness) we also need and seek out others, to "add" to or complement (and compliment) our unique selves.

This comfortable, antisocial and unenlightened illusion can be shattered by so simple an exercise as trying to describe that uniqueness of the self. For most of us our "uniqueness" comes down to the uninspiring statistics concerning the peculiar shape of our faces, the random contingencies of our birth, bearing and our more curious habits, the number of hairs on our heads and some coincidental configuration of facts about us (the only Irish Catholic accountant in the voting district). Even personalities fall neatly into "types," and it is only the most trivial details and gestures that set us at all apart. In desperation we can always point to each of our unique positions in the spacio-temporal order (compliments of the laws of logic and physics). So lovers at midnight proclaim the uniqueness of their love, but, of course, at the same time a million other lovers are doing just the same (with some allowance for time zones and local love rituals). It dashes our vanity and goes against much of what we want to hear but the truth is that there is nothing of any importance that makes every one of us unique. It is only in interaction with other people—and by loving and being loved in particular—that our individual existence has any meaning at all.

It is revealing that nearly everything we want to say about

ourselves, virtually every adjective that applies to us, depends upon other people. What makes us individuals, paradoxically, are our relationships with others. Even such straightforward facts about us as being tall or short, weighing 130 pounds, being thirty-four years old and born in Detroit state implicit relationships. "Tall" and "short" are comparisons; weight depends on a scale, based on comparisons, and why weighing more or less *matters* to us clearly depends upon the opinions of others, current fashions and an image of ourselves that is, even in the mirror, a reflection of how we'd like to be seen by others. What it means to be thirty-four and the advantages of being born in Detroit depend on where we are now and with whom and whether the Tigers are winning the pennant this year. Facts recede in the face of interpretation; what concerns us are not the facts themselves but their *significance*. It is easy to imagine a social context in which being tall is humiliating and having been born in Detroit a mark of sainthood. We are what is made of us, even if we have considerable say in then making something of what has been made of us. And one way we do this—often the most powerful and passionate way—is by falling in love.

Plato pointed out that love is essentially a seeking after the good, a redefinition of oneself in terms of goodness. Courtly troubadours sang the praises of love as a means and motive to self-improvement, and romantic poets in the eighteenth and nineteenth centuries celebrated love as the realization of a "higher" self. These claims may be aggrandized, but they contain an essential if somewhat more pedestrian truth about love —that it is fundamentally a matter of self-transformation, not as a secondary effect but in its very nature. Love embodies a reflective desire for self-improvement. In the simplest terms, to be in love is wanting nothing more than to show one's ideal self, to make oneself even better as well as to be loved for what one considers best in oneself. But the mundane wish to be "loved for oneself" often betrays an attitude of laziness or desperation toward love, an unwillingness to reconceive or reconsider oneself or a reaction to too many fraudulent self-presentations and their inevitably unhappy aftermath. The desire to improve oneself and *earn* the lover's love is a much better criterion for love. What makes the romantic creation of self so complicated and interesting is the essential indeterminacy of the self, so that it is not one's self *as is* that one presents but always the self as one would like it to be. Thus it is that we act and dress the part(s) we would like to play, to attract the person we would like to play with and, once a relationship is established, we develop and perfect those parts to the point where they seem as if they were completely natural, as if we were born into them. The creation of the self is, more than anything else, the establishing of a variety of *roles*, romantic roles in particular, in which the self is defined primarily in terms of one sensuous, intimate relationship. Sexuality is critical to this set of roles, but what is just as crucial is a powerful conception of *privacy* in which this special set of romantic roles can be defined.

Of all the networks of people and opinions that form our sense of ourselves, it is love that often proves to be definitive. Parental love is all-important in infancy; sibling love and rivalry in childhood, early friendship and "puppy loves" in school determine all but inalterably the basic framework of the self and what we think of ourselves. It is true that we also define ourselves in terms of our careers, our professions, our positions in the community. But our society and our lives are composed of so many crosscurrents of conflicting identities that our selves are never fully formed when we fall in love; it is this incompletion that makes love possible. Ultimately it is what we take to be the determination of the self, a self that is so intimate and private that one and only one other person may really know and be in contact with it. Love is not merely "added" to the self but inevitably alters and fulfills it. We are as we are made to think of ourselves by the person with whom we would spend our lives, share our bodies, our time and our minds. So many of our essential attributes are determined, not in public or by consensus, but by that single person who is "closest" to us. Whether one is ultimately sensitive, or lovable, or a "good person" is often settled only privately, alone with the one we love. The much-sought-after status of "good lover" is determined in the interchange between one's own sensuous sense of oneself and the supportive embrace (hardly just an "opinion") of just one other person. One can, at one's peril, attempt to settle the "good lover" question "objectively" by collecting a multitude of opinions. But the paradox is that even the most spectacular success in the public arena is an open invitation to uncertainty and failure, for the intimate embrace of a single person is far more certain and irrefutable than the votes of an ever-undetermined and largely indifferent casual audience. Don Juan is often presented as a hedonist, but the fact is that he lives a fearful existence. He can never be satisfied with his "successes" and he can be undermined by a single critical laugh at his expense. Two mutually devoted lovers define one another's qualities—and who else even has the right to make a suggestion? Some of our most important virtues—and in a romantic society being a "good lover" may be one of them—are so determined not by the public and not by ourselves alone but in intimacy with one's lover. In love the singular opinion of that single other person whom we have chosen (in part for that very fact) to love is trump. Love is this private, personal, mutual determination of virtues, of selfhood, of our proper place in the world, and that is why it is so vitally important to us. Love lasts because it comes to define our place in the world.

SEX AND THE SHARED SELF

It (love) does not hesitate to intrude with its trash. . . . It knows
how to slip its love-notes and ringlets even into ministerial portfo-
lios and philosophical manuscripts. Every day it brews and hatches
the worst and most perplexing quarrels and disputes, destroys the
most valuable relationships and breaks the strongest bonds. . . .
Why all this noise and fuss? . . . It is merely a question of every
Jack finding his Jill. (The gracious reader should translate this
phrase into precise Aristophanic language.) Why should such a
trifle play so important a role?

—ARTHUR SCHOPENHAUER,
World as Will and Representation

Why indeed? If love were nothing but protracted sexual desire, it would be difficult to understand the extent to which we
idealize it and give it such primary importance in our lives. But
along with this familiar reduction of love to desire, we also tend
to underestimate the role of sexuality in our lives. Sex is still too
often treated as if it were only a physiological urge, or a form of
recreation, or an intrusion (whether welcome or unwelcome)
into our otherwise rational lives. Plato distinguished desire and
reason, and his character Cephalus in the *Republic* declares his
great relief, late in life, at being freed from the chains of sexual
longing. Freud flatly juxtaposed sex against the better judgments
of the self and later opposed them as "id" and "ego." But sex is
not an impersonal or selfless "it," the manifestation of something
foreign and dangerous "in us." Sex is rather the body's definition
of the self, its most basic embodiment and expression. Where
sex is dangerous is where the self itself is dangerous, and sex is
not antithetical to the self except where we choose to make it so.
Our social roles are of limited personal significance compared to
the awesome power of sex in the determination of self and self-
esteem. Impotence and frigidity are far more damaging to self-

conception than failure or embarrassment, and we all know how the exhilaration of satisfying sex can temporarily wipe away the shadows of even the worst public or professional humiliation. Romantic love dominates our sense of the self in part because of the power of sex, but sex, too, is a pervasive determinate of the self, and the self in love and the self in sex are rarely very far apart.

Philosophers from Plato to Schopenhauer have pointed out that sex serves the deepest purpose not only of the individual but of the culture and the species—the continuity of oneself and one's kind into the future—"immortality" the Greeks called it (before that word was taken over by a more abstract and self-centered conception of continuity). It is sex that gets us in touch with eternity, and Plato's Socrates only embellishes this picture by suggesting that a higher form of "eros"—namely philosophy —would get us in touch more directly. For later philosophers, too, insofar as we are not isolated entities but members of a group—humanity—our selves are not just individual and constrained to the present; they are social, essentially tied to other people and, in particular, tied to other people through sex. It is in this spirit that the great pessimist Schopenhauer suggests that sex must be much more than mere sensuous desire. And, indeed, whether our immediate desire is just a one-night stand or the expression of lifelong love, the deep underlying impulse of the sex act is something much "bigger than both of us." For Schopenhauer it is nothing less than the cosmic "will to life" pulsing through us. Schopenhauer did not exactly say so, but much of what he says underscores the observation that sexual attraction is nothing less than our own blueprint for the future of humanity and life as such. Sexual desire is ultimately the desire for what we (as a species) want to be. And, finally, sexual consummation is not just an act of pleasure or self-gratification but the will to life manifesting itself through two people. When we "lose ourselves" in sexual ecstasy, we come to realize what is most ourselves. The joy of sex is in fact the joy of self, two selves enjoying themselves together by reaching out beyond themselves and enlarging themselves with each other.

Sexuality is something of a Rorschach test in that the same activity can be viewed in so many different ways, and each perspective dictates its own mode of expression. To view sex as the means to continue the species is inevitably to see it as something quite serious, an enormous responsibility and not to be taken at all lightly. To see sex as a means to pleasure and recreation, by contrast, is to insist on lightness and minimize responsibility, while to see sex as a physical and emotional union of two people is to add a much more personal dimension. (To see sex as the imposition and intrusion of one person into another is necessarily to view sex as a hostile act akin to rape—an attitude never wholly absent from conceptions of sex as conquest and as "scoring." Similarly, how one behaves in bed is not a mindless reversion to some more primitive mode of existence but rather the height of cultural education and sophistication. Most of the things we do to each other prior to and during intercourse are ingenious, to say the least, and few of them can be attributed to "natural" impulses (the grain of truth in the never-ending moralistic attack on "perverted" sex practices). Much of sex is expression—expression not only of desire and excitement but tenderness, respect, admiration, gratitude, timidity, trust, possessiveness and being possessed. It has often been written that sex is so close to the self because it is the medium in which so many of our most basic and primitive fears are expressed—the fear of intimacy, fear of vulnerability, fear of humiliation or impotence, fear of physical harm and fears about the appearance of our naked bodies. But this is too negative and one-sided. Sex is also the medium in which we realize our most basic desires and comforts—the desire to be held or stroked, the desire to hold someone else and caress them, the desire to be intimate, the desire, even against our fears, to be vulnerable (if only to overcome those fears), the desire to be looked at approvingly, aided by the ultimate cosmetic of mutual desire.

In sex we are naked, the most protected parts of our bodies exposed and open to another's touch. When excited we tend to lose our restraint, our sense of caution; we allow ourselves the rare luxuries of inarticulate expression and "shamelessly" move our bodies in the most sexually expressive and effective ways. In sex we feel free to want and even to expect (if not to ask for) just that which will please us the most, and in sex we are aware as nowhere else of our deepest fears of inadequacy and our sense of vulnerability. Not surprisingly, during or after sex we seem not only willing but quite happy to admit our darkest secrets, our most difficult anxieties. It is not just that sex provides a medium for intimacy; it also breeds intimacy, for the echo of that tightly shared self remains and, unless it is blocked, encourages the exchange of ideas and images just as readily as the bodies encouraged the exchange of sensations and pleasure. Sex itself may be momentary, but it is a deep philosophical mistake to think that therefore the significance of sexual intercourse is momentary too. In even the most transient sexual encounter, two selves become more than physically intertwined and it is always a wrenching act to pull them apart. In love that merging of selves is exactly what we want, and the reason sex is so satisfying in love is not because the sex itself is necessarily any "better" but because its symbolic consequences are so welcome to us. Good sex makes love last, but, more important, it is love that gives good sex its significance. In other words, one might say that it is love that makes sex last.

It is often suggested that sex is regressive, a "return" to our more bestial instincts or a temporary flight back to the physical simplicity and dependency of early infancy. (It is even suggested that "back to the womb" is a plausible motive for mature sexuality.) Of course sex involves the simple enjoyments and gestures of being held and holding, the simple fact of nakedness and freedom from all public roles and status. But sex is not unlearned and unintelligent, mere instinct or infantile habits or hang-ups harking back to some earlier stage of the self (though no doubt previous stages of the self influence our every sexual act and desire). Sexual expression is self-expression of the most profound kind, which is not to say that it cannot be abused and perverted so that all expression is foreclosed or fraudulent or that other forms of expression (whether buying flowers or writing poetry) might not be preferable to sex as an expression of affection or intimacy. But sexual expression is self-expression, and without sex it would be hard to imagine ourselves as we are or could be. Romance without sexual expression may on occasion prove to be extremely creative and even worthy of historical admiration, but it is always a truncated form of love, if only because it represents a truncated conception of self.

To say that our selves are sexual is emphatically not to limit ourselves to genital sex. Sex has to do with the whole self—the body, the personality, even the abstract mind. Plato used to delight in employing sexual metaphors to talk about the workings of the soul and its lust for knowledge, and so, too, our common use of sexual imagery for talking about sports, work and life in general as an indication of how central and pervasive we consider our sexuality. Sexuality is the feeling of potency or attractiveness one can have while walking down a crowded hallway, the vast system of significances that accompany the most innocent wink, the wonderful feeling of relaxation that comes with a back rub, a neck rub or a simple stroke of the hair. A couple in love radiate sexuality in every look and gesture, and this is true not only in the first days of an affair but even in the late years of marriage. Love is not sexual desire, we say again, but the neglect or denial of sexual desire is a sure way to undermine or diminish love. It may be a matter of physiological record that the desire (and ability) for frequent and vigorous sexual intercourse diminishes at some point with age, but here again it is a mistake to confuse sexuality with genital intercourse and, as one old saw has it, "what one loses in stamina one makes up for in style." Some sexual excitement is crucial to sexual performance, but it is not all that there is to sex, nor is it even the culmination of sex. One might just as well argue that sexual excitement and orgasm are preparatory for the calm and comfort that follow, that genital intercourse is no more than the temporary focus of a sexual union whose ultimate fulfillment is best manifested in a long, tender, motionless embrace and an evening of quiet, intimate conversation.

A few pages earlier we suggested that good sex helped love to last, and that sex was better in love. But what is "good sex"? As Freud often pointed out, it is not just a question of physical satisfaction; the psyche has to be satisfied too. We often hear that someone is "good in bed." What does that mean? At the very least it should be clear that "good in bed" has many different meanings and that a person who is "good in bed" with one person may not be with another, but it should also be obvious that being "good in bed" is not just a matter of skill or even (as one popular magazine would have it) sensitivity and attention, for the keen heed and devotion of someone whom one does not love can be humiliating or even disgusting. Two people who generally pride themselves on being "good in bed" may be an utter disaster together, and someone who confesses to "not being good in bed" may nevertheless—or just on that account—be a wonderful lover. He or she may honestly express affection and enthusiasm rather than exhibit the latest techniques and clichés. The problem is that lovemaking too often gets treated as a set of techniques and attitudes, which one has either mastered or not. This is not to say that clumsiness and lack of rudimentary knowledge are virtues or charms, and clearly there are skills and knowledge that are essential to making love just as there are skills and knowledge essential to having an intimate conversation—indeed, the two may not be so different. But sex is basically self-expression, not the technique of exciting another person or the thrill of being excited oneself. Being "good in bed" means, ultimately, being the right person for one's lover and expressing oneself and one's devotion without inhibition. Some skill and knowledge may be the precondition of satisfying sex, but the skill and knowledge alone, ready to be applied in any sexual situation, go against the very purpose of sex in the first place and turn it, as it now has often been turned, into a private form of athletics, a sport in which the rating of performance is as routine as it has become in gymnastics or wrestling. But truly being "good in bed"—if the term means anything at all—cannot turn on such an anonymous rating system. It must turn on the only thing in sex that really counts—not pleasure or skill or knowledge but the mutual expression of affection. And this has much more to do with what one has to express to this particular other person than it does with how one might perform more generally. In fact, until recently the idea of sexual performance was almost unknown. (If it was discussed at all, it had more to do with frequency than quality.) What was essential was the sheer *fact* of having sex with someone, and this had much more to do with desire and trust and romantic intentions than it did with any anticipation of the quality and skill of the performance. Nevertheless, sexual performance has now become an important (for some people the most important) feature of romantic attachment and love. What is actually important is to realize just how much this is still a function of self-expression and not merely a selfless set of skills.

In love and in bed with another person, the concept that seems to be most important is what I call *"sexual fit."* It is a way to understand just what role "good in bed" plays in love, for it is a rare case in which "being good in bed" isn't a reason—even an overwhelming reason—for being in love. The "bottom line," one might say, is mutual satisfaction, although it is clear that two people can be physically and even emotionally satisfied and still not be in love with one another. Nevertheless, sexual fit is an essential factor in love. Sexual fit is the way two people "fit" together. In fact, of course, almost all human bodies fit together by virtue of the clever design of nature, so "fit" in this sense must mean something more interesting than the coincidental coupling of concave and convex curvatures. Sexual fit has much more to do with comfort and ease, the degree to which two people allow themselves to conform to the will of the other, the extent to which sexual intercourse *means* something beyond the prescribed ritual of caresses and activities. Much of sexual fit involves prototypes, desires and expectations. Each of us has a certain comfort range in a number of sexual dimensions—the appropriate style, waiting time and subtlety of approach, the size of one's partner, how tightly one holds or is held, the need for and style of foreplay, the duration and vigor of sexual intercourse, the compatibility of certain sexual positions and, most of all, the amount of mutual attention and sensitivity that is involved. One does not have to be a fetishist to prefer a certain shape and size of body, breast, penis, hands, waist, hips or shoulders, and sexual fit is first of all the fit of body to preset desires and expectations—though it is remarkable how quickly these desires and expectations can be adjusted when the otherwise "right" person comes along. Nor is one necessarily hypersensitive if he or she requires an extraordinary amount of tenderness and attention—or insensitive if he or she prefers a rough and mutually self-absorbed encounter in which each partner gets carried away with his or her own sensations and activities and is only vaguely aware of the presence of the other. Here as elsewhere the criteria for sexual fit are personal and particular and not moral or prescriptive. They have to do with personal needs and tastes and not some abstract formula for "good sex."

But though it is most readily described in physical terms, sexual fit is not just physical; it also involves such traits as expressiveness, honesty, tenderness, affection, a sense of humor and a quick wit (to be employed sparingly during sex, to be sure). If one person believes in silent, eloquent sexual expression—a whisper, a sigh, a slight gesture of the chin and the lips—and the other believes in full-volume operatic oratorio, sexual fit will be negative, however well the bodies function together. If one person insists on every possible square centimeter of skin contact while the other prefers a light selective touch, there will be a bad sexual fit. If one enjoys prolonging sexual intercourse until the last bearable moment, while the other prefers a quick and spontaneous burst of mutual enthusiasm, there will be no sexual fit. In short, sexual fit depends on the (unspoken) agreement of two people on almost everything having to do with sex, not only "aim and object," as Freud suggested, but even such details as whether it is all right to moan or whether one ought to brush one's teeth beforehand. It is sexual fit that accounts for a person being "good in bed," but from this we can see that there is no such thing as one person's being "good in bed" at all. There are instances in which one falls in love with someone because of his or her sexual performance, but much more often—and much more dependable—two lovers are good in bed because they love one another. Sex is, above all, a medium of expression, and when love is what it has to express, its performance could hardly be bad.

THE IMPORTANCE OF PRIVACY

The need for privacy is a need for the protection against intrusion. . . . It is evident that the need for privacy is a socially created need. Without society there would be no need for privacy. . . .

—BARRINGTON MOORE, JR., *Privacy*

Romantic love is a very private emotion. It invites and welcomes seclusion. Sexuality also demands privacy. It has been pointed out by anthropologists that virtually every society considers sex to be a private activity, but the privacy that is critical to love is something much more sophisticated and peculiar than mere physical seclusion and staying out of sight of one's neighbors and family. Romantic love presupposes a very powerful and very modern conception of privacy. It is not that one cannot play the romantic lover in public, but public performance is secondary at best and, for many sensibilities, both unnecessary and distasteful. We too often think of privacy as a state of the isolated individual, but privacy is also the ability of two people to be alone together and, more important, to build their own world together, apart from and even indifferent to the larger social world around them. All societies may have some sense of privacy, especially in the performance of sexual intercourse. (The ancient Greeks, who were not shy about much else, nevertheless saw sex as a strictly private act and insisted that it be enjoyed out of the public eye.) But our sense of privacy extends far beyond such a limited set of public prohibitions; it includes an entire system of rights and, more important for love, it includes the radical right to define and evaluate ourselves in a private—rather than a public—context. Our selves—our "true" selves—are not the selves we present in public (a claim that would astound most of the world). Our selves are defined largely in private—with family and friends and, most of all, with the one person whom we choose to love above all others. Without our keen sense of privacy, our concept of self and society would be very different. And without that concept of self, there could be no romantic love, for romantic love requires this very private and personal sense of an underdetermined self that can be redefined and determined through the eyes and mind of a single lover. It is no small virtue and no small danger of love that it has this power regarding one other person who can re-create our self and has the power to utterly devastate it. Love allows for a private sense of self but it also renders us vulnerable to emptiness and destruction. Privacy is one of our civilization's most treasured inventions, but it is also one of our greatest liabilities.

The concept of privacy is, we said, a modern concept; one

finds little like it before the seventeenth century or so. It does not amount to the mere fact of being alone. That sort of privacy has always been the province of shepherds, hermits and the isolated rich and poor. It does not even consist of the *right* to be alone, although this, too, is a recent notion that could only accompany the new idea that privacy is somehow very important to the development of selfhood and not merely a deprivation. Societies have always designated some activities as private—that is, things to be done out of sight and in isolation, sex and excretion in particular. But this is not yet privacy in a much stronger sense, the right and ability of the individual to lead his or her own life and the right of two individuals to define each other on their own terms. What must be private, of course, is culturally variable: in modern Italy some romantic expressions are quite public that are considered strictly private in America, athough the American attitude toward public demonstrations of affection would still make a Chinese citizen blanche. And what is private need not be secret or, in an important sense, even hidden from view. It must be protected, kept away from public scrutiny, free from the demands and obligations imposed by outsiders. What is so special about our concept of privacy is that, whereas most societies recognized privacy only as exemption from, and subservient to, public interests, we see the private as primary (Barrington Moore, Jr., *Privacy*). We consider our private lives to be at least as important as public life. We criticize a successful public figure for having "no private life," but we do not worry excessively about, and may even admire, a person who is happy in his or her personal life but has no interest whatever in politics or other public questions. This is not to say that privacy has no obligations, but it is freedom from *public* obligations. Nor is it to say that privacy has no socially originated and learned structures, but only that the self that originates in privacy is a self that is protected from public scrutiny even if it is created according to rules and structures dictated by society.

It is within these structures and within the bounds of this

protection that we define and redefine ourselves in love through the romantic *roles* that we play. These roles are intrinsically private; indeed, the most striking single anthropological feature of our society is its sense of privacy—not the much-worried-about privacy guaranteed by the Constitution, but the more metaphysical kind of privacy—in which our "inner" selves are defined. Whether a person is sensitive or sensuous, for example, gets ultimately determined not by people in general but by only a small and intimate group of people, minimally, a group of two (including oneself). The role of lover is defined just between the two, and this becomes a public role only as a matter of perversion or parody. (The roles of attorney or professor, by way of contrast, can be imagined as private roles only by way of self-parody.) One is a lover not only in the spatial privacy of the bedroom but in the very special privacy of the self as well. There is good reason why lovers always want to be alone, and it need have nothing to do with private acts or caresses or even private conversation. Love gets defined in private, and it opposes the intrusion of all public opinion. Domestic roles, the role of housewife or househusband, for example, may require private space but nevertheless admit of public examination and evaluation and often interfere with romantic roles, which is why romance and domesticity are just as often enemies as allies. Romantic roles are private because they have to do with the private, intimate self, whereas domestic roles are public because they have to do with tasks and efficiency, getting things done in the world rather than *being* a certain person in a very private world of two. Romantic roles tend to be sexual, despite the fact that sex and gender roles tend to be public—one good reason to separate the romantic roles of love and its sexual expression from the biological and social conceptions of sexuality—male and female, masculine and feminine. In love only one other person need recognize a lover (though the signs may be unmistakable to others), and much of the excitement of love—and its anxiety—stems from the fact that one declares oneself (relatively) free from public opinion and puts one's self in the hands of a single other person. Of course in mutual love one also holds that person's self in one's own hands, too, a situation of mutual vulnerability that has led many social psychologists to formulate an "exchange model" of love in which mutual approval and verification are a matter of negotiation and mutual advantage. What the exchange model takes for granted, however, is the essential and most fascinating feature of love—the private definition of the self and the strong sense of privacy that is its precondition.

Privacy presents as many problems as it does possibilities, and it emerges in history as much the result of crisis and turmoil as the benign effect of any increasing awareness of the importance of freedom. The history of privacy is a history of revolt and alienation, a history of authority breaking down, a history of selfhood abandoned. With privacy comes the constant threat of loneliness, and with choice comes the ever-present possibility of foolishness. We often tend to treat such problems as "the nature of personal identity" as eternal philosophical problems, but the fact is that many of the questions we ask about ourselves would have been all but incomprehensible until modern times and personal identity in particular would not have been a problem at all. Romantic love could not possibly provide "the answer" to life's problems until the invention of those questions concerning the loneliness and indeterminacy of the self and the concept of privacy that made those questions conceivable. One of our most critical enigmas of self—the "identity crisis"—was not identified and named until the 1950s in America, appropriately, where such crises are far more prevalent than they have ever been in the rest of the world, where the self is fairly well fixed for life. Our ideal of "social mobility" is considered by most societies to be a sure recipe for chaos and loneliness. It is no surprise that the concept of an identity crisis should appear among people (and, first of all, in age groups) where social structures and status have become exceedingly unclear. Not surprisingly (and not as a mere matter of sexual maturation), it is adolescence, when the identity and direction of the self is most confused, that is the age at which one first falls in love and privacy becomes an explosive issue.

By way of contrast, there is no hint of any such institutionalized crisis of self in societies that lack that strong sense of privacy and individual selfhood, for instance, in Margaret Mead's Samoa, where growing up consists of a sequence of social responsibilities and roles, free of any period of "adolescence." Neither, however, is there anything like our concept of romantic love. Romantic love proves to be most important in societies and groups where social structures and attachments had become unclear or ambiguous. Romantic love, now the most bourgeois of emotions, had its origins among the more privileged feudal orders in the last days of feudalism. Only they had the luxury, not even the right, to privacy. So, too, it had its heyday among the aristocracy of the eighteenth century, by then in its final days and already unfashionable. This is not to say that romance *causes* the disintegration of societies, of course, nor does it imply that decadent societies inevitably turn to romantic love. But uncertainty and alienation lead to private reflection and resolution as well as the need for alliances and intimacy. Romantic love became big news in China in the chaos following the so-called Cultural Revolution when a small peek at privacy invaded Chinese communal life. Love has always been most obsessive in our alienated urban centers, even though the urban mythology of love often takes on a rustic romantic cast along with its sophisticated cynicism. (In the country, one imagines more privacy.) If love is born of the need for self-identity, then we should expect that love will become of increasing importance as traditional and established roles lose their authority or their significance and private roles become more important. The lover appears in history, and not just in Harlequin romances, in the midst of social decadence and disintegration. The self, which once was thoroughly determined by precise and specific social facts, is now left dangling, indeterminate, privately in search of itself. And our concept of love enters the world as a private solution.

ROMANTIC ROLES

She had her desire fulfilled. He had his desire fulfilled. For she was to him what he was to her, the immemorial magnificence of mystic, palpable, real otherness.

—D . H . LAWRENCE , *Women in Love*

What is the self? Every self is composed of *roles*, not as a front or facade, but as its very essence. It is sometimes suggested that the self is thereby merely a mask, a presentation of self behind which hides a vacuum (the view of the late sociologist Erving Goffman). More traditionally, it is supposed that the self is a soul that merely wears masks but is not itself a mask. I suggest the truth is that the self is rather the wearing of masks—nothing behind them, but not a vacuum either. It is the image of a true "inner" self that confuses us—the idea that the self can't be "just" presentation. But then we cannot seem to identify or locate that mysterious "inner" self either—the one that supposedly, and only very occasionally, comes bursting through the fronts and facades. Yet the self is neither inside nor outside; it is a set of dynamic relationships, "a network of relations" according to French author St. Exupéry. As we've alluded, the self is constructed in the roles we play for others and for ourselves as well. Sartre's exemplary waiter in *Being and Nothingness*, who plays at *being* a waiter in his every gesture, his mechanical walk, his exaggerated show of attention and efficiency, is no different from any of us except that he is clear and precise and exceedingly limited about what he is trying to be. The self constructed in love is a series of particularly private but by no means unique or individually created roles, especially those that have to do with our sexual being and courtship rituals. When we play the lover in love, we are playing a role that, very likely, we have been observing and possibly rehearsing most of our mature lives. It is a role in which, while losing ourselves in it, we feel that we have never been more ourselves.

One of the virtues of playing the lover is that we can recognize the fact that we are falling into a prescribed and common role but still feel that our expressions are very much our own. Thousands of flower shops stay in business supplying hundreds of thousands of grateful or generous lovers with the mandatory dozen long-stem roses, but every dozen has its own significance, just as every one of the millions of "I love you's" that gets uttered every day has its own meaning and its own essential place in a single relationship. Romantic roles are publicly defined but privately enacted—even when (through necessity, ignorance, vulgarity or vanity) they are performed in public. It is often thought that lovers, especially when desperate, "lose themselves" and break out of all roles, but the truth is that even the desperation and craziness of lovers is prescribed and predictable, a set of roles that are spelled out for us in detail even if played out on one's own private stage. The romantic suicide threat, the after-midnight phone calls, the proclamations ("I could never love anyone else") are predictable and even clichéd—not original at all. Romantic roles are completely familiar to us, as evidenced by every third-rate love story or situation comedy, but when we are in love ourselves those clichéd roles seem as fresh and as original as they would have been for Adam and Eve. The charm of love is that it does not matter that ten thousand couples are also sharing wine and flowers at this very moment, that they, too, are pronouncing the ritual formula "I love you," "I love you too," or that they are making love in more or less the same basic biological configuration that has been around since the Paleocene epoch or earlier. Romance creates its own private world and its own private, primordial self. Workers of the world may unite, and so may capitalists, too, but lovers are essentially and happily separated, off by themselves and all but indifferent to the fact that anyone other than they themselves have ever been in love.

The self is composed of roles we play (note "play") with other people, but there are different kinds of roles with varying scope and context. Most obvious are the roles that are strictly public or professional: one's role as a doctor or a director of a company or a skilled technician or a taxpayer or a criminal. But it is clear that we do not usually define our selves according to such roles; we make a major point of insisting that such public roles may show very little of the "true" self and, indeed, we often complain that all such public roles distort or perhaps even suffocate the self. The roles that we consider more important in the definition of self are personal and more private roles—the role of parent, grandparent, brother, sister, friend, neighbor, wife or husband. Thus we feel "most ourselves" with our friends and with (some of) our family, and we are extremely suspicious of someone — no matter how charming or successful in public—who is incapable of "being oneself" in such intimate circumstances. Most important of all, however, are those roles that are specifically concerned with love and living together. Some of these roles are domestic roles—the sort that one might also share with a roommate or any other family member, from such mundane necessities as daily chores and the division of household labor to such overriding roles as being the "head of the household," the provider, the center of attention, the troublemaker, the conversationalist, the one that everyone else worries about. Others are relationship roles, more intimate and less function-bound than domestic roles, the sort of roles that are typical of friendships, especially the closest friendships, mutually defined and (for the most part) mutually supportive, bringing out the best in each person and aiming to maximize happiness for both of them.

The roles that distinguish romantic love, however, are of a special sort, which we are (aptly but unoriginally) calling "romantic roles." These are roles mutually defined with sexual love and personal idealization at their core. As opposed to domestic roles, romantic roles are, from a "practical" standpoint, quite dysfunctional. They consist, for example, of such aristocratic, luxurious and useless activities as staring lovingly at one's beloved for indeterminate lengths of time, paying attention to features and activities not worth (by any other measure) attending to, touching softly and *without* any explicit sexual aim, walking through gardens and appreciating the aesthetics of nature without, perhaps, actually seeing much of anything. It is possible to "play" the romantic lover with any number of partners, of course; it is the world's oldest profession. But while the form might be generalized, the content is strictly particular, and to love is not just to play the romantic role as such; it is to define oneself by means of it, not in general but with reference to just one person. Indeed, one can adopt and play out the romantic role even without the cooperation of the other person—unrequited love is like this, and, as we all know, there may be no better performance of the romantic *Weltschmerz* than the unrequited lover who chooses devotion over happiness and the certainties of frustration over the possibilities of a real relationship. But what defines romantic roles is not so much the idealized role into which one casts one's beloved as it is the desire and idealizing itself, the way one behaves rather than the way one is behaved toward. To be loved is the desideratum of love but it is not its definition; to love is to play the lover, but like any role it is better played when it fits into a drama that others are playing too.

Not all romantic roles are directly connected with sex, even in a generalized way. A quaint but common illustration of the special kind of role-playing that takes place in love is the familiar use of "baby talk" among mature and sophisticated lovers. On the one hand, nothing could be more foolish, more weak and degrading, than a grown man or woman lisping or whispering pet names and childish private words. To be overheard in public would be humiliating. On the other hand, we would start to worry about intimacy in the relationship if such names and words never developed or—worse—if the attempt to use these was rebuffed as "immature" or "undignified." The use of nonsense names—"booby," "sweetness," "jou-jou" and so on—typically begins in the second half-year or so of a serious relationship and may enlarge in response to different moods and contexts as well as develop an entire vocabulary for all things sexual, sentimental or mutually meaningful. The process is significant, though rarely a subject for study or commentary. It signifies a quite conscientious attempt to diminish the self; in fact, the voice in which these terms are uttered is often a demure whisper, even a whine. A person who spoke to us like that in public would be the subject of pity or ridicule, but in love it is not only perfectly appropriate but almost necessary. Two witty, intelligent, verbally well-armed and possibly sarcastic lovers need to soften themselves, like two panthers making love or two porcupines ("carefully"). On the other hand, we are horrified to hear a couple in conversation address each other too formally. We do not think them sophisticated or strong, but defensive, less pliable, as if they have just had (or are just about to have) a fight.

We have several times alluded to the distinction between romantic roles, domestic roles and relationship roles, and much of the nature of love—and its duration—can be understood as a function of the interplay of these three sorts of roles. All of them are private, in the sense that they tend to be played by just two people together and defined by those two alone. In domestic roles these definitions tend to be rather routine, even if common sources of conflict. Domestic roles tend to be efficiency-obsessed and goal-oriented, and they are often covertly public as well (the desire to have a house or a yard that is "presentable"). Domestic roles require private space in the sense that domesticity presupposes the modern concept of the home, but although domesticity *can* be romantic and feed love insofar as it presents shared goals and activities, it is often distinct and even opposed to romantic roles and sensibilities. Goals and efficiency get in the way of the romance. Romance involves concentrated attention to each other; domesticity demands attention to tasks and deeds to be done, to the environment rather than the self. Domesticity is romantic to the extent that the performance of tasks and chores is something truly shared, not just in the sense of "equal distribution," but in the much more important sense that these tasks and chores are just another way of paying attention to each other and being together. Needless to say, this is often not a very efficient way of getting things done.

A relationship is also constituted by roles, but it is of particular importance that we distinguish—as well as one can—between the sorts of roles that constitute a relationship and those that are romantic. Romantic roles are those which distinctively further the process of two selves "merging." A relationship is an actual social arrangement between two people, whether that arrangement is limited to occasional sexual encounters or is as all-encompassing and committed as marriage. But a relationship is a private as well as a public arrangement, and a relationship is almost always the medium in which love gets to develop itself. Accordingly, we should not expect to get a very sharp or thorough separation of the roles that make up a relationship and the romantic roles that get played out through the relationship. Nevertheless, the two are quite different and it is the interplay between them that explains many of the vicissitudes of love.

Romantic roles are those that involve devotion and attention to each other, attention in particular to each other's emotions and feelings, to each other's bodies and expressions. The focus of all romantic roles is the idealized self of the other—"soul" if you like, as long as the soul essentially includes the body. Romantic roles accordingly cut themselves away from every public, practical and objective context. Correcting the other's speech habits is not romantic, and examining the other's body regarding some minor medical problem is not romantic either. Romantic roles consist almost entirely of rituals of expression, appreciation, seduction, whether the usual quiet dinner, loving looks and gift of flowers or the more spectacular poetic offering or death-defying demonstration of devotion. Romantic roles require leisure time together, time alone together, exclusive time not to be shared or repeated with anyone else. One reason why love may not last and may diminish as the years go by is simply the fact that we may not have the leisure or the aristocratic temperament to enjoy such unrestricted stretches of leisure time. We have to *do* something. We have to make a living. Or we just don't realize the absolute necessity of devoting this time continually to romance. It is worth noting well that the couples who most successfully carry their love full-blown into old age are those who early on learn how to make almost everything that they do romantic. They turn domestic chores into shared romantic roles. They share careers and interests, not for the sake of the careers or interests but for the sake of each other. Several author couples come to mind in precisely this context: Will and Ariel Durant, Irving and Jean Stone, Jean-Paul Sartre and Simone de Beauvoir. They made love last, not necessarily because they were "well-matched" but because they knew about romantic roles and knew that love would not last if left unattended while the tasks of life were taken care of.

Relationship roles are defined publicly even if—in some cases —that definition is in terms of privacy (as in a clandestine affair, for example). It is seen in the context of a family or a community, in a circle of friends or, in a limiting case, in the face of indifference among strangers—as when one gets involved with someone new in a new town, knowing no one. But where a romance is concerned solely with each other, a relationship is concerned with each other vis-à-vis the world. Relationships are contrastive ("Do you love him more than me?"), while in romance all such questions are out of order. Relationships consist largely of obligations, whereas romance does what it does as a matter of delight. Relationship roles involve shared interests, but the focus is on the interests, not the sharing. Relationships consist of doing things together, sharing conversation, expenses, but though there is mutual dependency there need be no shared identity. Two people get used to each other, even depend on one another ("Where will I go without you? What will I do?"). Two people in a relationship that lacks romance can have sex, of course, even exciting, exhilarating, satisifying sex, but it is not so much sex as expression, sex as as symbol of merging as it is sex as recreation that may even struggle to avoid the merging.

As we've said, romantic roles, relationship roles and domestic roles all flow together in any successful romance or marriage. The relationship provides the social substance in which the emotions of love can thrive; domestic roles provide the framework of efficiency in which the relationship can survive. But the relationship aims at stability, domesticity aims at efficiency, while romance aims at passion, the passion of union—anything to make us feel more together, even if it is destabilizing and inefficient. (Lovers' quarrels are more often than not strategies of emphasizing bonding, even by attacking them, rather than disagreements about the practicalities of the relationship or the household.) Love and the roles of being a lover redefine the self in a dynamic and dramatic way. They lift the self out of the ordinary, convert the world into a dramatic stage and keep us reaching for something "higher," an ever more noble sense of self, a sense of self inspired and expanded through this passionate connection with another person. The best test for love is in fact a role test, whether one still seeks above all else to improve him/herself in the eyes of the beloved. This secure vision, as opposed to the often fickle passing of passion and desire, is the ultimate measure of love, and the attitude that lets love last a lifetime.

THE DIMENSIONS OF IDENTITY ("DO OPPOSITES ATTRACT?")

The bond of Nature draw me to my own—
My own in thee; for what thou art is mine.
Our state cannot be severed; we are one,
One flesh; to lose thee were to lose myself.

—J O H N   M I L T O N , *Paradise Lost*

Looking into the temptation to generalize about love, we cannot help but stumble upon one of the enduring disputes about romantic dynamics, namely whether "opposites attract" or whether "like loves like." That is, whether we tend to fall in love with people similar to or different from us. In his dialogue *Lysis*, Plato made it clear that even in ancient Greece the two hypotheses were already the subject of popular discussion. In modern psychoanalytic theory, the favored hypothesis seems to be that opposites indeed attract, in Freud and Reik, for instance, on the grounds that one tries in love to "compensate" for one's weaknesses. Similarly, C. G. Jung developed a "shadow theory," according to which a person tends to seek out the "other side" of him or herself, sometimes a "dark side," which can turn love into tragedy but is usually an innocent complement that completes one's personality. In contemporary empirical psychology, on the other hand, the favored hypothesis seems to be that we tend to seek out those who are similar to ourselves, that differences (much less opposites) are more a matter of details than substance.

In favor of the "like loves like" thesis, there are always those popular instances of obvious narcissism—Rolling Stone Mick Jagger and his look-alike (ex-)wife Bianca are a fairly recent example. An artist marries an artist, an oldest brother an oldest sister. And then there are the cases of the "opposites attract" thesis: Marilyn Monroe marries playwright Arthur Miller, wealthy British dowager marries young punk rock musician. Well then, which is true? Do opposites attract or does like love like? The choice, of course, is absurd. At the very least it is usually within a framework of shared language, culture, background, religion, class, tastes and experiences that opposites attract. So they are, in one obvious sense, more alike than different. Romeo and Juliet may have been from feuding families, but they were both upper-class, healthy teenagers from the same Veronese neighborhood. Of course there is always the rebel who seeks out and chooses a love just because it is so in contrast with everything familiar and similar, who marries a person decades older or younger, of a different race, a different culture and, if it were possible, a different planet. But then again it is also possible to find that even within such dramatic differences the familiar is in fact doing all of the work—say, American men who marry British or Japanese wives who fit their conception of a woman's role more closely than their American peers, and upper-class women who marry working-class men who more closely resemble their favored conception of manhood.

On the other hand, within the context of similarity, two people in love might find the most glaring differences. They would meet one's observation that they are similar with a kind of dumbfounded amusement. Thus two compulsively neat people sharply distinguish between "the neat one and the sloppy one," and two quite socially skilled lovers see themselves as quite opposed introvert and extrovert. Two seemingly oversexed people may yet recognize that, within the context of the relationship, one of them is almost always more sexually aggressive, the other more passive and even coy. The point to be gleaned from this is that "like" and "unlike" are always comparative and contrastive terms and meaningless outside the context of the individual love relationships that they are brought in to explain. Moreover, the question of like and unlike is too often raised solely in the context of romantic *attraction*, but we have already argued that the basis for romantic attraction may be very different from the reasons for love. Attraction is significant only to the extent that it is a projection of the reasons that will (one hopes) make love work. One might be attracted to someone out of curiosity, because he or she is exotic or unusual, or one might be attracted to a kindred spirit because he or she shares one's interests, one's background, one's philosophy of life. But whether the attraction turns to love and whether love lasts depends infinitely more on the features of the relationship than it does upon the original reasons for attraction.

The initial attractions of love are often one- or two-dimensional—focusing on physical appearance or some shared skill or interest, but love itself is always multidimensional, covering virtually the whole of two people's life together. In this pervasive context, trying to simplify the many matching points that constitute the bonds of love in terms of similarity and difference is exceedingly simple-minded and misleading. If there is to be a match at all, there must be some substantial shared framework within which the relationship can develop. There should be some shared interests, of course, but what is much more important is that two lovers have an intense reciprocal interest in each other. Of course there will be similarities. For example, it is often pointed out that one tends to find attractive a person whose attractiveness is not such as to make one feel wholly unattractive by contrast. Psychologists sometimes call this the "equity hypothesis," and the simple plausible finding is that people tend to choose partners who are just about as attractive as they are, as long as we leave considerable room for compensation and individual exceptions (the homely genius who goes out with the handsome star). All of this ultimately is to say only that two people must share a world if they are to live in it together, and as one can demonstrate even at a two-hour cocktail party at which one feels "out of place," the dimensions of a shared world may be restrictive indeed ("I just couldn't stand being around all of those Republicans!").

But of course we can also find ourselves not only attracted but long in love with people different from ourselves—our "opposites" in certain dimensions. Jung and Reik are no doubt right when they say that this may be compensation for some weakness of one's own (a person who has trouble making decisions may welcome a partner who is decisive). But the attraction for "opposites" may also be a matter of entertainment. ("I'm too serious. I need someone who will amuse me"), a matter of continuing curiosity ("I never know what Harry's going to do next"), a matter of necessity ("Two people as domineering as I am could never live together in the same house"). Opposition, like similarity, is a multidimensional matter, and there is no simple generalization that will capture such complexities.

The big problem with all such inquiries about like and unlike is that they neglect the nature of love itself, which is neither similarity nor difference but *identity*. What holds a relationship together as a bond of love is a matter of overall fit and snugness. Of course not all features of two people will fit together, nor need they do so. A bond requires a matching of a significant proportion of two lives, and though the love bond will be stronger the more pervasive the match, it is inevitable that two people brought up quite differently will find that there are aspects of each life that are simply irrelevant, perhaps even strange or repulsive to the other. These aspects will not be "opposites" that help hold the relationship together but often a source of tension. In a successful relationship such features will be effectively buried or kept aside. (In an unsuccessful relationship they will be kept very much alive—whether on the table or resentfully suppressed, trotted out on occasion precisely to rub in the fact that this is a less-than-perfect match.) But in any affair that transcends the false enthusiasm of infatuation (false in that it fails to provide the shared identity that it promises), all attention will be aimed at those features best shared, that is, those that truly do bind the relationship together and make each lover a better person than he or she could possibly be otherwise, especially such other-directed virtues as sensitivity, generosity and caring.

The concept of shared identity should not be taken as an endorsement of the "like loves like" thesis; what is "shared" are not always similarities. Love is often but misleadingly described in terms of shared interests, and the success and failure of love are often explained by reference to those shared interests or to the lack of them. One couple breaks up because "we just didn't have anything in common anymore." Another makes it into old age on the basis of a shared passion for antiques, or rebuilding the house, or writing the definitive history of the world. But while there is obviously something to this, it fails as an account both of love and the success of love. Two people can remain very much in love despite different careers and hobbies as long as their primary interest is still in each other, and many people share many interests without being romantically interested in each other. Doing things together helps but is not the hallmark of love.

Shared interests, like similarities and the attraction of opposites, have been greatly overemphasized in the understanding of love and what makes love last. They are important, of course, but they fail to get at the core of the bonding of love. Shared interests may get a couple going in the same direction but they do not bind the two individuals together. It is shared selfhood that defines love, and shared selfhood has many dimensions that are not simply shared tastes and similarities. If we visualize the

Aristophanic metaphor, the two ripped halves of the primordial self will not fit together if their shared edges have the same shape (unless, of course, they were both completely flat and smooth). They rather *complement* each other; a protrusion here fits into an indentation there. Moreover, such complementariness is only partly characterized in terms of features of the individual lovers (tall, short, decisive, indecisive, sexy, homely). Much more important is the complementariness of *roles* in a relationship. Romantic roles typically require complementariness rather than similarity. (This is the half-truth upon which the "opposites attract" thesis relies.) Complementary roles do create that bond in the literal sense that it is impossible to have one role without its complement. For example, an insecure man needs nurturing; a strong matronly woman (who also needs someone to nurture) fits with him precisely. Or, within the context of this particular relationship, this man finds himself in need of nurturing and this woman finds that she enjoys nurturing (which is not to say that the nurturing relation is reciprocal as well). A woman who prefers to be irresponsible requires a man who is perhaps exaggeratedly responsible—both by way of contrast and as a corrective to her irresponsibility. Or, in this particular relationship, an otherwise responsible woman finds that she can afford to enjoy the luxury of irresponsibility, perhaps with a man who has never before appreciated the importance of "taking charge." Of course all complementarities presuppose some similarities as their basis, so it would be wrong to say that all roles are opposites. Many are simply reciprocal—complex matches of shared interests, similarities and complementarities. And many love roles are defined *within* the relationship; they do not proceed it. (Another danger of putting too much emphasis on romantic attraction as such.) Although every love affair has one or two roles that are readily identified as central, it also involves dozens of other roles (depending on the context), some of which might not work at all. Many a solid couple has tried some new activity in which they adopted roles that did not fit at all (kinky sex, or an emotional confession, or—a domestic example—both insist on taking command in the kitchen). The wise couple either works it out or jointly declares "We won't do that again." The self-undermining couple will leap to the conclusion that they have discovered some deep, dark conflict that they never noticed before, when in fact it is just one set of roles among many others that doesn't fit as well as it should. Roles often represent opposites rather than similarities, and when they work it is their opposition that helps create the bond of love.

Similar backgrounds and personalities, contrasting or complementary talents or traits, shared interests and mutually defined romantic roles all enter into the multidimensional identity constituted in love. But there are many other dimensions as well. There is the public dimension, shared social settings in which two people are identified publicly as a "couple," in which they make announcements in terms of "we" instead of "Chris and I." There is the all-important historical dimension, sheer time and experience together, moments and whole periods of life that could not possibly be duplicated with anyone else and so tie two lives together as no transient attraction ever could. There is the obvious physical dimension, the sensuous fact of two bodies pressed together, interdependent in their pleasures and signifying a "union" which nature as well as society recognizes as of ultimate significance. There is the too often neglected reflective dimension, the fact that two people recognize that they are in love, contemplate and announce that fact to each other (and, perhaps, to everyone else) and, in so doing, weave a conceptual bond that overlays the many other aspects of shared identity that already exist on a level of less self-awareness. (One form of infatuation consists of just this reflective weaving of a love story, but in the absence of any substantial ties to act as its basis.) And, in addition to romantic roles, there are dozens, perhaps hundreds, of other roles that two people play together, from such domestic chores as cleaning the house that they own together to the critical if rarely dramatic daily roles that bind together a relationship

—a good conversation, news of the day, a walk through the garden, an amusing grade-B movie together.

What constitutes shared identity is no one of these dimensions but some combination of all of them. Sexual identity may be the key for some couples but cleaning the house for another. Fifty years together may be the basis of shared identity for an older couple but a shared passion for collecting butterflies may be the basis for a new affair that has not yet even had time to be consummated. The essential thing to remember is that it is the identity itself that is crucial to love and its lasting and not one or two of the dimensions that may contribute to it. Sex may hold love together for a certain period but then get superseded by less passionate shared experiences and roles which nevertheless bind love with no less success, and it is tragic that we should so often confine our definitions of love to sexual passion and ignore the fact that the bond of love may be equally served by any number of shared and reciprocal activities and attitudes.

PRIVATE VIRTUES

. . . and you hear people say that lovers are seeking their other half; but I say that they are seeking neither for the half of themselves, nor for the whole, unless the half of the whole be also good. And they will cut off their own hands and feet and cast them away, if they are evil; for they love not what is their own unless it be good. For there is nothing men love but the good.

—SOCRATES (''DIOTIMA''),
in Plato's *Symposium*

To understand the lasting power of love it is necessary to understand its ultimate motivation. The primary motive for love is not sex or companionship or children or the convenience of a relationship but a sense of self-worth. Some self-worth may be gained simply by association with such a wonderful person, but this alone is never enough for love. To put it very crudely, when love succeeds, each lover feels better about him or herself than would otherwise be conceivable; when love fails, it is not usually because of flagging passion or infrequent sex or even fights and jealousy and it is not because of disenchantment with one's lover but rather because one no longer likes or can no longer tolerate the person he or she has become. Love (like most emotions) serves self-esteem, and what makes love last is not passion for the other person alone but the maximization of self-esteem. What makes love fail is the decimation of self-esteem, however much passion might be spent in compensation and whatever obsession or dependency might replace love in some states of self-degradation.

We are now in a position to understand why romantic love plays such an important role in the determination of personal identity and, consequently, why it occupies such an important place in our society. Personal identity is not just a matter of personal characteristics; it is also a measure of personal *worth*. The central thrust of our discussion in this chapter has been that our conception of the self and the worth of the self are not determined primarily in public, nor are they self-determined, but rather they are determined in our most intimate relationships, by those who truly know us well. The primary self is this private self, defined in a world inhabited by two lovers alone. Others may observe, but their opinions do not count, nor are they solicited. They may comment on the success of "the relationship" but they are rarely in a position to say anything about the love. It is in the first person plural—the "we"—that not only our most private and personal but also our most important virtues are defined, those that make us feel worthy as individuals—not in terms of our worldly success or public stature but in terms of our most intimate "inner" self. Here is where we will find the true sense of "merging" that the Aristophanes myth suggests, not just in the physical fact of intercourse, not in the social fact that two people are now a "couple," not just in the intertwined lives that result from a relationship, but in a mutual definition of self in terms of the self's most fundamental categories—the virtues. Indeed, love is itself a virtue in our way of thinking, perhaps the unifying virtue in which all the virtues find their home.

Everyone wants to be "a good person." This is not at all to discount the desire to be a rebel, an iconoclast, an eccentric, or even the desire to be evil. It is only to say that the self is not just a repository of facts and possibilities; it is also a core of values and ideals, ambitions and self-images—both desired and feared, and many of these depend on the opinions of others. Accordingly, negative images are often more powerful determinants of character than positive images. One person is terrified of appearing "soft" and will take on any guise of hostility or hardheaded stubbornness to avoid giving that impression. Another has a fear of being thought "pushy" or inconsiderate, and will let the world walk over him or her rather than risk such an image. Philosophers like Descartes and John Locke have described the self as an "inner" core of thoughts and memories, but the core of the self is established in conjunction with other people, and in our most intimate relationships in particular. Parents and siblings set up one's original sense of self-worth (if, that is, there are no congenital dispositions in this regard); friends and peers embellish and help it along. But in adulthood it is in the privacy of love that our sense of self-worth finds its essential dimension—even more than in such fundamental social measures as accomplishment and success. But what counts as being "a good person" is also socially defined. It is not just a matter of "pleasing ourselves" (a misleading way of saying that self-esteem is important). It is only a certain kind of society that respects and honors private virtues fostered in intimacy and isolated creativity (the artist in the attic or the writer in the cellar). Aristotle would not have understood what we are talking about; the idea of a personally good man who was not so on the basis of his work and status in the larger community would have been unthinkable to him. But the contemporary distinction between public and private virtue —with a strong emphasis on the private—is essential to our thinking about ourselves.

Virtues are the most treasured attributes a person can have. What distinguishes them from such desirable benefits as wealth or health or success is the fact that they are intrinsically valuable not only to oneself but to others as well. They are, as the Scottish philosopher David Hume says, "qualities pleasing to oneself and others." They are, as Aristotle wrote long ago, those "excel- lences" which represent a person at one's best. The virtues are such attributes as honesty, generosity, kindness, trustworthiness, tenderness and sensitivity. It is the virtues that make one "a good person," which, despite the banal connotations of that phrase, make up the heart of our ethics and our values. It is our virtues (and vices) that ultimately make up the self and, not unrelated, most traditional notions of the soul. The soul is not well-dressed or charming or chic, but the soul can be moral, compassionate, full of faith and hope. Being a good person is the humanist equivalent of having a good soul, and it is—however perversely pursued—the ultimate goal of being in love. That is why Plato so pursues the idea of love as "the pursuit of the Good," a lesson that is repeated often in the following twenty centuries and be- gins to dwindle only with Freud's romantic pessimism in this century.

What are one's virtues? It depends on where you are, and it depends upon whom you ask. It was a virtue in ancient Athens to be loud and boastful, a warrior and a killer. It was a vice (or simply pathetic) to be humble, and to be a pacifist—unthinkable. One cannot imagine virtuous Odysseus sitting down to dinner and conversation with twelve Christian apostles. The virtues of the college classroom are not the virtues of the football field, and the virtues of the boardroom are not the virtues of the bedroom. There are virtues, we are told, even among thieves. We all want to be virtuous, but what counts as a virtue varies indeed. The banality of the phrase "a good person" attests to this ambiguity. Some people think that a good person is bland as Wonder Bread; others think he or she should be as raunchy and as raucous as a barroom brawler. But this conclusion leads to another, even more curious: the same person might be a good person in one crowd and a creep in another. Given the fact that most of us tend to populate at least two or three worlds per week, this naturally tends to cause considerable commotion in the quest of self-identity.

This variety of virtues is an essential condition for love. One can imagine sexual attraction and even sexual obsession without a sense of virtue, but it is part of love to feel right if not righteous, to see oneself as well as one's lover as a paragon of virtue. The great illicit lovers of history and literature—Lancelot and Guinevere, Anna Karenina and Vronsky—have always seen themselves in the right, no matter how guilty they may have felt or how horrible they may have seemed to the rest of their worlds.

What is special about the private virtues of love is that they are *created* in love. It is not that "I love you because I trust you" but "I trust you because I love you." Love invents virtue where it cannot find it, and whether found or invented, virtue is thereby confirmed. It is not the least attraction of love that it tends to confirm what we want to like best in ourselves. This is not to say that love is illusory or that it "blinds" us to the faults of the beloved. It rather insists that love doesn't just allow us to "see what is best" in another person but also to bring out and inspire virtues that may not have been evident before. The private virtues are *indeterminate* as far as the public is concerned. Whether the world thinks that one is sensitive or loving is of little importance, and whether one thinks oneself sensitive or considerate may be of even less importance. Such virtues are determined in intimacy, with one's closest friends or with the one person to whom one delegates this awesome power over oneself. Our inmost virtues (whether or not we can be a good person or not) depend on them—and horror is choosing a lover who cannot give approval or offers only criticism and abuse. In the face of a critical or unappreciative lover, there is no success that can compensate for the damage. On the other hand, love can make the otherwise vicious person devotedly virtuous, at least within the confines of love.

It is no secret and no embarrassment that we choose our friends with at least half an eye to manifesting our virtues—that is, exercising those attributes that are virtues in that shared context and having them recognized as such. Smart people befriend smart people, sensitive people sensitive people, successful people successful people. However, a smart kid in high school might quickly learn that being smart, while an advantage in school, isn't a virtue; toughness is more important in certain groups, and he or she will downplay the one virtue in pursuit of another. A stupid or an ugly person, instead of accepting the alleged "fact" of stupidity or ugliness, may well seek out those who instead see "naive insight" or "nobility," or may seek out those who take stupidity and ugliness as virtues. The facts restrain us, but they never define us. As long as we can move, our identity is in our hands. It is a matter of whom we choose to judge. In love, accordingly, we pick a single, supreme judge who alone has the power to acknowledge and encourage what we ourselves see as our most noble attributes, our most important virtues, even if the whole of the rest of the world fails to appreciate them.

The single most important feature in the choice of a lover is not his or her beauty or charm or intelligence or accomplishment; it is, as we've said, the choice of a lover who will "bring out the best in us," who will recognize and encourage our best sensibilities and discourage (which is different from chastising or nagging about) our vices. One of the most common tragedies of love concerns the choice of a lover who, though requiting, nevertheless does not provide what is most essential—approval of one's virtues. Susan, who's a brilliant philologist, moves in with a man who couldn't care less. She consequently feels worthless about what she does and wonders why being in love does not make her happier about herself. Ferdinand, whose one evident virtue is his sense of humor, marries a humorless woman who respects only seriousness. He loves her madly, tries tirelessly to get her to laugh and enjoy herself but ends up wondering why he feels so frivolous and insignificant as a person. Such examples are legion—but interpreting such cases in terms of "self-destructiveness" or "masochism" explains very little. What such cases show us is that we do not always know who we are or what our virtues are and we often reach for virtues that are not ours at all. In love we often want to be acknowledged for virtues *not* approved of by everyone else. The great wrestler wants to be found sensitive. The wimp wants to be recognized as assertive and domineering. Love is not just a vehicle for proving what you are; it is also a device for trying to be what you are not. At its best this explains the self-improvement that is often a part of love, but at its most tragic this same reaching for what one is not explains that failure of love. Thus in the *Symposium*, Plato has Socrates argue the extreme thesis that one loves what one lacks, and Jung and Reik more recently argue that we love another by way of compensation for our own inadequacies. But some virtues emerge by way of contrast ("domineering," "tolerant") while others thrive in their own setting—honesty breeds honesty, and generosity breeds generosity. When one looks for a lover, one looks for shared virtues as well as contrasts, and what is important is not similarity or difference but rather wanting and getting what one needs.

We tend to fall in love with a person who maximizes our virtues. It is not quite as Socrates insists—that we seek only someone who is good and a shared self that is good, but this is certainly the ideal. Sometimes, however, we seek someone who will maximize our virtues by way of contrast, make us seem strong in contrast to their meekness (real, feigned or imagined) or smart in contrast to their modest intelligence. And sometimes we seek someone who will actually bring out the "bad" in us—rebelliousness or defiance, cynicism or cold-bloodedness—underscoring once again the confused state of the virtues in our society. But in general we choose a lover who will maximize what we take to be our most important virtues. This effort does not always succeed. Sometimes it succeeds in the short run but not for long. Sometimes one set of virtues gets maximized to the disadvantage of others that may prove to be more essential, as when devotion eclipses integrity or generosity eclipses prudence. Some virtues are sufficiently public so that private definition is illusory: no love affair will allow someone who is phobic about mathematics to think he would be a great accountant, but of course the encouragement and confidence of love can help overcome enormous psychological obstacles, and, where looks and personality are involved, that one private opinion may count immeasurably more than the whole of combined public opinion. This is true of the core of private virtues—such virtues as sensitivity and understanding, being sexy, charming, funny or generous; love is the context in which such virtues are best nurtured and acknowledged, where other people's opinions just don't count at all.

This is possible because the private virtues, like the self itself, are largely underdetermined. Whether or not one is virtuous cannot be settled simply by reference to "the facts," nor is it merely a matter of personal opinion. As an illustration of this, consider the personal question "Am I generous?" The truth is that sometimes I am extremely so—giving, outpouring, gracious. I leave 50 percent tips, give gifts spontaneously, volunteer my time. Other times I am stingy, cheap, miserly, petty. I undertip a decent waiter; I bring an on-sale Blanc de Blancs to a friend's dinner party instead of a good Chablis, or I give a bottle of J&B instead of Glenfiddich for a Christmas gift. True, I feel guilty, I feel cheap, but character is built on action, not retrospective feelings. And even when I am generous, there is always that nagging question, whether I am so out of generosity or vanity, whether generosity is indeed the source or is it rather my desire to appear generous? What could establish this? Of course one can and should always go beyond the single incident and look for the pattern, the long-term record, but the record is undoubtedly mixed, an irregular curve from magnanimity or miserliness that is remarkably independent of the curve marking such indisputable realities as my financial well-being at the time or whether the recipients of my tips or gifts deserve them or whether or not my generosity is motivated by vanity. The problem is that any accusation of miserliness seems irrefutable. The accusation sticks—or at least it is always a nagging possibility, available at any time to my enemies or detractors or an unsympathetic or cynical public—and to me.

Love resolves this indeterminacy. It provides a single source of appeal to settle all such uncertainties, and, just as important, it provides a self-fulfilling sense of this resolution. It is not just that my lover's recognition of my generosity makes it seem real; it also inspires me to be more generous, and it is with this in mind that Phaedrus in the *Symposium* comments that an army of lovers would be invincible, for each would rather die a thousand times than be a coward before his beloved. Our virtues are solidified and inspired by love, and this is true not only regarding such underdetermined traits as generosity, fairness and good humor but also such overall traits as sensitivity and understanding and, most of all, "being a good person"—that overall balance of the virtues versus the vices. But most of all it is in the privacy of love that the specifically private virtues are defined, being a "good lover" (being sensual, understanding, considerate, fun, sexy), and also the related vices (being insensitive, cold, inconsiderate, a bore, a "cold fish," etc.). If my lover thinks that I am a sensitive lover, I am—and that is the end of it. This is hardly a virtue that one can simply endow upon oneself (though many seem insistent of trying), but neither is it a virtue that is best demonstrated with a large number of lovers, much less in public. It is a virtue whose truth is manifested in a singular situation, with a single lover whose opinion is absolute. (The wrong lover, of course, is a disaster, and multiple lovers offer the risk of being deflated, even by one out of a thousand and one—the problem of Don Juan and the advantage of sexual exclusiveness.) This is why it is so dangerous to parade intimate virtues publicly, for they are bound to be judged harshly and unsympathetically. It is why the privacy and exclusivity of love is so important, for without them the determination of the virtues is no longer an intimate issue.

The privacy of love is a liability as well as a benefit to the self. Having given a single person the terrifying power of judgment over us, with little objective or public standard or limit to the use of it, our self-esteem can be ground to fine powder—whatever our public proof of virtue and lovability. If abandoned, one can suddenly find oneself as if without any virtue, or any identity at all. Love is so explosive because two people have this power over each other, and the violence of domestic fights has much to do with the escalating mutilation that is possible as they each start retaliating for every brutally cutting aspersion of character. The orgy of mutual celebration that typically begins love can turn into a devastating defensive battle for self-esteem as each tries to save the self by demolishing the other. Sex, of course, provides a prime battleground for such attacks, for while many of our virtues have at least some public corroboration, our sexual virtues—no matter what one's past experience—seem tightly tied to the present and the private. A couple can protect their high sense of themselves through the privacy of love, but they can also butcher one another without mercy and without the possibility of an outside "objective" balance. This is how a person surrounded by supportive friends and family can be thrown into a suicidal funk by love turned sour, for that one other person has had the power to wholly undermine a lover's sense of self. And a person who is entirely devoted to love and otherwise very much alone in the world may have no outside perspective and no possibility of salvation.

Plato and Aristotle and their friends could not have understood our sense of private virtue, and, consequently, they could not have understood our concept of love. The Good for them was an objective quality, and the idea that a person's virtue has anything to do with what he or she and a single lover or friend want to believe they would have found balmy. To us a man might seem to be utterly unscrupulous in his dealings with the world, but if his wife and loved ones declare him a saint, we may be tempted to reconsider. For Aristotle a family's opinion of a man's private life had very little if anything to do with virtue— though it might still be a good topic for gossip and scandal. Of course we might have our doubts in particular cases, when discrepancy between private sensitivity and public reputation becomes too great. But the point is that we can even raise the question: the idea that a person's true self—true virtues—are to be found in his or her private life and emotions rather than in public performance alone is one of the most profound conceptual transformations in history, and it is on the basis of this transformation that we can make sense of love. Love is the pursuit of the Good, as Socrates says, but love creates—it does not merely find—the Good in us.

FROM DIALECTIC TO DYNAMICS

And why? Why should we consider ourselves, men and women, as broken fragments of one whole? It is not true. Rather we are the singling away into purity and clear being, of things that were mixed . . . the admixture of sex in the highest sense surpassed, leaving two single beings constellated together like two stars.

—D . H . L A W R E N C E , *Women in Love*

The idea that love is concerned with selfhood might suggest that love is essentially self-love, casting love in the role of a vice rather than a virtue. And the suggestion that love is essentially the reconception and determination of oneself through another looks dangerously similar to some familiar definitions of narcissism. But self-reference entails neither cynicism nor narcissism. Although one does see oneself through the other, and although as in narcissism the idea of "separation of subject and object" is greatly obscured, love as mutual self-defining reflection does not encourage either vicious or clinical conclusions. Unlike narcissism, love takes the other as its standard, not just as its mirror, which is why the courtly lovers called it "devotion" (as in devoting oneself to God) and why Stendhal—himself an accomplished narcissist—called "passion-love" the one wholly unselfish experience. Love is not selfless but it is nevertheless the antithesis of selfishness. It embodies an expansion of self, modest perhaps, but what it lacks in scope it more than makes up for in motivation. And in today's climate of personal greed and "self-fulfillment" it is for many successful citizens one of the last virtues left standing. We trust someone who can love, and we do not trust someone who cannot love. To love is to transcend selfishness, even as it redefines the self in a noble new way.

It must not be concluded, however, that love and selfhood stand in an easy, comfortable alliance. Romantic love is a powerful emotional ally—better than indignation and resentment—in breaking down the isolation that has become the dubious heir of some of our favorite traditional values. But we remain staunch individualists, and love will always conflict with its own presupposition. It is folly to think that one can continue to live a complete life of individual success and self-fulfillment and at the same time maintain the devotion of love. Of course it is possible to live a life of success and have the benefit of someone wholly devoted *to you*—the assumption of most successful men until the present century and now the goal of a number of successful women and men. But being loved is not the same as loving, and the convenience of having someone devoted to you is not the same as being devoted and in love. The latter takes time, and if it is to succeed at all, it must be the top priority of one's existence. Otherwise, it soon becomes just a "fling," a temporary vacation from worldly ambition and seriousness, perhaps dismissed as "infatuation" on the grounds that it never really was serious after all. Love demands attention, and love requires breaking down just those barriers and pretensions that make social success and status possible. Love and individuality are necessarily in conflict even while they mutually support one another. This is the dialectic of love, and it is, for each one of us, also a matter of choice and compromise. One can be individually independent; one can love and be in love. Insofar as one chooses one, there is fundamentally less of the other. But, on a more positive note, the choice of love puts independence in perspective, while success without love almost always seems fragile and inconclusive.

The dialectic of love is the tension between individuality and the shared identity of love. It is this dialectic that also explains the dynamics of love—why love tends to be so passionate at the beginning (when individuality must be overwhelmed; fusion requires great heat and excitement), why love tends to breed crises (fusion goes so far, then individuality inevitably has its say again), why love can get so immensely comfortable with time (when two selves so adapt to each other that there are few differences unresolved, when the sheer weight of history and familiarity makes continued fusion a matter of simple assumption rather than an object of great effort) and why love is always an open question (individuality never fully resigns itself to be merged, and there is nothing guaranteed about the merger that is never fully completed). Shared selfhood is the goal of love, the aim of its every word, caress and gesture, but it is a partial, ultimately impossible goal that must always coexist with the reality of two very different people, each with their own histories and backgrounds, their own battles in life, their own personalities. But it is often two people who have particularly strong selves who also have particularly strong love for each other, not because they fit so well together, but because fitting together requires so much of themselves. They will probably fight, perhaps a lot. They will often disagree, and critical disagreement may even be one of the structures of the relationship. (Fights and arguments must be distinguished from that petty nagging and quibbling whose only purpose is to cause friction, not to resolve differences.) Two lovers with little character, on the other hand, might find love quite easy but wonder what all of the fuss is about.

Love that lasts does not abandon this struggle but thrives on it. And the best love, as D. H. Lawrence always insisted, is that in which there is neither the pretense of total fusion nor the isolation of complete individuality, but rather the delicate dialectic (hardly anything so genteel as a "balance") between the two.

5

....

THE DYNAMICS OF LOVE: MAKING LOVE LAST

CARING AND THE MYTH
OF SELFISHNESS

Most people see the problem of love primarily as that of *being loved*, rather than that of *loving*, of one's capacity to love.

—ERICH FROMM, *The Art of Loving*

Love may be a matter of self, but what defines the self in love is first of all *caring* for another person. Love is an expansion of self to include—and even to favor—the other. It is the antithesis of selfishness, and it is caring that marks the opposition between them. "Tough-minded" thinking aside, it is caring that is closest to our natures. We are not by nature selfish—only limited in our vision and our understanding. The dividing line is not between self and others, not even between "us" and "them"; it is between the personal "we" and the abstract "others," which is why justice and fairness are a problem for us. But not in love, where caring is quite sufficient.

It will strike future historians as a matter of considerable curiosity, if not perversity, that many Americans today seem to take it as a philosophical axiom that every person is first of all concerned with his or her own interests—not necessarily to the exclusion of others but with an attitude that begins with "If I don't watch out for me, who will?" Consequently, many people believe that they have no choice but to practice a belligerent solipsism in which the very concepts of success, happiness and contentment are defined in terms of the satisfaction of personal goals, private ambitions and self-contained individual desires. But this is a sure recipe for failure and that nagging dissatisfaction that can find no source for itself except the meanness of the world ("It's a dog-eat-dog world out there") when in fact the meanness begins with oneself. The perennial theme of best-selling "self-help" books is that one should *be* oneself by breaking free, by being independent and by knowing how to say no and not feel guilty. These may be soothing images for a harried clerk or a frustrated homemaker, but they are hardly conducive to helping or understanding one's true self. The self is defined not by its defensive boundaries but by its expansion in *caring*, by saying yes and not no, by attachment and not by separation. It is selfishness and not love that is the product of insecurity and frustration, a retreat into what is poorest about the self rather than a reaching out for what is best. Selfishness is a learned pathology.

One is what one cares about. Caring only about oneself is a conceptual short-circuit that leaves only empty goals and burns itself out. The self is not made up of needs so much as it is a matter of being needed, by someone, by something. One learns and grows by caring, by expanding one's interests outward, by making others not the *object* but the *subject* of one's own interests, by making their interests one's own. *Caring* is the basic (but not the only) bond of love. Caring establishes the most important and usually the most durable bonds of identity between persons.

"Caring" is one of those terms that gets bandied about as if it were entirely unambiguous and unproblematic in love. It is worth remembering, therefore, that Mephistopheles punished Faust by making him care, and at least one major dictionary (Random House, 1980) starts out defining "care" as "an uneasy state of mind, as arising from burdens or anxiety." It is not an easy flow of affection but a kind of cramp in consciousness, holding it down, restricting its freedom. This is not at all to say that care is negative or undesirable, but let's at least begin with a little realism. Caring is a responsibility as well as a virtue.

There are at least two distinct and quite different meanings of "to care," with a spectrum of meanings in between. There is caring for someone in the sense of an active engagement (as in "caring for the sick" or "caring for a child"), which entails responsibility and possibly custody but need not include any particular state of mind or personal concern. Then there is caring as a state of mind, a kind of concern. The former is typically taken as proof of love—why else would one offer such a devotion of time and energy—but it is the latter that is usually mentioned as the stuff of love itself. But notice that one can care a great deal without doing or being inclined to do anything whatever. Such a state of mind may be merely a question of investment, such as the fact that I care about the Gillette corporation because I own 400 shares of their stock or care about a certain obnoxious student just because I have put four years into his training. Care can also be distinctively neutral or negative ("Of course I care what happens to him. I'd like to see him hang"). Care can be worry, or care can be benign "wishing well." To care for someone can be to value them highly, but without any personal concern or responsibility whatever (as one might value an artist or a teacher). Love may involve any or all of these, but none of these suffice to distinguish love as a kind of care.

Care in love is something more than mere investment and abstract involvement or worry. Like most emotions, love is impatient for expression—whether an urgent "I love you!" or an opportunity to save a loved one's life at great risk to one's own. It is all well and good to be concerned about people and wish them well, but love requires action or, in the absence of any possible action, that kind of awful paralysis that can come only from desperate frustration. The lover who moons and sulks is, in a sense, acting out his love, for that may be the only action available to him at the time. Writing poetry may be an expression of love, but so may be helping with the dishes. It is important to distinguish, however, between helping out of love and helping out of a sense of fairness or obligation. The latter may be noble (and it is certainly not incompatible with love) but it is quite different from an expression of emotion. To care about a person is to be motivated to help and encourage without the aid of more general principles or concerns. Caring precedes fairness and morals, which is why it is so important and indispensible in love.

We need a deeper definition of care in its relation to love. To care is more than investing in or worrying about another person. It is expanding one's *self* to incorporate and include the other and his or her ambitions, needs, desires and self-concerns. Care is not just the antithesis but the refutation of selfishness. Whereas the apostle of selfishness suggests that each of us is (inevitably, naturally, prudently) out for ourselves, the fact that we care shows that the self is not so self-enclosed. Rather, it is expansive and open. You are what you care about and that can be quite a lot. Care is not just concern but an expansion of self; love is in part (but just in part) this elaboration and reaching out of the self to include another. Caring is the Golden Rule internalized: treat those you care about *as* yourself, because they are.

In a delightful little book, *Caring*, some years ago, Milton Mayeroff analyzes "caring" as "helping to make the other grow," and "experienc[ing] what I care for [a person, an ideal, an idea] as an extension of myself and at the same time as something separate from me that I respect in its own right." We might be cautious about the pop-cult jargon of "growth" and restrict ourselves to the question of caring for a person (not an idea or an ideal), but Mayeroff captures the dualistic nature of caring quite well: you are an extension of myself but also separate. Because so many of the examples in his book are examples of caring about an idea or a creation, such as a novel or a symphony, and such tutorial relations as parent-child and teacher-student, however, Mayeroff does not consider the explosive if not impossible tension between identity and distinctness in the sharing of selves that is romantic love. The danger of extending one's self, one of my Freudian friends is fond of saying, is that it can get cut off. The danger of identifying with another, as Freud himself often said, is that by doing so one opens oneself up to the nasty vicissitudes of reality, the possibility of rejection, frustration, and worse. The advantage of caring about children and students is that one has decisive advantages—authority and experience. One is (within limits) in control. Caring about another adult is a confrontation between two independent and experienced selves, one or both of whom may resent the caring and have their own ideas of what should be expected or demanded. We know what "growth" means in a three-year-old or a beginning piano student; it is not so clear in what direction a thirty-five-year-old is to "grow."

Caring for another person, in love, is not like caring for one's own creation, for love requires the independence as well as the bond with the other. In caring for novels and symphonies, ideas and ideals, we have a distinct advantage. No matter how difficult the process of creation may be, no matter how it may take on "a life of its own," there is an obvious sense in which ideas, novels and symphonies do not fight back, do not resist the identity they are given. As an author I would be the last to deny that ideas, novels and symphonies (not to mention children) have their own ideas about how things ought to be and often fall short of our expectations. But any would-be writer who thinks that wrestling with a half-finished novel is like struggling through the painful months of a mutually frustrating love affair probably shouldn't write a novel. Caring about another person is the most difficult kind of caring—and the most necessary. What another person cared for can give us—or not give us—is caring in return. The saintly among us may insist that such reciprocity is to be neither required nor expected, but the rest of us know better. To care without being cared for in love can be the very essence of damnation.

Or as the Lady Yakamochi has written,

> *Ai omo wan*
> *Hito wo omouwa*
> *Odera no*
> *Gaki no shirie ni*
> *Nukazuku gotoshi.*
>
> (To love somebody
> Who doesn't love you

Is like going to a temple
And worshiping the behind
Of a wooden statue
Of a hungry devil.)

It is often said that lovers take the interests of the other as more important than their own. In a strict sense this is incorrect: lovers take the interests of the other *as* their own. One's joy at the other's success, or sadness at failure, is not a bit less than one's joy or sadness at one's own success or failure—and ideally unmixed with envy or glee. This is not a verbal quibble, but a basic question about the experience and the nature of love. Insofar as one person cares about the other, one does not just "look after" his or her interests or sympathize with them. As Mayeroff nicely puts it, "The meaning of caring is not to be confused with such meanings as wishing well, liking, comforting and maintaining, or simply having an interest in what happens to the other." Caring is a matter of one's own identity, not a spectator sport. Caring is an absorption of (or by) the other, not simply a matter of watching over and expressing concern. It is inextricably sharing the risks as well as the rewards, not safely helping out, not being willing at any difficult moment to say "Well, it's your problem." Caring is essential to love, and it is no small virtue in a relationship that, no matter how bad things may be, two people continue to care for and about one other. A relationship without caring cannot long be love, but in any decent relationship it is caring that makes love last.

We have said a great deal about the creation of the self, but the simplest formula for self-creation is that, insofar as we create ourselves, we do so by caring. We care about our parents, brothers, sisters and children and thus are part of a family. So, too, we define our social selves by caring. We enter into a profession, turn a job into a career, become an artist or a writer or a golfer or a stock-car buff by caring. We form the inner circle of friends that determines our character by caring. And we form the most important and exclusive identity(ies) of our lives, in love, by caring. Life has meaning not because of what we have or what we know or what we are "in ourselves" but because we care about something. Popular melodrama aside, meaning is not deep inside of us but on the outside, in the ideas, things and people we attach ourselves to and their attachment to us. The meaning of life as well as the meaning of love is to be found, first of all, in the ways we define ourselves by caring and by being cared for by other people.

Caring, however, has its conditions. There is a dramatic difference between caring in relationships already established (as in a family) and caring when the relationship itself is open to decision and debate. Home, according to Robert Frost, is where you can go when you have to and they have to take you in. In romance, by contrast, getting there is the hard part and, once you leave, you can rarely go home again. Romance is reciprocal and sometimes fickle, founded on coincidence and always subject to extensive (if rarely explicit) negotiation. Most forms of love evolve between people who find themselves together—mothers, fathers and their children, brothers and sisters, neighbors and members of the same religion or community. Between gratitude, necessity and familiarity we make the best of it—and the best of it is love. But in romantic love two full-grown adults *meet* each other, perhaps as strangers (and in any case as strangers to love) and inevitably experience a clash of established identities coupled with the awareness—not available to, say, parents and their children—that this relationship is strictly *voluntary*. Caring may be essential to love, but the dualism of caring in romantic love confronts a formidable challenge. Initial proclamations aside, it is the kind of caring that makes demands as well as offers, threatens as well as promises and begins with a set of unspoken conditions and expectations that make most business contracts and political treaties seem casual by comparison.

The problem with talking about "caring" is that the word itself connotes an attitude at once both simpering and superior. But there is little room for simpering in the dynamics of love and no place for superiority in a relation that is emphatically between equals. What's more, talk about caring tends too often to remain on the plane of a general attitude and not deal with specific needs and desires. As soon as we start to look at the particular conflicts of a relationship, however, the gloss of all pious talk about the importance of caring quickly fades away. Two lovers may really care about each other and honestly accept the other's needs, in general, as their own. But when these mutually contradictory needs come into conflict, "caring" turns out to be a pretty poor instrument for understanding the intrigue and conflict that make up love. "Care," yes, but let's not get the idea, almost built into the word, that care means devoted concern, like an idealized priest watching over his flock. Love is caring. But let's not paint our picture of the world with such a limited palette that we fool ourselves into thinking that life is either selfishness or selfless devotion. Love, in particular, is the kind of caring that one knows in a ferocious but also delightful battle between equals. It is not that concerned but superior attitude of custodianship that one has with children or a book in progress. Indeed, in love, this attitude signals the end and not the essence of romance. Caring, in other words, is foremost among the virtues of love, but it is hardly the whole story.

LOVE AND TIME

Because if it didn't work out, I didn't want to blow the whole day.

—FOOTBALL SUPERSTAR
PAUL HORNUNG
*(when asked why he had decided to get married
in the morning)*

Love is too often described as a transient state—a feeling or a passing passion—that by its very nature cannot last more than a few weeks or months at most. Then the question comes up—

with a note of despair: "How, then, can love last?" But love is not an emotional state, it is a dynamic emotional process. There are emotions that can have their say in fifteen seconds—in a burst of spontaneous anger, for example, but love takes weeks, months, ultimately years. And it is not just that it takes that long to establish a firm and stable relationship; love itself takes time, like good wine. It may be love at first sight, but it continues to develop as love for possibly a lifetime. In one sense it is wrong to ask "How can love last?" for the fact seems to be that lasting is the nature of love, even one of its preconditions. The question should concern why love so often doesn't last. The answers are many—because we have such unreasonable expectations of it, because we confuse love with the relationship and allow the latter to wholly eclipse the former, because we take the dynamics of love as problems instead of as essential ingredients.

How can an emotion be so tied to time? In part it is because love, unlike most other emotions, involves reciprocity with another person, and this means months or years of learning and adjustment, weaving a shared self that is not just a projection of hopes and old frustrations but a self that is solid and based on what is most intimate in both people. Furthermore, love, unlike many emotions, has a story behind it, a narrative form that lovers, knowingly or not, must more or less follow. One can find societies where other emotions (e.g., anger, in "vendetta") has such a narrative structure, and one can find many societies where sexual love does not have one. But for us love is first of all a "romance," a story, and to pursue this story—which we hope will turn out to be an epic and not a short story—takes time. Love takes time.

Love is a philosophical experience, quite apart from the (dubious) quality of the many philosophical rhapsodies produced by so many untutored philosophical lovers. The logic of love is in many ways the logic of an idea—or rather two different versions of the same idea being played out over time. It is a dialectic of conceptual change, from a world of individual values and social demands to a world in which individual needs and desires are inextricably tied up with the needs and desires of another person. Accordingly, love is rightly referred to as a voyage of discovery. The speculative verbosity of love that is so familiar to us is not so much an expression of new affection as it is an attempt at exploration, not merely of an inner sensation but of one's "true" self as well as of another. And, again, one might direct an emotion *at* another person in an instant, but the exploration that is part and parcel of love is complex and consuming.

The experience of love not only takes time, it is very much an experience *of* time. Most of the structures of love we have been discussing are the structures of love at any given time, but there are also structures over time, and love, as such, looks not just to the present but also to the past and the future. This is part of the reason that love has such a perplexing sense of time, sometimes impatient beyond tolerance, sometimes almost in a state of timelessness. It is never simply awareness of the moment but always exquisite awareness of the fleetingness of that moment. No sooner have two lovers begun to learn about one another than they begin to seek out or invent a past and plan a future. The geographic search begins: "Have you ever been to . . . ?" or "Do you remember what it was like in . . . ?" and proceeds to "Oh, did you ever run across so-and-so?" and "You weren't by any chance at the Altamont Rolling Stones concert, were you?" Even in cases of extreme incompatibility there are at least the chronological touch points: "I was just beginning grade school then" or "I wasn't born yet." A couple has no sooner been together a half dozen times when the "remember when we . . ." game begins, and it doesn't matter whether it is played with a bit of nostalgia, as a bit of teasing or a memory test, the essential function is being fulfilled, weaving what few shared events and memories there are into a narrative, a love story, with as much humor, import, foresight and adventure as the events will bear. As love develops the past does too, sealing the shared identity as a zipper moving through time. Old experiences are reinter-preted: a chance meeting becomes an omen; an almost forgotten sentence becomes prophecy. Evenings get spent piecing to-gether and filling out earlier items of the story—when it was not clear that there was a story (or which one it was): "Do you know what I thought just then?" "And then didn't you say to me . . . ?" This is not just the chatter of a relationship, but part of its es-sence, the stuff that gives it temporal substance. Likewise, a love that denies its past may have little basis for a future.

Planning a future is more difficult than weaving a past. For one thing, it has no guideposts, no undeniable events or memo-ries to show the direction. In place of such fixed events there are fantasies, promises and the established cultural narrative with its expectations—marriage, children, a house, old age together and death. But these are abstractions, devoid of detail and therefore without concrete significance. The imagined child (or children) that we *will* have together has, beyond the vague "I bet she'll look just like . . . ," no identity, no personality, no problems, no pecularities, no smile, no eyes, no giggle, no habits. One cannot putter around in an imaginary house, paint a nonexistent wall or relax in a merely possible future yard. Old age is all but unima-ginable to those who have not been there, and, given current divorce and death rates, the likelihood of two young lovers reaching that stage of their projected drama makes it unappeal-ing as a point of focus. Nevertheless, it is by projecting ahead to such abstract possibilities that a couple builds a future together and gives meaning to the present. Love, no matter how enthu-siastic, is never simply for the moment. As an identity it must always be "forever," not because the future is in any way assured, but because an identity cannot conceive of anything beyond itself.

Love is identity and identity is, in part, time together. Whether it is real time or imagined time together is not nearly so impor-tant as the fact that it is time together, moments shared in memory or imagination, events coauthored (or cosuffered) as so many plot elements to hold two lives together. It is said—usually after love has ended—that "time heals all wounds." The happier truth about time is that it nourishes and builds, not only heals. It is the medicine of growth as well as recovery, and love without time is desperately deprived. In their few days together the tragic Romeo and Juliet managed to reconstruct their whole family history, get married, consummate their marriage, have at least two major misunderstandings and imagine an entire if unrealized future together. Love, no matter how brief, cannot settle for less.

Romantic love is often confused with mere novelty, but romantic love can last a long, long time, yet at the same time there is a sense in which romantic love is always new. Love gives us a spectacularly keen sense of the preciousness of the present even while it reweaves or relives the past. It is the newness, the excitement of love, that makes it seem "romantic," but newness isn't just a matter of time, for that sense of excitement (that is, excitement as enthusiasm, not as "thrill") can go on for years or a lifetime, and on rare occasion it actually does. What is significant about newness is the fact that it is fresh, not just another novel experience, and the enthusiasm of first love is a function of the pregnant present—a present overflowing with desires for the next few moments or hours and filled with fantasies for the future. In our enthusiasm we quite understandably fail to see the purpose of all of this lust and excitement, the retelling of time and rebuilding of the future, but it does indeed have an essential function—to destroy the old self and re-create a new one. Not surprisingly, this is a process that takes time, and one does not begin to build a life together without the intention of finishing it.

This is not to say, however, that only love that lasts is "true," the real thing, love that has proved itself. We already noted that Romeo and Juliet, in their few days together, managed to cram in a truncated lifetime of experiences in which—in the absence of time—their fantasies for the future had to suffice. It is one thing to deny (quite properly) that the week-long flirtation of a Don Juan is true love; it is something quite different to deny love to a tragic young couple who meet death only days after their first meeting. Sometimes love doesn't get the time it demands, but this does not make it any less love. What is essential to love is not that it must get the time it demands but the fact that it demands it. Don Juan, after a week, has had all the time he wanted. Lovers after a lifetime still want more.

Love as a narrative dictates to us a series of culminations, a series of choice points or, if you prefer to accentuate the negative, a series of predictable crises in love. It is not hard to spell out the earlier and more obvious ones:

> first meeting
> first conversation
> first date
> first kiss
> first sexual experience
> "I love you"
> meeting best friends
> meeting family
> first trip together
> moving in together
> first fight
> getting married
> first child

Of course several of these might happen at the same time (first kiss and first sexual experience, moving in and getting married) and often steps can be rearranged or drawn out—e.g., sex can be postponed or a couple can live together before taking any further steps for fifteen years instead of fifteen months. But each of these, at the time, feels like a culmination, a plateau of experience, although after a brief sense of calm a crisis may begin to

emerge—first with anxiety ("Have we let it go too far?") and then
the decision: whether to go on. The fact that one might be so
enthusiastic that he or she cannot even imagine *not* going on
makes it no less anxious and no less a crisis—the sleepless night
is a universal phenomenon, whether prompted by joy or despair.
Love has a "timetable" that cannot be avoided or denied, and as
much as we would like to say that we "make up our own rules"
nevertheless we are bound by it whether or not we recognize it.
Sex seems to be virtually obligatory after a certain period of
romantic attention or flirting—and it is not just the infamous
hormones and consequent impatience that is responsible for
this. The difference between courting and coquetting is respect
for time, and while it would be absurd to expect a general rule of
morals or etiquette in this regard (we no longer have strict rules
about "kissing on the first date" and there is no longer any such
period as "the proper length of an engagement") there is a point
in every incipient sexual relationship where the appropriateness
of the next step is simply obvious—or should be. Its presence is
often announced by a dramatic momentary silence. Or, more
awkwardly, one shyly initiates the familiar query that begins
"Don't you think that it's time that we . . . ?" So, too, an affair
becomes a relationship after a certain amount of time. Asked
why they got married, couples will volunteer a dozen familiar
reasons, ranging from the romantic to the urgently pragmatic,
but the most common reason, so evident that it may often go
unrecognized, is simply that "it was time."

The various steps of love are often presented as a matter of
"taking a chance." Of course this is true, but *not* taking the next
step is also taking a chance, and though we would like love to be
such that we are assured of success, the truth is that such assurances seem possible only in retrospect and even the most enthusiastic lovers blunder, if quickly, from step to step and may only
postpone the crisis that is sure to come with reflection. (Here is
a possibility: "Doesn't it seem crazy to you now that we did all of

that so fast without even thinking about it?") The steps of love are not just steps *into* love nor are they the consequences of love. They constitute the temporal structure of love, its narrative applied to each individual case. It makes no sense to claim that you are in love if, at the same time, you want to by-pass or abort the timetable. There may be modifications—e.g., the rejection of marriage, which is a relatively new entry into the romantic schedule anyway, or the prolongation of celibacy, which is one of romantic love's oldest tricks. But it is usually an argument against love if one denies and foreswears sexual expression altogether, expresses no interest whatever in meeting the other's friends and family, insists on always traveling alone (unless, perhaps, there is some very dramatic reason for this). And while it is important not to tie love and marriage too tightly together, it seems fairly obvious today that one must have fairly strong objections to and arguments against marriage for it not to be an essential step in the process. Lack of interest or indifference alone will tell against love, even if there is passion elsewhere in the relationship. ("Marie suggested that we get married, and I said all right, if you want to. Marriage is an important decision, she said, and I replied, 'No.' " —Camus, *The Stranger.*)

Each step in love's timetable brings with it new rules, new expectations, new obligations. Dating carries with it no proper expectations for regular contact, but the obligatory phone call the day afterward has become almost a cultural cliché with us. Sex alone does not dictate fidelity, but marriage certainly does, and so do any number of less formal living arrangements. One of the more popular if incoherent arguments of the sixties insisted that sex and love carried no obligations, but the fact is that even sex has its more or less automatic obligations—at the very least an obligation to be attentive and caring. (Obligations are not democratic; it is no refutation of this to point out that so many lovers today fail in such obligations.) Also, most of the steps carry with them the expectation of continuance; they are for the most part initiations, not achievements. The purpose of a date is not "to have fun" but to audition and pave the way for more dates. Having kissed a person once, it is usually presumed that one will do it again, and having made love once, there is something odd or at least very unusual (or suspicious) if there is not the repetitive urge to do it again. Having said "I love you" once, it is expected that one will say it again—and again. Getting married, of course, is not just *getting* married, it is the obvious definitive step to *being* married, a role that, properly played, goes on for a lifetime.

Each step also indicates a new level of "seriousness"—i.e., a new level of self-involvement. Or, to use the somewhat hateful but seemingly unavoidable financial metaphor, each step is a new level of investment in the relationship. One has invested that much more of oneself and cannot simply withdraw. Indeed, one might say that the timetables of love are essential schedules for the gradual transformation of self, first by way of casual conversation and time together, sharing interests and insights, an occasional secret or two. Then the sharing of sensual delights, the physical union of two bodies with more and more comfort and familiarity, then sharing more time, deeper secrets and confessions, celebrating triumphs and accomplishments together, seeing the world together, sharing and eventually merging friendships, then families, then an apartment and finally a family of one's own. One might ask where at these various stages does love begin—but the question is mistaken and there is no single answer. Love is the process, the whole development, and not any particular "feeling" at any particular stage. "I love you" is but a step in the process, not a description of a state achieved.

If there is anything obvious about the temporal dynamics of love, despite the pious harping on static eternity, it is that love is explosive, that lovers are hypersensitive and that Stoic indifference is the very refutation of love. Our Identity Theory of Love says that love is a sharing of selves. But "sharing" sounds so civilized, so agreeable, so secure, so—unromantic. Our domestic image of a shared self is quite at odds with the terrible tensions suffered by our romantic heroes, and quite at odds, too, with the tragi-comic image of a self split in two imagined by Aristophanes. It is possible for two selves to grow together into a remarkably harmonious synthesis, but this is a rare achievement and in any case comes rather late in a long process of adjustment and reaction.

Instability is the mark of love—as opposed to the stability of friendship, for example. Love may last, but it typically does so by way of convulsions rather than mere stasis. We can tolerate much in friendships, even be amused, but it is a familiar experience in love that the very virtues that inspire love in the first instance often provide the fault lines that lead to the collapse of love later on. Whatever else it may be or become, love is not as such a stabilizing force in our lives. The self shared in love is a cauldron of forces in tension that threaten to blow love apart even as they hold it together. Love might appear stable but it is, in fact, "metastable"—if we may borrow a term from chemistry and from Jean-Paul Sartre—at every moment courting disaster. Imagine a waiter in a cafe precariously balancing a half dozen full cups of hot coffee on his arms as he walks across the patio. But at any moment a single slip, a single drop of hot liquid on tender skin—and total disaster. So, too, with love. It seems secure, even eternal, but at any moment a single ill-considered comment, a moment's silence, an evening's neglect . . . but then the two lovers begin to realize how much is already at stake, and swallowing pride, they go back to try again. They "make up" (a remarkable psychological ritual) and continue the dynamic of love.

INTIMACY

Those who have never known the deep intimacy and the intense companionship of happy mutual love have missed the best thing that life has to give.

—BERTRAND RUSSELL

The dynamics of love are defined by intimacy, one of the features that most distinguishes modern romantic love from most other forms of sexual attachment and enthusiasm. Intimacy presupposes the very strong sense of privacy that we discussed in the preceding chapter. Intimacy is quite explicitly self-conscious, a matter of keen, immediate awareness. Intimacy is always shared—if one finds that his or her feelings of intimacy have not been shared, it is not that one person has been intimate and the other not; there has been no intimacy, only misunderstanding. Intimacy, accordingly, is not just a feeling; it is a shared experience, usually a beautiful, rapturous experience, but for that reason, too, it can be quite frightening. To make matters more complicated, it also seems that there are two quite distinct conceptions of intimacy—neither complete—which we might (cautiously) follow Francesca Cancian in labeling "masculine" and "feminine" conceptions. The masculine conception involves "instrumental and physical" activities, doing things together, and sex. The feminine focuses rather on emotional expression and talking about feelings. Since the latter (which, of course, is hardly a uniquely female trait) is usually taken as the definition of intimacy, it is often concluded, wrongly, that women are more capable of intimacy than men.

Such misconceptions about intimacy produce problems in relationships. If intimacy is expected to be expressed only in confessional conversation, then many intimate gestures and activities will escape notice, and because intimacy is thought to be essentially self-conscious, these gestures and activities will not count or contribute to intimacy at all. A man might perceive his sharing of his professional secrets with his lover as the most intimate activity imaginable, but if she perceives this as nothing but "shoptalk," the attempt will probably turn into a source of friction instead of intimacy. If a woman sees her account of an early, humiliating sexual experience as an extremely intimate piece of shared information, "in order to really understand me," but he fails to see the point of such a confession, the effort is worse than wasted and may become something of a humiliating experience itself. Intimacy is the immediate shared experience of that sense of shared identity that constitutes love. Anything that fosters that shared experience can be intimate, whether something so ritualized and routine as a candlelight dinner or an occasion so rare and difficult as some shared humiliation turned to good humor.

Perhaps the most serious misconception of intimacy is the common supposition that it consists wholly in "making oneself vulnerable." Vulnerability in any other context means weakness, being open to attack. Intimacy, so conceived, consists of confessing one's innermost flaws and failings and opening oneself up to abuse, embarrassment or humiliation—the condition being, of course, that one trusts the other enough to know that the attack will not come. We too often read that intimacy is "the ability to reveal innermost feelings, thoughts and emotions to someone else without becoming anxious or afraid" and "to reveal yourself without fear of reprisal." To think of intimacy in this light is pathetic, and it wrongly precludes the possibility and the desirability of a sense of intimacy based on feeling good and strong and on top of things. Intimacy means togetherness, a feeling of fusion, not vulnerability toward each other. There is a reason intimacy is regarded as one of the most valuable experiences available to us, but as long as we think of it in terms of vulnerability without fear of reprisal, we are never going to understand why it should be so valuable.

The idea that intimacy is self-revelation is one-sided, as if intimacy is an act that one person does to (or at) another instead of an experience shared. It also tends to put too much emphasis on verbal expression, on confession, on conversation. The focus on revelation—the transfer of embarrassing information to a willing and sympathetic listener—misses the point of intimacy. One can easily imagine, for instance, a stranger on a train pouring out to us the gruesome story of a life gone wrong, affairs ended in disaster, a personality twisted with pain, character corrupted. We can imagine—given a certain gift for story-telling—that such an experience might be extemely moving and engaging, or at any rate entertaining. But it is hardly intimacy. Indeed, such confessions can easily be manipulative, repulsive or, as in Camus's brilliant short novel, *The Fall,* a device for seduction—to bring the innocent listener down into the depths of depression suffered by a charming but pathological confessor. In a relationship this confusion of intimacy with vulnerablity and verbosity can too easily provide an excuse for mutual embarrassment or a justification for vehement accusations ("I'm just telling you how I feel"). One such well-known abuse is the elaboration—in gory detail—of previous affairs or relationships. It provokes an impetus for too much talk when a hug or caress would be much more appropriate. On the pretext of intimacy, many a relationship has suffered a sad and slow demise. Intimacy—which should provide a shared sense of vitality and strength—gets confused with whining, and in its name love can degenerate into mutual bitching and sniveling against the world.

None of this is to say, of course, that intimacy doesn't *involve* vulnerability and verbal expression. But vulnerability is consequent to intimacy, not constitutive of it, and verbal expression is its vehicle and not its substance. Anything that has as much at stake in it as love is going to involve uncertainty and risk. What creates vulnerability is not our failings or weaknesses but the sheer fact that so much is at stake, and this is true whether we are talking about the exhilarating but uneasy intimacy of early romance or the trusting easy intimacies of a long marriage. A small part of intimacy may be the ability to share our fears and the great relief one might experience when confessing an awkward secret, but this is surely not the key to intimacy nor even a necessary part of it. The same must be said of that sense of "telling everything" that is so often confused with intimacy. It may be true that, with one we love, we have that overwhelming temptation to say everything that has ever come to mind—total "transparency" Rousseau called it. But this is a product of intimacy, not intimacy itself—and it is a product that should be monitored—or at least edited down, for while openness is a virtue, garrulousness is not, and there is much that should not be said or revealed, even between—especially between—people in love. Intimacy consists of those actions and statements that bring two people closer together, and in the delicate hypersensitivity of mutual intimacy it can be far more important *not* to say certain things in candor.

So, too, we should minimize the usual emphasis on *trust* in intimacy. Of course trust is extremely important in love (or in any relationship) and a certain amount of trust is something of a precondition of intimacy—you do not share your inmost self with someone who might well turn on you at any moment. But the trust that foments intimacy may be only temporary, even a brief lapse in a long history of *dis*trust. Some of our most intimate (and surprising) experiences of intimacy emerge with people of whom we once were afraid or awed, and indeed the intimacy may be greatly heightened by the contrast. Of course the other side of this is that such intimacy with people we otherwise distrust can quickly give rise to a profound sense of betrayal, disdain or self-contempt. The trust presupposed by intimacy may be temporary, but the sense of involvement may yet be profound. The appeal of a brief affair with a stranger is thus, that it superimposes an illusory sense of intimacy over ignorance, feigning trust where there is no ground for it. Not surprisingly, the emotional aftermath is not usually the development of love but rather suspicion, fear, resentment or contempt.

Intimacy is first of all a willingness to share one's joys and triumphs. Making love, of course, is such a mutually shared experience, but it is easy to overemphasize this connection and fall into the common verbal equation between the two ("to be intimate with" meaning "to have intercourse with"). But sex can be an alienating and distancing experience, and mere physical proximity or interpenetration is not enough for intimacy. Thus when Desmond Morris tells us that intimacy is "lavish bodily contact, replacing lost intimacies of infancy," we have to say that such contact *can* constitute intimacy but need not, and in any case must be part of a larger experience. And yet sexual contact clearly does contain its own urge to intimacy, and it seems that one must make an effort to *avoid* intimacy in sexual encounters rather than make an effort to create it—but it must be said that men in particular (though now more women too) have developed a number of defense mechanisms to allow them to enjoy "casual" sex and at the same time block the impulse to intimacy. These include the limiting device of the "one-night stand," the emotionally distracting emphasis on "sexual technique" and the more subtle tactic of total self-embodiment—getting so excited by the sex that one becomes conveniently oblivious to the reactions and feelings of the other person. Indeed it may be, as Rollo May argued twenty years ago, that one of the dubious accomplishments of the sexual revolution was to sever once and for all the established connection between sex and intimacy. On the other hand, as Rubenstein and Shaver argue in their book *In Search of Intimacy*, "deep intimacy tends to be physical." But how are sex and intimacy connected—or are they not the same thing? For most of us, touch and sex are *expressions* of intimacy, but the question then is—what is it that gets expressed?

The word "intimacy" is also sometimes expanded to include any unusually heartfelt conversation or shared experience. Between these too narrow and much too broad interpretations there is much room for confusion. Is sexual excitement itself intimate? (Many men seem to think that it is.) Is sexuality an obstacle to true intimacy? (The women who live with the above-mentioned men often complain that it is.) Part of the verbal problem is the varied usage of "intimate" as a verb. Intimacy is clearly shared but "to intimate" is something that one does. One of its meanings is "disclosure," thus encouraging the tiresome interpretation of intimacy as confession. ("To intimate" also means "to hint," which at least has the delightful suggestion of teasing built into it.) The word "intimacy" comes from the Latin "intimus," meaning "inmost," but this too easily shifts the proper emphasis to something "deep inside" instead of something essentially shared. We do, of course, talk about intimacy in terms of inwardness, but the idea is not that intimacy is itself inward but rather that what intimacy shares is "deep" in the sense of being basic to one's true personality. This is presumably what Bertrand Russell had in mind when he praised "the deep intimacy and intense companionship of happy mutual love" but not the same as what Barbara Fast seems to suggest in her characterization of intimacy as "mutual sharing of inner feelings and private emotions."

The metaphor that is most central to intimacy, however, is not depth or inwardness but "closeness." (For example, psychologists Rubenstein and Shaver vaguely define intimacy as "a complex combination of psychological and physical closeness.") It is obvious what it means to be physically close, but it is not at all clear what it means for two people to be close mentally or spiritually. We often talk about "feeling close to someone." What does this mean? Feeling close is the experience of a certain kind of attachment or bonding. It may be only temporary, and it may be only a momentary experience. ("Just then, I felt so close to you.") This sense of "close" emphatically does not mean "similar," for one can feel attached to someone who is very different in every relevant respect. But notice that this will not do as an analysis of intimacy, for one can *feel* close without *being* close. What distinguishes intimacy is that it must be mutual and not just a feeling that one person has. It is a shared *experience*, the experience of sharing. It is not uncommon for soldiers in battle, for example, to describe their shared war experience as the most powerful feeling of intimacy that they have ever known. But the experience does not consist of their various individual feelings (fear, for example); the experience itself is what is shared. So, too, in love, though the context is limited to two people and usually less dangerous, the experience of intimacy is the situation experienced, which includes a complex of shared emotions that tie them together in each other's eyes.

Intimacy is an experience of mutual *availability*. It is not just openness of expression but an openness of the self to share and to change. It is a momentary sense of exclusiveness (which is not to say that intimacy must be exclusive), as if "we two are the only ones in the world." The experience of intimacy can, as most of us know from experience, be wrong or misleading, for it may well turn out that the person with whom we were so intimate only the night before turns out to be very different from what we believed, someone surprisingly cold and distant. Such experiences should be a warning against thinking of intimacy alone as any sort of assurance or road to knowledge. One can be intimate with a person of whom one is almost totally ignorant, nor need one learn anything about a person through intimacy, as many of us have found out, often with a rude shock, the following day. But this is not to say that intimacy is nothing more than infatuation either. Infatuation is also an intense momentary experience of love, but infatuation keeps its distance (not always by choice), and infatuation, unlike intimacy, is always (as the very word tells us) wrong about love. Infatuation is contrasted with love; intimacy is essential to love.

We began by noting that there are at least two quite different conceptions of intimacy, which we hesitantly called "masculine" and "feminine." In fact, however, as we've gone on to discuss, there are quite a number of competing erroneous notions of intimacy, from the intimate conversation to sexual intimacy. On a larger scale, there is the experience of the first blush of romance, when intimacy seems miraculous and an exhilarating discovery, and then there is the comfortable intimacy of a long relationship, when little need be said just because both know all so well, and know that they know, and every experience quietly reverberates with the deep echo of years of history and shared experience. These examples conflict and rub against one another. But on closer look, these images of intimacy are not and should not be opposed, and, despite differences of novelty and adrenaline level, the intimacy itself is the same in both of them. Part of the problem is the confusion of intimacy with sexual enthusiasm; familiar and tender intercourse is not necessarily any less intimate than the thrilling discoveries of first love, and, in fact, thrills can sometimes distract from intimacy. Intimacy can be exciting, but it is not the excitement that constitutes the intimacy, and if the intimacies of a thirty-year marriage are no longer so exciting, they are therefore no less intimate.

The rapid admissions of early love are the attempt of intimacy to tie together two selves, to weave a web of mutual knowledge and shared, if largely vicarious, experience. So, too, the early passions of sex are not just the thrills of discovery but a conscientious effort of intimacy to weld two bodies together. But there is a paradigm that will serve us much better than the sexual paradigm or the paradigm of the intimate confession, and that is the example of *looking*. The organ of intimacy, if not of love too, is the eye. It is the *glance* that determines intimacy, not just an expression of intimacy, but intimacy itself. The intimate glance includes an exchange of information ("I want you" or, separated by a particularly garrulous guest at a dinner party, "Isn't he just an obnoxious bore?") but "the look" is much more than a silent but limited device for communication. It offers access to the other person's soul; it thereby opens up a particularly immediate kind of "vulnerability"—not that of weakness or being open to attack but rather that naked sense of being seen, or being seen *through*. It is in the tear-filled, swollen, mutual looks of a couple newly in love, or the confident, familiar, slight smiling glance of an elderly married couple, that one understands the nature of intimacy. It is not through confession or the rigors of sexual intercourse that one comes to understand the meaning of intimacy, not through the mouth or the body but the eyes. So, too, it is in the most subtle gestures, the seemingly most innocuous phrases, the simple pleasures of simply being self-consciously together that intimacy is most in evidence. The idea that intimacy is always a traumatic breakthrough, rather than the basic experience of togetherness, is perhaps our most persistent misconception about it.

This stress on intimacy as an experience that might be momentary leads one to ask what, then, is meant by the expression "an intimate relationship." I think that this is a secondary significance, meaning that it is a relationship that involves—or perhaps is based upon—intimacy. But intimacy is episodic. It is an experience at a certain time, with a certain duration. Indeed, it is hard to imagine how it could last for a very long time. Because it involves total attention, it is hardly compatible with the many urgent demands of life outside of love. It may repeat itself, and indeed one should be suspicious of an intimacy that occurs only once and cannot be repeated. Intimacy is never a mere disposition, a potentiality; it is always *there*, acutely present, immediate. To be intimate with someone, in general, is to have shared intimate experiences. (In the same way to say two people have a sexual relationship doesn't mean that they make love all of the time.) Love, on the other hand, is not episodic; it involves much more, and much more time in particular. Indeed, one might reasonably say that intimacy is the immediate shared experience of what love is. When the relationship ends, love may continue but not the intimacy—for intimacy, unlike love, requires the immediacy of being together. On the other hand, the intimacy may continue in friendship, even more intimate than love once was.

Intimate behavior is motivated by an intense but particularly open form of mutual self-awareness that is contemptuous of any "put-on" performance and which cannot be dependably guided by any particular technique or strategy. Intimate behavior does not consist of particular actions and gestures but of acts and gestures motivated by intimacy: e.g., a gentle caress, flowers in the evening, a few affectionate words, may be symbolic or traditional, but they are empty and not intimate at all without the right motive. It is "not the act but the thought that counts." On the other hand, almost any self-consciously mutual activity can be the height of intimacy. A friend tells me that her (ex-)husband was never so enraged or jealous as when she would be laughing boisterously on the telephone with an old boyfriend. "I think he would have rather I'd just slept with him." Laughter breaks down barriers; it is a powerful shared experience in itself, clearly mutual and (if no one else knows or understands the subject matter) aggressively exclusive. And intimate behavior is never habitual —even many years down the line. The "put-on" of first dates is dramatically opposed to intimacy (indeed it may be the collapse of that performance that signals the birth of intimacy). Paradoxically, it may be just those times when we feel most in love that it is *hardest* to behave intimately together, just because doubt and uncertainty overwhelm the sense of being together, and the loved one becomes a painful question instead of one's intimate other half. But this is also why intimacy is so resistant to ulterior motives (other than intimacy itself). Intimacy may be a mask for power, but it thus becomes a form of betrayal. (It is worth noting that men often find it easier to be intimate when they're down and depressed; the jargon of self-reliance comes out when they feel good.)

We said many chapters ago that the main and most disastrous misunderstanding of love was our Platonic tendency to think of it as a state instead of a process, as static instead of dynamic, as tranquility instead of an unstable, tension-filled, always tentative harmony. So, too, we tend to think of intimacy too much in the terms in which it sometimes presents itself—as a peaceful, quiet experience not unlike religious communion. But it is important here also to emphasize that intimacy is not a steady state, and even in the most intimate relationships it must be relatively rare and not too predictable. H. L. Mencken, no Fogger when it came to love, wrote, concerning monogamy, that it "forces the contracting parties into an intimacy that is too persistent and un-mitigated; they are in contact at too many points, and too stead-ily. By and by all the mystery of the relation is gone, and they stand in the unsexed position of brother and sister." We can appreciate the too rarely noted advantages of a relationship re-stricted by formalities (e.g., the prototypical Victorian marriage or courtship). The brief bursts of intimacy are all the more pow-erful because of their rarity and the contrast with the stiffness that surrounds them. A momentary mutual glance across the forbidden ballroom floor might be traumatic enough to last for the rest of the evening. By the same token, we moderns who so easily confuse intimacy and familiarity with slovenliness and in-difference often find that, even in the most intimate circum-stances (e.g., scantily dressed, in the privacy of the bedroom), intimacy is not forthcoming.

Intimacy, too, is dynamic. It is always the tension between the awareness of identity and the awareness of difference. It can be so exhilarating precisely because of that tension and the contrast with the distance and alienation that make up so much of our lives. But even if intimacy is as such a momentary phenomenon, it can nevertheless feel like the most solid and permanent feature of life. What a shame it is to comprehend intimacy as vulnerability and pathos when the truth is that there is no experience that sends us soaring so magnificently to the top of things.

EQUALITY AND THE PROBLEM OF POWER

> Among unequals what society
> Can sort, what harmony or true delight?
> Which must be mutual, in proportion due
> Given and received.

—A D A M, in John Milton's *Paradise Lost*

Romantic love, as we've said, presupposes the equality of man and woman. This distinguishes romantic love from so many forms of asymmetrical love—the love between parent and child, teacher and student, master and servant, God and his flock. But the supposition of equality is not an easy proposition. For example, while a parent and a child are clearly unequal in their knowledge, ability, sheer physical power and legitimate authority, we would certainly want to say—at least in this society—that children are equal to their parents in several senses: their interests are (at least) as important as the parents' interests and most of their fundamental legal rights are the same, for example. But at the same time, despite our egalitarian prejudices, it is obvious that two people in a relationship are not always equal in all ways either: one person's career is considered to be more important (and not only because he or she brings in more income), one person generally makes the decisions or, most important, one person is more in love or more dependent than the other. Indeed, some theorists would insist that it is only in the very rare case—and then often for a very short period of time—that the power in a relationship is equally distributed. Differences, of course, are not the same as inequalities, and even the fact that two people view love and each other quite differently need have nothing to do with equality. This makes equality a hard quality to measure, however, and different ways of behaving romantically may misleadingly appear as inequities. The fact that one chooses an apparently subservient role does not necessarily mean that he or she is getting the short end of the relationship. On the other hand, different roles sometimes do exemplify inequality ("masculine" and "feminine" roles are sometimes said to do so) and it is an essential question whether such role inequities are or are not a crucial component of love.

Our answer is that love does indeed *demand* equality and romantic roles are strictly egalitarian. This is not to deny that "masculine" and "feminine" might enter into the definition of some romantic roles, but these two oversimplified categories are not in themselves inegalitarian nor are they essential to the delineation of romantic roles as such. What counts as "masculine" and "feminine" (as opposed to the biologically defined distinction between male and female) is culturally determined, and in our culture it is a distinction that is being rapidly and radically revised. It is no longer the case that so many men feel (whether or not they also think or say) that they ought to be "the boss." Not so many women still think and say (even if they no longer feel) that they ought to "serve" or "stand by" their man. Much of the seeming inequity that is blamed on romantic roles is in fact a displacement of public inequities—unequal job opportunities and pay scales, discrimination on the basis of "image" in many gender-associated jobs and outright sex-discrimination. But the presupposition of romantic love is precisely that form of privacy that is cut off and protected from such public comparisons and contrasts, and though it may still be true that "the personal is political" (as some feminists argued), it is private politics. A husband might claim dominant status because he makes more money or is physically more powerful, but insofar as he does so he thereby loves that much less. Social advantages can always be used as leverage in love, of course, but when they intrude into love they interfere with rather than define the love relationship.

Domestic roles may be equally or unequally assigned, but, as we've said, they, too, are something quite other than the romantic roles that define love. One person might do all the work, the other none of it. One person might take all the credit, the other none of it. But though inequities in the household will almost always cause tension that will then interfere with love, domestic inequities themselves do not undermine love and domestic equality is not what is involved in romantic equality. More complicated are relationship roles, which sometimes define outright inequalities—e.g., the sexually submissive and the sexually aggressive partner. But what is critical in the evaluation of such relationship roles is their connection with romantic roles and choices. Is this sexual asymmetry the preferred choice of both lovers, for example? Does it allow them to express themselves in love better than the alternatives? It is surely no expression of love, for example, to force a shy but appreciative sexual partner into an aggressive role in which he or she feels only awkward or embarrassed.

How does one measure equality—as "feeling like equals" or by some more objective calculus? We are bound to be disappointed if what we expect is some explicit general agreement about commensurable roles and responsibilities or some androgynous neutral position in which all sex- and gender-defined characteristics are ignored. This uneasy sense of equality, however, was evident even to Adam and Eve, at least according to John Milton. When Adam asks God to make him a companion, he explicitly insists on an equal, for only an equal can be a true friend. But she must also be different, for love, Adam recognizes, cannot be mere servitude or self-reflection in another. But if male and female are different, with difference comes the threat of inequality. Commentators have often criticized Milton's male chauvinism in such lines as

> Not equal, as their sex not equal seemed;
> For contemplation he and valour formed,
> For softness she and sweet attractive grace;

But Milton also recognizes that equality (and its two antipodes, superiority and inferiority) are not constant but rather in constant renegotiation. When Eve contemplates her new and forbidden knowledge, before she has told Adam, she muses,

> Inferior, who is free?
> More equal, and perhaps—
> A thing not undesirable—sometime
> Superior.

The battle between the sexes is no doubt endless, and so long as men and women frustrate and resent one another there will always be the temptation to generalize ("You men!"; "Why do you women always . . . ?"). But it would be a serious mistake to take such accusations at face value or to engage in the thankless evaluation of the advantages and disadvantages of each sex in the question of traditional romantic roles. It is also a mistake to confuse the public political questions of equality with the private romantic questions. It is a biological fact, for example, that men still tend to be physically larger than women, and men usually *choose* women who are smaller than themselves (who accordingly choose men who are larger). Historically, men have traditionally mustered the educational resources and credentials of society for themselves and, consequently, they have had not only tradition but the working definitions of superiority on their side. Superiority then gets defined in terms of public power and expertise, in terms of rationality and professional abilities. Inferiority in turn gets identified with private "pettiness," emotionality and domesticity. Accordingly, men have often been quite happy to admit women's "superiority" in "matters of the heart and home"—thus separating public (real) power and status from domestic responsibility (also providing a convenient excuse for in-house and romantic irresponsibilities). This is why equality in love gets so complicated (as if the political notion of equality were not complicated enough). Questions of gender and the "war between the sexes" intrude and confuse the political and the personal. Of course the personal is affected by political structures, and the differential status of men and women is written into habit and custom even if it is (halfheartedly) denied by law. But the point again is that there is a sense of equality that is specific to personal relationships and distinct (if not free) from public, political considerations. And this sense of equality is something more than an equal chance to express emotions—including, of course, feelings of oppression and dependency. It is true that freedom of speech is sometimes little more than compensation for the deprivation of other freedoms no less precious. But, without broaching the multitude of questions about sexual equality in the public world, there is no sense in which gender has anything to do with equality in love.

The notion that man and woman face each other as equals in love is, of course, a hard-earned historical victory. When we look at the history of love and marriage, it is shocking to see how little sense of equality there is, and not just in the sense that the husband remains "boss" to his wife. In many countries and in some states still the laws of adultery and murder are grotesquely unequal, so that a husband can kill his adulterous wife with impunity but a wife is obliged by law to forgive an adulterous husband. Marriages were often arranged on the sole basis of a gentleman's preferences, with no question whatever concerning the woman's sensibilities—as long as he was "appropriate." The now partly corrected inequities in job opportunities and advancement are almost innocent compared to the inequities throughout most of history in terms of such basic rights as the freedom from physical abuse, the right to say no to sex and unwanted children and the right to express one's emotions and opinions. For much of history the man was legally "boss" and equality wasn't even an issue. Accordingly, neither was love, except in that very different and dubious sense in which a servant and master might come to love one another.

Reading back into the *Symposium*, we find that beneath the elegant praise for eros and the witty turns of thought and phrase, there is a pervasive contempt for women and the love of women —"vulgar" is the word that appears most often. Love between man and wife is not even worth discussing, much less praising, and although some of the speakers do not object to using the same word for the love of women as for the love of men, they make quite clear that it is in a degraded sense and in no way to be confused with the enlightened and elevating eros that can be between men alone. But love between men could not have been romantic either, in part because the love between men was asymmetrical love between man and youth, between tutor and tutee, and therefore not love between equals. (It is not even clear that the sentiments of man and youth should both be called "love"—a term that is appropriate to the lover but not to the beloved.)

It is with courtly love, with the Renaissance, the breakdown of feudalism and the birth of the concept of "the individual" that equal status for women starts to become a real possibility, and that possibility is first manifested in love, in the right as well as the willingness of a woman to "give her heart"—as opposed to being sold or traded without her consent. Indeed, the central feature of courtly love—the courting itself—was a measure of the woman's autonomy, of her ability to decide for herself whom to accept and whom to reject. Of course there was still a sharp distinction between peasant women, whom male courtly lovers merely slept with, and women they loved; only the latter were to be considered equals. And while the approach and courtship might vary depending on class (Andreas Capellanus's dialogues on love are obsessed with the question of the relative class of the man and woman), love itself becomes the great equalizer. By the time of Shakespeare we find the romantic equality between men and women accepted socially—however much may remain of traditional sex and sexist roles and differences. At least in the game of love, Shakespeare's characters exchange roles and change parts. Men dress as women and women as men, and the decision to love is equal on both sides. In the nineteenth century the roles themselves begin to disappear: e.g., in Tolstoy's *Anna Karenina*, Vronsky's falling in love is described in "feminine" language and his symmetry with Anna is essential to the development of their tragic love. Today all such roles are blurred and confused, as women insist on "sensitive" (but still strong) men and men insist on strong (but still "soft") women. This is a healthy sign of historical role change, as love frees itself even further from the traditional and typically unequal economic and social gender roles that now stand in its way.

To understand both the origins and the nature of romantic love, we must come to grips with this very difficult notion of equality. Equality is not just given or guaranteed but must be demanded and fought for. Equality in love is not a "natural" state of affairs but a dynamic equilibrium that almost always requires negotiation, compromise, threats and fights. Equality is not merely equivalence or "balance"; it is always a struggle. It is in one sense given, but in another, it must be earned.

Equality is given in love in the sense that it is a precondition, a presupposition, and if it is not there from the beginning (e.g., as in a relationship between a boss and her secretary, or between teacher and student), it very soon forces itself upon the relationship. Thus Stendhal says that "love creates where it does not find equals," and we noted in Chapter 1 that Cinderella must become a princess in the eyes of her prince in order to love and be loved by him, not as a matter of propriety but as a precondition of romance. If two people have very different social status then love will either force social equality upon them (one of the social functions of marriage) or it will—as in the illicit affair of Lancelot and Guinevere—deny the legitimacy of society in general, though for most of us this denial consists of little more than seeking some quiet privacy. The equality that is demanded by love begins with this refusal to be measured by any "external" standards. Social power, wealth, public acclaim or popularity, physical strength and attractiveness are all rendered irrelevant to the mutual evaluation that takes place in love. They all disappear in favor of the very different concerns of intimacy and private virtue. But this, in another sense, does not guarantee equality at all; it only places the determination of equality (and inequality) in the hand of the lovers themselves.

Equality means first of all that a love relationship begins without any prior or a priori advantages or authority. The boss who falls in love with her handsome assisitant leaves her authority behind, indeed may make special compensatory gestures to assure that they meet on equal footing. The teacher who becomes involved with a student quickly elevates him or her to an equal —whether this is warranted or not—and the role of teacher becomes an insignificant role in a script that is primarily romantic. Romantic love can here be contrasted with parental love—which continues with a built-in superiority and authority (no matter how often abrogated) or with the love between a queen and her subjects—where again superiority and authority define the very nature of the relationship. In romantic love there are no such definitions, and they are emphatically irrelevant. This is why the contrast between social roles and romantic roles is so often so dramatic. It is also why mixing parental and sexual roles is in almost every society *taboo*. This has to do with elements other than simply the genetics of the species or sociobiology or the repression of the Oedipal complex; it is enough to explain it in terms of an intolerable and insolvable conflict of roles. The authority of a boss or a teacher or even a prince or princess can be compromised or set aside for love, but the authoritative role of a parent is too important, too mythical. Any attempt to combine parental and romantic love will therefore lead to a clash of equality and authority that cannot but make any human relationship impossible.

To so insist on equality, however, is to say that equality may be no more than an absence, a lack of prescribed status, a breakdown of traditional hierarchies and family power structures. Where there is no delegated authority, there is, accordingly, the presumption of equality. This is why, in the "state of nature," equality is sometimes assumed, despite the fact that there is no law of nature under which we can all be equal and despite the numerous ways in which we are all "naturally" unequal in strength, intelligence, talent and resources. There are a number of familiar arguments that make equality seem like the "natural" order of things between man and woman. It is pointed out, rather obviously, that "it takes two to tango"—and a "no" from either carries equal weight and is sufficient to end the liaison. It is often said that sex is the great equalizer: two people in bed are stripped of all public roles and power. Momentarily, at least, their status vis-à-vis each other is self-enclosed and mutually defined. (Thus the shocking sense of disorientation and/or intimacy when first making love to someone with whom one is already involved in well-defined social relationships.) But it would be wrong to think of equality as nothing but the absence of all external measures. Equality is, in any meaningful sense, not a "natural" concept but relative to the relationship. It is deeply bound with a sense of *power* that is also quite distinct from social and public power. There are people who are publicly powerful and have great presence but are pathetic or impotent in privacy, and there are people who are shy in society and submissive in social gatherings but overpowering in private intimacies. It is that private form of power that is at stake in love, and it need have little correlation with more public forms of power. (It is worth noting that social roles are sometimes reversed by sex and sexual desire through the degradation or desperation of an otherwise powerful and respectable person by a lover of considerably lower social status—Professor Rath in *The Blue Angel* or Lady Chatterley.) It is a form of power that has often been in history the resource of great women deprived of more direct public influence, and it is power that every beloved has over a lover, the power of being desired, the power of being depended upon for the lover's very identity, and the ultimate power—the power to say no, the power to destroy.

The British philosopher Thomas Hobbes argued that we are all equal in the unhappy sense that we share an ability to kill one another. But Hobbes's general claim about human nature has a rather specific application to the power everyone has in the shared vulnerability of the bedroom. A feminist friend of mine explains the continuing distrust between men and women on the model of an ancient warrior, invincible in battle, sleeping in a postcoital stupor next to the woman he has recently captured and raped, his sword lying by. He is as vulnerable as a sacrificial lamb. It is a paranoid image, but it makes the Hobbesian point about equality with brutal clarity. Where there is so much intimacy, even Conan the Barbarian is vulnerable. And though murder in one's sleep is not the worry of most nervous lovers, an emotional analogue is indeed just as threatening. It is the power of the beloved to stop loving, or in its most dramatic (nonhomicidal) manifestation—the power to leave.

The equality demanded by love is in part sexual equality, but this is often misinterpreted in unrealistic ways. A strong-willed woman friend recently told about her current love, a highly charged sexual relationship in which she "for the first time" could allow herself to feel "totally in his power"—but only in the bedroom. At all other times, she insisted, there had to be absolute equality, but some of our friends were nevertheless outraged. Giving in to such submissive sexual feelings, they argued, undermined the equality of the entire relationship. No, she said, it only underscored her trust in him. But the issue is not the question of sexual submission. The predilection of publicly powerful men for subordinate, passive and even degrading sexual positions in private has been a familiar paradox for centuries, and we should not be surprised if now the notion of publicly powerful women wanting similar degradation is getting attention (often presented misleadingly as "rape fantasies" and "masochism"). On the other hand, many if not most men seem to feel the need to feel dominant and powerful in sex, which may provide some women with one more reason for distrusting men. For others, however, it seems to characterize nothing more than the traditional (if unfortunate) role in which the male has been conceived and evaluated on the basis of some fairly obvious physiological differences. But this has nothing to do with love or equality, and if sexual equality meant equal desire and symmetrical nondominating sexual roles, then it would have to be said that rarely do we find sexual equality even in love. What seems to be at stake in every case is not equality of desire—which varies in all of us from time to time—nor even questions of domination and submission but rather equality of respect for the other's needs and desires. And this means that sexual equality is not equality of sex but equality in a more general sense, equality as persons, specifically as lovers. Equality is mutual respect for one another's needs and desires, even if these may be asymmetrical and if one person makes more of the demands. And this can be generalized as an essential feature of romantic roles: the concern of lovers is never competitive even when the roles are contrastive, and it is the will of one's lover as one's *own* desire that dominates—even when, paradoxically, the other's will is to be utterly dominated.

In the politics of equality, there is always the obvious problem —the fact that some people are "naturally" stronger, smarter, more talented and capable, and in every relationship one person is bound to be in better shape, a bit more intelligent, more at ease in public gatherings, more willing or capable of expressing intimate feelings. Do such inequalities create inequities—that is, endow superior rights or status to one person or the other? In most activities superiority in relevant skills is and should support special authority, and so, too, in any romantic relationship we would expect some degree of "specialization"—preferences and abilities at one activity or another. But in love, unlike most joint activities, there can be no boss, no supervisor, no captain. There may be dramatic differences in skills and virtues and admiration thereof, but love does not recognize superiority. The champion skier may win the admiration of his lover but does not feel superior to her. The great artist may enjoy the praise of her lover but does not compete with him with her talent. (Love is often jeopardized when two people share a competitive career. It is hard not to internalize the possibility of being compared.) In love all else becomes inessential to the love itself. Alternatively, in love all skills and virtues are shared, and so the notion of competition does not arise.

The equality that love demands is the equality of interests, the equality of status within the relationship. Nevertheless, it is clear that we cannot simply deny or ignore such differences in skill and virtue. The denial of advantages in love—a not uncommon occurrence—leads to the sad and sometimes tragic "leveling" of a relationship, the lopping off of virtues for the sole purpose of reinforcing equality—and not coincidentally solidifying mediocrity and mutual frustration. A man who will not allow his wife to pursue her promising career, a woman who disparages her husband's hobbies or makes fun of his skills, this is love at its worst, prompting many writers to argue that it cannot be love at all, for love is wanting the best for and from one's lover. I certainly

endorse the sentiment but have to reject the conceptual point—
that love cannot be so damaging. Quite the contrary, it is this
essential feature of love—its insistence on equality—that creates
such restrictions, however unhappy or tragic. The man who is
jealous of his attractive wife and consequently will not take her
out in good company or arranges outings that will not show off
her beauty (camping trips, darkened theaters) is enforcing equality by eliminating all possible competitive situations. A woman
who will not let her husband play sports because it makes her
feel "unathletic" may indeed love him, so much so that she will
take such steps to insist on their equality—even if she will jeop-
ardize the relationship to do so.

One cannot and should not deny one's lover's superiorities,
but the point is that there can be no superiority as such *within*
love. But, having said this, a number of problems become rather
obvious. First of all, every love affair is riddled with competitions
in which two people may not be at an equal advantage *within*
the relationship. For example, one person may be more articulate, better at argument or more capable of expressing emotions
—essential skills in every relationship and sometimes straightforwardly competitive—in fights or disagreements, notably. One
person may be much more sexually experienced—introducing
an unavoidable "teacher-student" relationship into the love affair (the alternative being frustration and/or resentment), and
even such standard domestic skills as cooking and keeping house
tend to provoke competition and competitive evaluation (one
reason traditional household tasks were so strictly sex-segregated
and specialized). But most basic of all, one person may simply
need or love the other more than he or she is needed and loved
in return. To say that equality is the precondition of two people
loving one another is not to say that they necessarily love each
other equally.

A further complication is that, to a certain extent, outside
successes and failures inevitably enter into the privacy of any

relationship. The distinction between "public" and "private" is itself a public convention, so it is not surprising that one's public conception of self heavily influences one's private sense of self. A man who feels unattractive in the world is going to be slow accepting the fact that he is attractive to his lover, and this in turn produces that strange sense of competition that is not about "Who is more attractive?" but rather by way of a challenge: "I dare you to make me feel attractive." So, too, a woman who feels like a failure in her profession may have a difficult time feeling successful in love—even with an admirably understanding lover —and, whenever possible, contrasting her failures with his successes. Where there are real inequalities between two people in the world, there are bound to be shadows of those inequalities in the private world of love. Of course the more distinct one's public and private lives and the more distant one's spouse or lover from the concerns of public success and failure, the less the pressure will be on love, for the less such concerns will have any effect whatever on notions of equality or inequality in the relationship. This is why two people in the same competitive career or profession—while such similar interests and concerns obviously feed each one's sense of mutual identity—face the specter of enormous conflict *within* the relationship based on wholly *external* considerations—who is more recognized, who is better paid, whose article got published by *The Quarterly*, or, as in the classic Tracy-Hepburn film, who is going to win the case.

Where there are inequalities in public life, love tries to neutralize or compensate for them in the bedroom, at the kitchen table, in the privacy of a walk in the garden. One of the marks of equality—as well as a source of great confusion—lies in the fact that different people are superior in different ways: one is more analytic, the other more intuitive; one more sexual, the other more sensuous; one more compassionate, the other more efficient. And what we mean by equality in a relationship is obviously not equality in each of these aspects but rather an overall balance, and not so much in aspects but in mutual respect for one another as equal persons.

To put this all together, the concept of equality in love might be analyzed as a series of steps:

Equality of love means, first of all, that there is no pre-established hierarchy in the relationship. Insofar as there is such inequity, the emotion in question is not (romantic) love. Asymmetrical Greek love between man and youth does not qualify. Wives bought in auctions, no matter how loved, do not qualify.

Second, it means that both partners' emotions get taken equally seriously. One person in fact might be moody and moving from depression to mania and back again while the other's emotional weather is smooth as the sea, but they are given equal weight (in proportion to their frequency and significance), and the obvious fact that one person's feelings are almost always a topic of concern while the other's never are is not a matter of inequality. If, however, the usually calm partner has a crisis or an impulsion of passion that is ignored by virtue of the habitual self-absorption of the other, than that breaks the requirement of equality.

Third, equality means that two people are equally dependent and equally independent, that they share decisions affecting both of them, that even if it is generally understood by both people that one of them will make all the decisions, *this* decision must be a mutual one. ("Harry, you know I make decisions all day at the office. You decide where we're going for dinner.")

Fourth, equal importance is given to the needs and desires of each—for example, the need for attention, time for conversation, the desire for touch, caresses, sexual intercourse. (It was a big step in history when a woman could turn down a man's proposal because she didn't *like* him, and when a woman could turn down her husband for sex because "she didn't feel like it.") Of course these needs and desires themselves are not always identical and, unfortunately, few couples succeed in really treating each other's needs and desires as equally important. The crucial point here is not that romantic couples automatically find themselves in equilibrium but that the standard of equality is always presupposed. It is always the basis of a legitimate complaint ("How come we always have sex when *you* want it, never when I decide that I want it?"). It is the *ideal* of equality that is guaranteed by love. Its realization is a matter of constant conversation and effort.

Fifth (now moving from the private into the public realm), equal attention and respect are due to each partner's place and roles in the world. This is not emphatically to say that romantic love forbids a woman (or a man) to forgo a career or that an entertaining hobby should be given equal practical weight with the job that provides all the income. It does not dictate roles in or out of the home. Indeed, one serious complaint against the recent tradition of romantic love is that it tries to decree a conservative attitude toward "traditional family values" and the purely domestic role of the woman in love. But love is a radical and not a conservative emotion, and what equality means is the very opposite of traditional, unequal roles. Practical priorities are one thing (her law school professorship pays the mortgage; his ceramics provides only some spending money); respect and equality are something else. (A bad day with the clay is as much a matter of personal concern as a bad day at the courts.)

Lack of pre-established hierarchy or authority, equal emotional status, joint decisions in all matters, equal attention to needs and desires, equal respect for each other as persons in the world—these are five central categories of equality. They manifest themselves in hundreds of small and continuous issues in love and relationships and ultimately determine the durability of love itself. It has often been pointed out by tyrants that the most stable society is an inflexible dictatorship, where the volatile will of the people is not allowed to interfere with public order. So, too, it may well be that the most stable personal relationships are those that are defined by authority, structured according to inflexible rules and freed from the whims and insecurities of the two people left to fend for themselves as equals. But we reject the tyrant's idea of a stable society and no one ever sensibly insisted that stability was the virtue of love. One of the reasons why love can fail to last, we might suggest, is precisely that ideal of personal equality that is one of love's foundations, an ideal which demands constant vigilance and invites continuing struggle. When equality goes out of a relationship, love must go as well.

But perhaps the best way to end a discussion of equality in love is to point out an important sense in which *inequality* is an entirely desirable aspect of a love relationship. Consider yourself choosing a tennis partner: would you choose someone clearly inferior, superior or about the same? There are advantages and disadvantages to each. You can beat the inferior person with little trouble, but it's guaranteed that you won't improve your game. With an equal the competition will be keen and fair but, again, it won't elevate your game, only increase your practice. But with a superior you learn, you admire, you reach higher. So, too, with love. There are so many people who pick someone inferior in so many ways—social skills, sexual experience, education and intelligence—just in order to feel superior themselves. Unfortunately they don't learn very much, often get bored and do not find love a very uplifting experience. The sense of equality that love requires gets experienced as a "drag," a lowering of self. Others mistake the precondition of equality of status in love for the equality of skill and accomplishment, and while such relationships are typically stable, they often tend to become overly competitive and, again, do not elevate themselves very much. But loving a superior—and not just a superior in particular skills or accomplishments but a "spiritual" superior—

can be an experience of a very different and very special sort. Consider the following quote from May Sarton, *At Seventy:*

> I have been wondering why it is that Americans must insist on "equality," not on the political scene where it is valid but in private relations where it is not. I cannot imagine thinking even, let alone saying to Basil de Selincourt, Jean Dominique, Virginia Woolf, Elizabeth Bowen, or my teachers Anne Thorpe and Katherine Taylor when I was a child, "We are equals!" I was too aware of all I had to learn from them and through them, and I gladly gave them love and homage.
>
> For me at least, one of the most rewarding emotions is that of feeling in the presence of someone whom I admire wholeheartedly and from whom I know I can learn. It is a very pure emotion. There is no envy in it, nothing but aspiration. The reward is in the feeling itself.

Or as John Stuart Mill wrote at the beginning of the women's liberation movement over a century ago. "When you have true equality, you have the luxury of 'looking up to' your partner."

POSSESSION AND
POSSESSIVENESS

In real love you want the other person's good. In romantic love you want the other person.

—MARGARET ANDERSON

It is one of our favorite tenets of libertarian love that lovers seek nothing more than the freedom and autonomy of the other and respect for him or her as a distinct and separate person. The truth, as usual, is more complicated. As unpopular as it may be to say, one of the central features of romantic love is a powerful sense of *possession* of one's beloved. It is built into our thought and language, from simple possessive pronouns ("You're *mine*") to such straightforward gestures as grasping, clasping, hugging and holding. And while, no doubt, one should insist that this sense of possession should always be balanced by respect for the other's rights as an individual, when there is serious pressure on love it is often the respect, not possession, that is relinquished. That is what we call "possessiveness."

Possession—perhaps we should call it "ownness"—is actually a perfectly normal and even essential part of love. In *Lysis*, Plato argues that one can love only what "one makes one's own," and he often talks about love (like knowledge) in terms of "grasping" and "possessing." The idea that if you love someone you will let them (this already assumes a certain authority and control) do whatever they want to do is as naive and unrealistic with lovers as it is with children. To love a child is to care not only *for* the child but *that* the child does this as opposed to that, not only for its own good but also for the sake of the relationship and the parent as well. To love someone is to invest oneself heavily in that person and his or her feelings, and one cares not just in the sense of wishing well but also in the self-interested sense of watching one's own fate in the hands of another. What he or she does is not a matter of benevolence or indifference but of one's own survival.

What does it mean to say that love includes a sense of possession? We are obviously not talking about the standard capitalist, private-property notion of ownership. It is this sense of ownership that rejects "possession" utterly, as a form of slavery or, at least, mere "objectification." But if we do look to the origins of the capitalist property theory, we find the English philosopher John Locke arguing not so much an "entitlement" theory but also a theory in which the key is that we legitimately possess something when we "mix our labor with it." He was talking about land, of course, but the theory adapts to relationships in an illuminating way. We use the economic concept of "investment" perhaps more than we would like, but it is a key concept in both economics and emotions. One invests one's *self* in something, in a person, a cause, a principle, a situation. In love one paradigmatically invests oneself and, in an important sense, one's labor in love, in the relationship, in the other person. The possession that is part of love is nothing other than this sense of investment —time, energy, attention and emotion put into a life with another person. Such personal investment carries with it certain rights and expectations—as well as obligations in return. The ideal of allowing one's lover total autonomy, absolute acceptance without expectations, ignores the obvious fact that love is not merely a spectator's emotion. The self is deeply involved in love, and with that involvement comes an inevitable and blameless sense of possession and control.

To a certain extent the sense of possession may seem to be no more than a feeling of familiarity. After living in a house for a couple of years, one feels at home—as if the house is his or her own—quite apart from the legal question of ownership. Further along, one might even come to feel *entitled* to the property, a very strong claim of possession and one clearly recognized as legitimate in common law. So, too, we feel with each other a sense of familiarity over time, a sense of being "at home" quite apart from any real questions of possession. With more time we start to feel entitled to the other, a feeling which may never be evident only because it is never tested. But when one longtime lover threatens to leave the other, you can be sure that entitlement claims will be flying fast and loose, and not just such tangible allegations as "I put you through law school." The sense of betrayal—rather than mere disappointment—that usually appears at the end of love is a sure sign that entitlement rights have been violated. It is not just the sad end of a comfortable or enjoyable arrangement; it is a breach of trust, a violation of some sacred expectations.

"Possession" does not mean the crude sense of ownership in which one legally owns a house or a motorbike. Possession of a lover in love is not the same as slavery and does not imply the sacrifice of all human rights and the threat of being sold at auction. Possessive pronouns indicate attachment, an aspect of identity as well as ownership. I can refer to *my* boss, by which I am certainly not suggesting that I own him or her. I am indicating that he or she stands in a special relationship to me and my interests, and in one obvious sense defines my identity as far as this job is concerned. So, too, when Porgy says, "Bess, you is my woman," he is not necessarily being patronizing or in any way indicating her servitude or inferiority. But neither is the possessive merely a mark of affiliation. The sense of possession involved in love has much to do with expectations. "You're mine" means first of all that I expect certain things of you—a modicum of attention, care and affection, and special treatment and consideration. And "I'm yours" indicates that you can and should expect the same things of me. So conceived, one gets a certain sense of possession and being possessed even just after first intimacies—at least the expectation of a phone call, some courtesy and consideration. After years of a relationship, the sense of familiarity has long since become a set of established expectations, and expectations over time tend to become claims of entitlement. One might challenge these claims in any particular case, but there can hardly be any objection to the idea that a sense of possession is all but inevitable in love.

The place of possession in love is nowhere more evident than in sex itself. What could be more possessive than the total enclosure of the most vulnerable part of a man or the physical intrusion of a woman, which, no matter how much desired, is an invasive act even before we take into consideration its deeper psychological consequences? Deromanticized and devoid of pleasure, the sex act would appear to be nothing other than a struggle for possession. Familiar feelings in love—"Take me"

and "I'm yours"—make the role of possession fairly unmistakable, and we might note that the pronouncement "I want you"
is also a clear indication of possession. We can also appreciate
how sexual intimacy, beyond the physical motions, prompts the
sense of possession. At least for a moment, that one person is
very special, even the whole world, and sex contrives a powerful
sense of temporary dependency. The interruption of the sex act,
especially if one's lover "turns off," can be the most devastating
rejection in the world. That vulnerability breeds insecurity,
which quickly generalizes beyond the immediate sexual context.
It is not just lover's enthusiasm that cries out for continuation,
for an extension of that kind of closeness beyond the exhilaration
of intercourse. It is the focus of sexual passion that makes it so
profound in love, and that focus inevitably carries with it a sense
of exclusion and possession. When that sense of exclusion is lost,
when the specialness of being a lover is spread around, it quickly
loses its significance. Thus the intimacy of sex dictates the desire
for the exclusive attention of the other even outside of the sexual
context, and it is here that the sense of possession is most pro-
nounced. Sexual possession is not the whole of the sense of
possession in love, but it is surely the very core of it. One can
share friends without diminishing the friendship of any one of
them, but one cannot share lovers without loss.

This is the place, obviously, to say something about jealousy.
A generation or so ago it was commonly claimed that jealousy
was a "bad" emotion, antithetical to love. But behind this claim
was the unreasonable idea that love was "total acceptance" of
the other person and whatever he or she might want to do and
the mistaken insistence that the sense of possession involved in
jealousy was nothing other than ownership, making the other a
virtual slave. The idealism may have been admirable (when it
was not just rationalization for infidelity and even cruelty) but it
was conceptually confused both about love and about the nature
of possession. Jealousy is (in part) the fear of loss of something
to which one feels entitled, and one does feel entitled to a certain

significant amount of respect and affection from a lover. To feel threatened and outraged when that respect and affection are compromised or taken away is not antithetical to love but its natural consequence. What counts as a threat may vary considerably, of course, and so will what amounts of respect and affection are expected. This is not to say that jealousy cannot (like all emotions) be unwarranted and even pathological, nor is it to say that jealousy is, after all, a "good" emotion—as many situation comedies would have us believe, where the presence of jealousy is proof of love. It is only to say that jealousy as such is a legitimate emotion and intricately tied up with the sense of possession that love demands. To love without any such sense is not so much saintly as foolish, and to love without at least the possibility of jealousy is most likely not to love at all.

The sense of possession in love is an aggressive set of desires and expectations. Love is too often said to be the tender emotion, but though love has more than its share of soft sentiments, love is a hungry, territorial, grasping emotion. This is not to say that love is brutal or bestial (we give too little credit to tenderness in the rest of the animal kingdom as it is), but only that love is not the sweetness that the more tender-minded poets and philosophers have sometimes suggested. In love we make extravagant and extraordinary demands, the demand for exclusivity, the demand to be thought of as "special" and more important than anyone else in the world. Of course this may be mutually accepted by both people, but it is no more modest for that. In the days of courtly love it was said that love is necessarily "jealous" (in the sense of possession). No matter how elegant, demure or controlled love may be, it is always a kind of grabbing, a reaching out and a deep and possibly desperate concern for one's own interests, even before the well-being of the other person. It is possession that gives love its hard edge, its intractibility, its unwillingness to compromise, sometimes even to listen. Love is not just caring and admiration but a powerful sense of "mine!"

So some sense of possession is a natural and normal part of

the shared identity of love even if our strong sense of individual autonomy resists any such notion. *Possessiveness,* on the other hand, is this sense of possession taken too far. Possessiveness is not an expression of love but an accusation, a violation of love. And yet it is based on just that same sense of possession that is always present in love. One difference between the two is that possession is rarely in evidence when all is going well. When you are holding on tight to someone it is hard to take offense that he or she is holding on to you. Mutual possession is taken for granted in most relationships, like the coupling of two trucks in tow or the leash of a sleeping dog, which is not even noticed until it is pulled too far or too hard. But possessiveness intrudes at every opportunity; it does not settle for possession but insists on a continuing display of exclusive attention and affection. It makes demands without desire; it makes a show when none is required or appropriate.

Though a sense of possession is intrinsic to love, it does not follow that possessiveness and love are easily compatible. A possessive husband gets infuriated whenever his wife even talks to another man. It is not that he is jealous—he never lets her out of his sight, so there is no room for suspicion or legitimate doubt. Does he love her? Possession may be part of love, but when love becomes possessive the urge to control overpowers not only respect for the other's freedom and autonomy but also one's sense of caring and many of the very virtues that were attractions for love in the first place. There are men who want and look for a "wild, independent woman"—apparently just to "tame" her, and though one might well speak of love in the courtship stage of the relationship, one can hardly use the same word for the domesticated prison that emerges here when courtship is completed. Possession indicates an investment of identity; possessiveness is that sense of possession gone wrong, thereby degrading identity. It is particularly objectionable when men do it to women. (It is more pathetic when women do it to men, indicating that possession and possessiveness have much to do with power.)

Possessiveness invents a universe of threats and, as often as not, undermines the very sense of possession from which it emerges. We would hardly say that a lover is possessive if he or she objects when a lover threatens to go off with another who is "more exciting, and he makes me happier." Indeed, we would consider grotesque—or at best uncaring—someone who would not object but could reply—without hurt or anger—"Well, if that's what you think you want, then go ahead." But there are real threats, and then there is paranoia. The man who "refuses" to allow his wife to go back to school because he is afraid that she *might* meet another man, or cultivate herself to the point where she *might* look down on him, is being possessive. Likewise, a woman who interrupts any conversations between her husband and a younger woman, on the grounds that there is always a *chance* that he might be attracted to her, is being possessive. Possessiveness is often just such an exaggerated sense of insecurity, but sometimes it is a matter of sheer control, the sense that one can and should dominate the other's behavior, not because of what *might* happen but just for the sake of control itself. That, too, is possessiveness, and it is something much more than the more innocent sense of possession that is an integral part of love. To love is to make something "one's own," in Plato's words. That does not mean that one should imprison or crush one's lover.

The sense of possession can be quiet and subtle but it can also be extremely aggressive. It can take the form of gentle social reminders ("Can I get your coat for you?") or such simple social leashes as a grappling "honey" or "dear" or a light touch on the arm at just the right time. Or it can be threatening ("If you speak to her, don't expect to go home with me!"). Sometimes possession can be expressed by silence or omission, as when a person barely even speaks to his or her lover at a party, spending the time mingling, making it quite clear that one's claim is so strong that there is no need to insist on it. Perhaps it is true that men tend to be more bossy, threatening, women more subtle, demanding—but this is a matter of social power, not sex or romantic roles. But possessiveness in either sex is not known for its subtlety, and possessive lovers tend to exercise brutality openly and excessively. It is possessiveness, not the legitimate sense of possession, that often lies behind violence and cruelty in love. One causes pain—not as the expression of contempt or frustration but rather because one is not sure of his or her power. As the Marquis de Sade was fond of pointing out, lovers may feign pleasure but they rarely fake pain. Violence may be the antithesis of caring and tenderness and so seem the very antithesis of love, but violence may be the straightforward expression of threatened possessiveness, which has its origins in love.

If possession is an essential part of love then so, too, is being possessed, and, indeed, we often talk about love as being possessed in a variety of senses—from the witchcraft notion of "being taken over" to the more common sense of "belonging to someone." Indeed, the passive "belonging to someone" is often the stated goal of love, more than active possession as such. On the other hand, some lovers insist on possession but resist being possessed, but this, too, is an incomplete sense of romance. In the movie *Choose Me*, the heroine comments, "He doesn't belong to me, and I don't belong to anyone"—with a bitterness that is audible and obvious. Possessing and being possessed are complementary and ideally reciprocal, of course, though they are not necessarily symmetrical; it is much more common for one person to be at least slightly more possessing and the other to want to feel more possessed—a feeling that in love is usually called "a sense of security."

A previous generation tried hard to get rid of obligations in love, reducing love to fellow feeling and shared sexual pleasure. It was an essentially flawed effort, grossly underestimating the sense of possession that is intrinsic to love and the enormous range of special obligations and expectations that are involved. Now there seems to be a backlash, emphasizing love as responsibility but thus eclipsing spontaneity and much of the romance. (Perhaps that is why the *word* "romance" is so much back in fashion.) But love is necessarily both autonomy and obligation and that is why questions of "How much of me is yours and how much of me is mine?" inevitably arise in every love relationship, whether in very difficult matters of sexual fidelity or such mundane domestic concerns as keeping appointments and making time for one another. Possession in love is always uncertain, not because love is fickle or unpredictable, but because it always stands in an uneasy position vis-à-vis that dialectic of autonomy and shared identity. Too keen a sense of possession violates one's lover's sense of independence and becomes possessiveness, but too little sense of possession violates one's rightful expectations as a lover. A sense of possession is not by itself a proof of love and it may not always be one of the more "romantic" aspects of love, but it is, nevertheless, a key to the dynamics of love. Anyone who would still like to think that love can last with the same light innocence of the first few weeks has probably failed to come to grips with the question of possession and the dangers of possessiveness. And this is crucial, for any love that lasts must be love that has faced these questions and dangers head-on. It is easy to be "laissez-faire" in the initial weeks of love, when all that one wants is a positive response. But it is impossible once one has invested one's self in love, and what seemed like innocence can now be viewed in retrospect as indifference, a lack of any real emotional investment, despite the desperation of the moment.

THE IMPORTANCE OF FIGHTS IN LOVE

The large, powerful female mantis may in fact become more amorous with her mate, after she has eaten his head.

—ROBERT A. WALLACE, *How They Do It*

We all know at least one couple, very much in love, who fight all the time. They make up, of course, and their making up is unusually passionate, as if to "make up" for the verbal violence they have just been inflicting on one another. But it would be utterly wrong to think that the fights are nothing but an excuse for the passionate "making-up" sessions, and there are many couples who seem to thrive on the fights alone, without the sexual apologies and reparations (George and Martha in *Who's Afraid of Virginia Woolf,* for instance). Young couples sometimes fear that their first fight is the beginning of the end, as if love begins with fusion but then disintegrates through fighting. But the truth is the very opposite—that the initial fusion of love is largely fantasy. Fights force the actual integration of two tangibly, even belligerently, real and independent selves. Fights contribute mightily to the fusion and the mutual definition of love, perhaps even as much as sex and all of those pleasantly shared interests that allow a couple to enjoy each other in so many ways. Fights are not in themselves threats to love or dangers to a solid relationship. They are part of love's essential dynamics.

Of course there are rules, though the rules may vary from couple to couple. "Don't say something you'll later regret" might be an essential rule for tender-minded folk who have long memories, but it could be irrelevant to a couple who need the slash and burn of vindictive hyperbole to get themselves really going. (Without fury and outrage, a fight just seems like a domesticated disagreement.) What the "rules" say, in effect, is that the function of a fight—no matter how disruptive—is to help build and not to destroy the relationship. This is not always easy to keep in mind at the time, and fights can be, obviously, deleterious to a relationship. Indeed, around the climax of a fight it seems more plausible to think "This is it! I don't need this aggravation!" But that, too, is essential to the nature of the fight—fights define the limits of a relationship, the parameters of love. Fights emphasize the individual autonomy of each partner even while holding a couple together, "at arm's length," within range for touching but opposed face-to-face instead of embracing. It is often said that fights "clear the air" of accumulated resentments and frustrations, but they also raise issues which, though matters of conflict, nevertheless represent important bonds in the relationship.

The subject matter of fights may be frivolous or trivial, but their real content is always the structure of the relationship and the limits of love. A fight over a household bill is inevitably a fight about the whole locus of financial responsibility in a relationship; the battle over who takes out the trash on a rainy Wednesday night is almost always a covert discussion about the overall distribution of obligations. Fights about sex are typically the most painful and mutually humiliating, but they, too, have a function—not just to make sex better (which sometimes results) or to ease the pressure of unfulfilled sexual demands or expectations (which usually happens) but also to put sex in its place in the relationship, limit its importance and, though this again might not seem evident at the time, underscore the importance of other aspects of love. Not surprisingly, such arguments almost always do generalize and "get out of hand," not because people who fight are irrational, but because the fights themselves are about much more than they can conceivably settle in an evening or, for that matter, in a week. Fights are the aggressive manifestation of the tensions that are not only inevitable but an essential part of love. But they are also more than this. No two individuals fit together as neatly as Aristophanes's image suggested, and those rough and protruding edges, pressed together over time, cause considerable friction. Shared identity is the development of a shared self despite enormous personal differences and contradictions. Fights are not just the "airing" of differences but the effort to make those differences themselves part of the relationship, to turn love from a subject of mutual fantasy into a set of bonds hardened by experience and time together.

We too often see fights as a sign of weakness of love, or as proof that we are letting self-interest get the better of mutual affection. But again fights are a sign of strength in love. Couples who don't fight are only rarely those in perfect harmony; more often they are two people who have too little shared identity to care. In the beginning of love the fantasies may be powerful enough to ignore reality. Toward the end of love two people might be so exhausted that it is just easier to let it be. But neither oblivion nor indifference is a mark of love, and the strength of a relationship is precisely the extent to which both people care, not just about the other person but about themselves and what seems to be a violation of their own self-interests. Love *is* self-interest, in the sense that the self is deeply involved, and it is the assertion of one's individual autonomy in love that makes love possible (as opposed to mere dependency). The fact that love is a remaking of one's self in the eyes of the other does not mean that one jettisons all interest or responsibility in the making of oneself. To the contrary, the moving force behind love is precisely the desirability of that resultant self, and nothing is more contrary to love than self-contempt mixed with resentment. Love endures because the self that emerges from love is a better self than the self that was alone, and love typically fails—let us say it again—not because one is disappointed with one's lover so much as because one becomes disgusted with the self that he or she has become. Fights are the means of monitoring and correcting the growth of the self in love, in which we refuse to accept a self that is too submissive or diminutive, too burdened with responsibilities or too unappreciated. Fights reassert independence at the same time that they wear down the differences that keep two people apart. Fights play off the different roles that we adopt with each other. Household battles may remind us that domestic roles are starting to eclipse romantic roles ("You expect me to pick up after you?"). They are a way of putting the frustrations of everyday life back into perspective, and keep them from overpowering love. Fights also challenge relationship roles, throw them into question, challenging a difference that has been accepted as a "matter of fact" but in reality has only recently developed in the relationship. Fights break the flow in routine, provoking a crisis that can best be resolved through love. They are the other half of the dynamic of love, opposed to (but also conducive to) intimacy, the built-in brake on the temptation to total fusion, which would—if it were possible—displace our individual, autonomous selves altogether.

FRIENDSHIP AS
THE FOUNDATION OF LOVE

It is not lack of love but lack of friendship
that makes unhappy marriages.

—FRIEDRICH NIETZSCHE

In the ancient world it was common wisdom that "He who throws away a friend is as foolish as he who throws away his life" (Socrates) and "No one would choose to live without friends" (Aristotle). Even in medieval times, friendship was considered something holy—an ideal secular exemplification of Christian love. In the twelfth century (about the same time when courtly love was beginning to blossom) there were Christian cults of friendship. St. Thomas Aquinas writes that

> the happy man needs friends, not indeed to make use of them, since he suffices himself, not to delight in them since he possesses perfect delight in the operation of virtue, but so that he may do them good, that he may delight in seeing them do good, and again that he may be helped in his good work by them. For in order that man may do well, whether in the works of active life, or in those of contemplative life, he needs the fellowship of friends.

Friendship was clearly recognized as one of the unmixed blessings of life, and we are not surprised that love and friendship were often referred to with one and the same word.

Today, by way of contrast, we have books teaching us "how to be our own best friend," extolling "the virtue of selfishness" and reminding us to be "looking out for number one." Friendship has become something of a commodity, and a cheap commodity at that. We call a casual acquaintance or colleague "friend" or even "one of my best friends." We abandon our friends for a business deal or a casual romantic interlude. We too easily treat friendship as banal and relatively unimportant, at best as a weak form of love ("Let's *just* be friends") and in any case quite distinct from love. And yet love and friendship would seem to have much in common, particularly the crucial element of personal *choice.* The most noteworthy exception to this current degradation of friendship is the recent rediscovery of the importance of friendship among women, which some might describe as a personal and intimate substitute for the more political and aggressive notion of "sisterhood" that held the stage for the last decade. Unfortunately, this very positive movement too often drives the gap between love and friendship even further apart. This image of a refuge from romantic relationships is particularly vivid in the reinstatement of the Victorian notion of "romantic friendship" —by the poet Margaret Atwood and others—which makes clear the competition, both literary and political, with romantic love. "Intimacy without sexual domination" seems to be the theme, but it must be said that neither love nor friendship benefits much. Friendship is indeed one of the most important features of life, much too important to be another piece of disputed territory in the war between the sexes, and much too important to love to be so contrasted with and opposed to it. Friendship is not always love, and love is not necessarily friendship, but they complement and reinforce one another. They are sibling passions, almost twins, usually of the same mind and temper, occasionally engaged in bitter rivalry. The degradation of friendship and the elevation of love—or vice versa—damages them both.

Is friendship essential to love? No, but it is essential to love's lasting for it is the foundation of love. The problem is that couples usually begin as lovers, not as friends, or when friends do become lovers, the dynamics of love often overwhelm the friendship. The question, then, is how to incorporate friendship into love. Without that, love too readily tends to be possessive or slip into habit, perhaps ceases to be love at all. It is friendship that makes love last and lack of it that makes love falter. The reason is not just the much-repeated observation that sexual desire and attractiveness dwindle while time together goes on. It is rather that sexual desire and satisfaction don't *mean* anything without friendship. The other side of this is dramatically evident when two old friends do make love, especially the first time. What is so overpowering is not the sex but the meaning of sex, which is why sexual friendships can (but need not) turn so readily and so successfully into love. But friendship has other virtues which it adds to as well as shares with love. Friendship is loyal, caring, trusting, wishing the other well. Friendship also involves intimacy, and inspiration, and the sense that one's life is not complete without the other. Thus friendship reinforces love, and love friendship, and even when love does not work out, friendship is the only desirable residue. Indeed, if love doesn't turn into friendship, that might just mean that it wasn't love.

One thing that we might notice is that there is no unrequited friendship, as there is unrequited love. This suggests that friendship, unlike love, is more of an objective state of affairs, like a relationship. This would explain one way in which love and friendship are different. It is not that friendship is a "weak" form of love or a calm emotion where love is a powerful and turbulent passion; it is rather that friendship as such is not an emotion—as a relationship is not just emotion. Of course "feeling friendly" may be a quite distinctive and essential emotion. But friendship is essentially a relationship and must be mutual, no matter how strongly "felt" by one person or the other. This would also explain why friendship is so essential to the success of a relationship but so readily distinguished from the emotion of love. Of course a friendship, like any relationship, may be asymmetrical, unequal or unbalanced in power or mutual feeling, but, like love, it demands reciprocity and insists on equality. Unlike love, friendship always assures as well as demands equality, and so becomes the ideal model and foundation for love.

Friendships overlap and reinforce each other, whereas love can be combative and competitive. Friendship is necessary to complement and pacify love, and love without friendship can be nasty, brutal and short. Friendship mellows love—which we should not confuse with making it less exciting or more routine. It retains that valued sense of possession while blocking the temptation to possessiveness. It reduces anxiety and mutual distrust and belligerence (thus the apparent "loss of passion"). It reinforces caring while introducing a necessary note of tolerance and thus increases independence even while also giving greater reason for mutual dependency. The tension in love between possession and respect for the other's autonomy and freedom is soothed in friendship, for in friendship, unlike love, there is little possessiveness and the other's autonomy and freedom are in no way a threat or a danger. On the other hand, the growing desire for possession in friendship is a telltale sign that friendship is turning into romantic love.

In his discussion of friendship in his *Nicomachean Ethics*, Aristotle distinguishes three levels of friendship. The first is, in our language, simply two people "using" one another, and it is accordingly the lowest level of the three. A friend of this sort—if we would soil the word in such an instance—sticks around only as long as we continue to provide the tennis lessons, or the free dinners, or the transportation to and from work. And we, of course, tolerate his or her presence only because we enjoy the complementary tickets to the theater. The second level of friendship is companionship, enjoying one another's company and doing things together. This is a concept of friendship that we readily accept. But friendship of the highest sort, according to Aristotle, is a friendship of mutual virtue—that is, two friends who are mutually inspiring and "bring out the best in each other." Love is by no means superior to friendship of this sort; indeed this is both love and friendship at their best and, we might now note, the level at which they are indistinguishable. (The Greek word "philia"—which means both love and friendship— is sometimes reserved for just this.) We might also speak of love when two people are "using" one another for sex—and the fact that it is overwhelming and extremely passionate sex is no argument against this. We might speak of love when two people are constant companions, fully enjoying each other's company in every romantic way. But our ideal of love—and our ideal of friendship—is and ought to be "higher," beyond utility and enjoyment and deep into the most basic questions of who we are and would be. And to do this, love alone is not enough. It takes friendship, too, and, in return, friendship can make love last as love alone will not.

Friendship soothes and solidifies love, but we must nevertheless recognize their differences. Friendship, like love, involves identity, but because we do not think twice about the possibility of having several or even many friends, the share of one's identity that is tied up in any particular friend is only a relatively small proportion, far less than that demanded by romantic love. Of course this proportion can vary, and in the special case of two "inseparable friends"—or a romantic friendship—many of the exclusive and all-or-nothing features of love may emerge. But in general we do not make the absolute demands of friendship that we do of love. The interesting question is why we do not, and to reply that we make fewer demands because we have more friends is just to repeat the question in different form. Why are we so exclusive and demanding in love? The most obvious answer might seem to be the inclusion of sex in love, but nonexclusive sexual friendships are hardly rare in our society. Yet the fact remains that even the closest friendship—with sex or without—raises fewer expectations, is more tolerant and easygoing than the most open romantic relationships.

One suggestion is that friendship may involve intimacy but it does not include obsessive desire, not just sexual desire but a multitude of romantic desires. These include possession (not possessiveness) and other "grasping" emotions not necessarily derived from sex but that may in fact be expressed through sexuality. In an important sense, however, this is untrue; friendship may well involve desires just as powerful as those in love—including especially the subliminal sexual desire for each other. The difference is that these desires are not defensive, not necessarily exclusive and do not present themselves in the same desperate, combative role. In friendship, at least on Aristotle's third level, the main desire is for the other's well-being. Quoting Aristotle and Aquinas again:

> We may describe friendly feelings toward anyone as wishing for him what we believe to be good things, not for your sake but for him, and

trying your best to bring these things about. A friend is one who feels this and excites these feelings in return. . . . Those then are friends to whom the same things are good and evil, and by wishing for each other what they wish for themselves, they show themselves each other's friends.

—Aristotle

. . . not every love has the character of friendship, but that love that is together with benevolence, that is, we love someone so as to wish him well. . . . Yet neither does well-wishing suffice for friendship, for certain mutual love is necessary since friendship is between friend and friend, and this mutual well-wishing is found in some form of communication.

—St. Thomas Aquinas

When Margaret Anderson quipped that "in real love you want the other person's good," she captured in part that Aristotelian-Thomistic insight. If we interpret "real love" as friendship this would characterize the difference rather well. Our problem is to overcome that difference between "real love" and romantic love.

The trouble is that, for us, love and friendship are not the same. We have friends whom we adore and might die for but do not want to have sex with or spend our lives in the same bed with. We might say without hesitation that we love them but— one might add—"not that way." And it is obvious that one can and often does fall in love with a person who is not at all a friend, shows no prospects of becoming a friend and does not with time become a friend. Friendship is one good reason for love but it is clearly not the dominant or most persuasive reason. Two friends of mine—who are inseparable friends of *each other*—have spent the past six or seven years together and are as intimate and as happy as any romantic couple. One of the activities they seem to enjoy most together—or at any rate spend the most time doing together—is lamenting their individual difficulties in finding a decent lover, someone they can trust and get along with as well as get excited about. All of us—their friends—have made the obvious suggestion: that they have just this already, and why don't they just get it together and stop their whining. But though they love each other, find each other extremely attractive and in fact have spent years of time together, and despite the fact that they have both found every other relationship in their recent history to be disastrous (to put it mildly), they continue to insist that they do not love one another "in that way." They know each other too well, they explain; they think of one another as brother and sister. They are both romantically hungry, even while enjoying a most delectable friendship. Why is this not enough for "love"?

This separation of love and friendship starts early, indeed at the beginning of our romantic careers. In Chapter 1, I mentioned the comment of a thirteen-year-old girl who had just started dating. In search of an escort for the end-of-the-year prom at her junior high school last June, she went through a list of favored candidates with her mother, who suggested one of her oldest and favorite playmates. "Not Jimmy!" she cried in alarm. "He's a *friend*." That is, one does not try or expect to try to form romantic entanglements with a person who is already a friend. Why this is so, is one of the most tantalizing—and infuriating—problems in the study of romantic love.

An obvious explanation is that one does not want to risk a good friendship with the uncertainties of romance. One has a dear friend of the opposite sex, a close confidant and delightful companion who is also sexually attractive (though one avoids acknowledging this as much as possible). But sex or even just sexual suggestions would or might "change things," presumably for the worse. Yet then, if love is so good and so important, why not take the risk? Because, perhaps, one knows in advance that it probably wouldn't work out—and then one has lost a good friend as well as a lover. But, of course, one doesn't know. Indeed, one would have to say the odds for two friends getting along romantically—especially in the long run—are far greater than those for two strangers who know nothing about each other and are attracted mainly because of their mutual attractiveness. Still, we doubt the success of love between friends because they know so much about each other and suspend judgment about strangers because of their mutual ignorance. It is, ultimately, not a very convincing argument.

Another explanation is that sex is inappropriate with friends. The argument behind this invokes a rather ancient conception of the different levels or "faculties" of the soul, such that sex is of the lowest, friendship of the highest. Thus Plato, getting old and puritanical, expressed in his *Laws* a certain disgust with men who expressed their love for each other in a "bestial" way. So, too, thought the medieval philosopher Marcilio Ficino, who was primarily responsible for the late medieval concept of "Platonic love." Love and friendship were divine, "but not that way"— from which we get our current, quite vulgarized conception of "Platonic love." But this view presupposes a truly despicable view of sexuality, hardly the view that is involved in romantic love. Not surprisingly, the resultant view of friendship can be made so ethereal that it is hard to imagine what (besides theology and metaphyics) one might be able to talk about with a "friend." But more to the point, it is usually true that overt questions of sexual attraction and desire and the complications of "sexual fit" are irrelevant to friendship, though the more complex truth is that one can have sex with a friend—even magnificent sex—without that relationship crossing over into romantic love. Of course sex can and probably will be a complication in any friendship, but the contrast we're analyzing here is not with sex, it is about friendship and love.

One thing about romantic love is its newness—not just ignorance but a sense of adventure, the idea of building a relationship from scratch, a different *kind* of relationship. Part of this, we can surmise, is the standard love story, which clearly specifies "boy meets girl" as its beginning. Indeed, whether or not we buy into the possibility or desirability of "love at first sight," it is clear that we tend first to think of love as starting anew, only second-arily as the transformation of an existing friendship (although it seems that the transformation of hatred into love, the conversion of a mortal enemy into a lover, is one of our favorite traditions). One argument against loving friends, then, is the fact that it deprives us of the chance to start something new.

What makes a person a good friend is not at all what makes them attractive as a lover, much less a good lover. What attracts us to a friend, so the argument goes, is his or her loyalty, intelli-gence, our shared interests (perhaps just a single interest of con-siderable importance), more personality than looks. What attracts us to a lover, on the other hand, is a certain sexual charm, a set of fantasies, more looks than personality. But what-ever brings lovers together, the factors that keep them together may be quite different, and the most important of these is friend-ship. On the other hand, many very close male-female friends have tried to be lovers—perhaps have been lovers for several months or years—only to find that it didn't work out. They have remained friends, and the friendship, by contrast, hums along smoothly. There may be no less intimacy, no lack of expression, just fewer demands and expectations. Love is not friendship, and friendship is not romantic love. One may succeed where the other fails, and friendship may be more than compensation for the failure of love. Where love is compensation for the failure of friendship, however, there may be real trouble.

Because we usually have several friendships, these together circumscribe our identity rather than define it as love does. Friends provide examples for us, but a lover supplies a definition. Friendship is supportive but love is something more, something all-embracing but therefore restrictive and exclusive too. For that reason we need both love and friendship (and if we had to choose, just the latter), love and friendship together in love, but also friendships that surround and on occasion provide a haven from love. At the end of *Women in Love*, Lawrence offers us his own vision in the words of Birkin in conversation with his wife, Ursula:

> "Aren't I enough for you?" she asked.
> "No," he said. "You are enough for me, as far as a woman is concerned. You are all women to me. But I wanted a man friend, as eternal as you and I are eternal."
> "Why aren't I enough?" she said. "You are enough for me. I don't want anybody else but you. Why isn't it the same with you?"
> "Having you, I can live all my life without anybody else, any other sheer intimacy. But, to make it complete, really happy, I wanted an eternal union with a man too: another kind of love," he said.
> "I don't believe it," she said. "It's an obstinacy, a theory, a perversity."
> "Well—" he said.
> "You can't have it, because it's false, impossible," she said.
> "I don't believe that," he answered.

THE MEANING OF FIDELITY

> Never damage your own character. To have a love affair breaks a bond between husband and wife—and even if your partner doesn't know about it, the relationship must be less open, so something very important will never be the same.
>
> —LAUREN BACALL

Fidelity is an abused word in our language. We confuse fidelity with sexual fidelity—as if sexual exclusiveness were the only measure of romantic integrity and devotion. We also confuse it with monogamy, which is not a state of mind or a moral precept but a social arrangement which is ethically neutral and whose evolutionary advantages are by no means anthropologically obvious. Historically, monogamy has been not only the setting but the excuse for sexual infidelity—marriage being one thing but sex and romance another. Sexual fidelity has often been a matter of politics and etiquette rather than personal integrity, for considerations governing sex used to be safety and social status rather than scruples. (Safety is once again a crucial concern.) There was fidelity, loyalty, devotion—and then there was the question of sex. Looking back to some of the more famous marriages in history before the seventeenth century, one might conclude that a good mistress was one who did not get in the way of the marriage, and a good marriage was one that did not put obstacles in the way of the mistress.

Fidelity as such is rightly viewed as a virtue, but it is something quite different and much broader than sexual fidelity (limiting oneself to having sexual intercourse with one and only one person). Indeed, the criterion for intercourse—"going all the way" —is often humorously precise and arbitrary. For many illicit and premarital couples, anything less than the insertion of a penis into a vagina is still utter innocence—no matter how many shrieks and orgasms may accompany that innocence. We chuckle at such conventions in adolescents, but we ought to laugh at these contortions of logic even more in ourselves. For the truth is that sexual fidelity is significant only insofar as it is a matter of feelings, intentions and intensities, and one can be unfaithful and adulterous—as many from St. Paul to Jimmy Carter have attested—in a passing thought or feeling even without making so much as a gesture. A conversation over coffee can be more of a betrayal than a kiss or caress, and many couples who regularly stab one another in the back still paradoxically think that they've been faithful just because they didn't express affection to anyone else.

It is true that one of the greatest delights in love is that sense of bursting desire aimed entirely toward and inspired by that singularly alluring and totally satisfying person right before us. (You can tell that something is totally satisfying when you can't get enough of it.) But this is not the essence of fidelity, and to confuse sexual exclusivity with fidelity is to limit and largely deny the scope and importance of fidelity. The ideal of sexual fidelity is that one person can inspire as much passion and desire as either lover can handle, but this may be a matter of mutual low libido rather than fidelity as such. As Nietzsche pointed out vis-à-vis much of morality, "Thus it is always, the emasculated man as the good man." The lack of desire for anyone else may not be a compliment but rather a symptom. On the other hand, the sublimation and redirecting of desire may in fact be the most honest and effective means to sexual fidelity. It is in no way admirable to make love to one's lover while "having to imagine someone else," but there is a more metaphysical sense in which the person with whom one makes love becomes all men, or all women, *as well as* him or herself as a unique and individual lover. The naturally wandering libido is too often taken as a sign of rejection—"You don't want *me* anymore"—when in fact there is nothing about desire as such that is intrinsically competitive or exclusive. And without for a moment underestimating the power or symbolic significance of sex, it is worth asking why we think that sex with another person constitutes infidelity while the most awful conduct with one's lover still counts as fidelity. To limit the possibility of "betrayal" to the act of sleeping with someone else—whether casually or with deep affection—is to make a prohibition out of fidelity instead of an expression of love and devotion.

One way to look at sexual fidelity, accordingly, is to view it as a kind of gift, suggests the French writer Mme. de Lafayette. One does not pretend to be uninterested or unexcited by the possibility of other sexual adventures, but rather one grants to a lover an ultimate sacrifice by refraining from acting on such desires. Indeed, the fact that one wants an adventure increases the value of the gift, the cost of the gesture. This is quite different from the (often hypocritical) suggestion that one is sexually faithful because one "can't even think of sleeping with anyone else." One can and one does and this is why the refusal to do so means something. But even so, it is not the gift but the thought that counts, for exclusivity accompanied by resentment and resistance is no gift at all but will surely destroy the love it is meant to gratify.

Fidelity—as opposed to sexual fidelity—is to a relationship as integrity is to personal character. Fidelity is all-embracing good faith, a refusal to hurt or betray, an insistence on doing right in all things having to do with love. Fidelity is not the same as caring, but caring is certainly one aspect of fidelity. Fidelity has long been taken to be the hallmark of true friendship—and we should take it to be the hallmark of true love as well. It is not the same as commitment—which is more explicit and more like a promise than whole-hearted absorption in the good of another and the flourishing of the relationship. Fidelity entails honesty, but it is not the same as honesty and, sometimes, it may require well-meaning dishonesty and even deceit. Fidelity is devotion, but devotion reflected in a keen sense of self as well. No matter how successfully deceitful, the "sneaking around" that is so often a part of sexual infidelity virtually guarantees that the other will become an obstacle instead of a partner and that resentment may at any moment eclipse love.

Discretion, not prohibition, is the better part of fidelity. What is the difference, one might ask, between being discreet and being sneaky? The first is part of fidelity, taking trouble not to trouble or betray one's lover, keeping one's actions straightforward and one's manners above reproach. The latter is a device for evasion, necessarily secretive as opposed to merely guarded and self-aware. In terms of action alone, the two might be indistinguishable, but in terms of intentions, they are quite opposed. Discretion is always being conscious of one's lover as a partner and ally; being sneaky is being aware of one's lover as an obstacle, an opponent, a threat. Extraneous sexual relations do not always betray love, but (as in politics) the "cover-up" may be much more damaging than the deed itself. One good argument for honesty is that, even when there is hurt and disagreement, discretion at least remains an issue within the relationship. Being sneaky, on the other hand, is always outside, or rather underneath, undermining it. It is an open question whether any given relationship can or will tolerate extraneous sexual encounters or affairs, but what is not open is the extent to which any relationship is threatened by deception. The strangely mixed message "You can do whatever you want but I don't want to know about it" is a paradoxical attempt to bridge the gap between tolerance and a sense of security. It requests discretion but as it does so it muddies the distinction between discretion and deceit and adds to the danger of misunderstanding and conflict.

None of this is to say that sexual exclusivity (what it should be called instead of "fidelity") is undesirable or, silly or not, essential to mutual peace of mind in a relationship. It is rather to point out the differences between devotion and prohibition. To think of sexual exclusiveness in itself as a moral obligation or a social restriction is to deny the only truly desirable motive for such exclusivity—and that is that it is dictated by devotion and desire itself "from the inside" and not imposed from without. One of the dangers of monogamy and the strong social emphasis on sexual fidelity is that sexual exclusivity gets interpreted as an imposition, a seemingly oppressive cultural convention opposed to which adultery and even promiscuity will seem "natural." It is only insofar as sexual exclusivity is taken to be our own decision, as the rules by which we will run our romance, that there can be none of this sense of imposition, but only a real sense of personal integrity and fidelity. And it is only insofar as the urge to exclusiveness is a matter of desire and not prohibition that it will be essential to the relationship and not simply a boundary within which one feels confined. Where there is no desire, on the other hand, sexual exlusiveness is hardly the most worrisome problem. "Fidelity" then becomes the rather desperate denial of the possibility that someone else may provide what this love has already lost.

Fidelity, rightly construed, is the total sense of one's own needs as well as the needs and desires of the other. A friend suggested an unusual example of fidelity: a very sensual woman's husband suddenly became impotent. There was no warning, no apparent cause, but this condition continued for almost a year, then it went away, as suddenly and as inexplicably as it had appeared. During that entire year she never mentioned it, never reacted with either contempt or pity, never altered her affectionate behavior toward him, never gave him the least reason to add guilt or embarrassment toward her to what could have been the most humiliating experience of his (and her) life. My friend said, "That is fidelity." It is not necessarily total honesty, nor is it being "honest about one's feelings"—for presumably she was experiencing considerable frustration and even disappointment at the very least. She exhibited care and devotion, but the fidelity itself was something more too—a kind of discretion and concern. My friend added that she did not know and did not care whether or not the same woman may have needed, wanted or accepted other sexual contacts during that period. Her fidelity was not measured by sexual exclusiveness but rather by her faith in the relationship.

One might have mixed reactions to this example, but this much seems exactly right: fidelity is ultimate concern for the person and the relationship. There is little question but that sexual exclusivity simplifies life and increases the focus on a single relationship, that it reduces distraction and risk and eliminates the most usual source of jealousy, insecurity and suspicion in love. The danger is that it comes to be treated as the most essential single feature of a relationship—by way of a warning instead of a desire, a limitation instead of inspiration, and thus turns love into a restriction instead of an expansion. In recent years monogamy has become a new religion, in part romantic, in part convenience, in part fear, but mainly it is a rejection of romantic tension and a reassertion of managerial efficiency in relationships. The argument against adultery is usually not fidelity but rather that it "takes too much time" and energy and almost always leads to covert behavior and deceptiveness. If "fidelity" is to mean anything, it cannot be out of mere passivity and indifference, any more than "integrity" can be considered to be achieved by staying alone in bed all day. And it cannot mean just honesty either, for it is perfectly possible to be truthful to a lover and say nothing affectionate, encouraging or loving. On the other hand, one can protect love by not confessing every negative feeling. Romance is a perspective; truth is not. Truth is important to love only insofar as it fits the framework of love. And, finally, fidelity is not just being devoted to a person but to a relationship. On occasion one might even have to hurt one's lover for the protection of love, for the feelings of love are not nearly so important as the love itself.

THE WANING OF LOVE, AND KEEPING LOVE ALIVE

Happy families are all alike; every unhappy family is unhappy in its own way.

—T O L S T O Y , *Anna Karenina*

Tolstoy was wrong on both counts; there are many varieties of happiness in love, and though the details of the loss of love may differ, the forms are finite and familiar. Of course love and happiness are not the same thing. Love may make us miserable— even when (and because) it is requited—and it is possible to maintain a happy relationship for decades after passionate love has been forgotten. But there can be no doubt that love can be the most important ingredient in a happy relationship. We *want* love to continue, and love has built into it its own impetus to last and go on, to the limits of our imagination. And yet it seems to be one of the most familiar facts of love that love does not go on forever, that love like youth wanes and ages, that love that really lasts is rare and admirable good fortune. Indeed, it is often even argued that passionate love *cannot* last, because it is by its very nature new and novel, because it is based on physiological "highs" that cannot be maintained for long, because "familiarity breeds contempt" and because the illusions and delusions of love cannot long survive the *dis*illusionment of a long relationship. I think all of these arguments are unsound but the facts must be faced—that love ends as often as it lasts, and it often ends between just those poeple who seem best matched and most in love. The waning of love, then, cannot be simply the unsuitability of two people who "got it wrong." It must be something inherent in love itself, which threatens love even as it makes it possible.

Why does love wane? The argument that passionate love depends on novelty confuses the initial excitement of "falling in love" with the nature of love itself. Of course novelty as such wears off, but if the passion (which is not always easy to distinguish from anxiety) diminishes too, we conclude without hesitation that the initial excitement could not have been love. It may have been flirtation or a challenge. It may have been just a new sexual conquest or an exciting way to spend a week's holiday. But love is not novelty—even when new. It is a structure that extends indefinitely into the future, and if it does not last, that means that the structure itself has been somehow damaged. The argument that love must wane because it depends on psycho-physiological stimulation and all such stimulation has limited duration is unsound as well. It misses almost everything essential to love—that it is more than mere excitement, that it is excitement *about* another person and a relationship rather than simply excitement as such, that the enthusiasm inherent in love has a much more solid basis than the vicissitudes of the brain's physiology. Love concerns the whole self of the lover. And, ironically, such explanations as these of why love wanes begin with a concept of love such that love isn't much worth having in the first place.

The idea that "familiarity breeds contempt" provides a much more ominous explanation of love's waning, lending itself to the usual aphoristic dialectic that would also explain how "absence makes the heart grow fonder." But like most paired pieces of folk wisdom, these are only half true. Familiarity also breeds respect, admiration, devotion and love, and the risk of absence is "out of sight, out of mind." There is no doubt that love suffers any number of small disappointments and disillusions when faced day to day with realities of a relationship—the cap off the toothpaste once too often, the embarrassments of ordinary bodily dysfunctions, the first night of sexual frustration, a stubborn insistence on an obvious error, a refusal to say "I don't know." But no love ought to get lost because of such disappointments; instead, it is the work of love to absorb these into its context, to rearrange one's conception of the other (and of oneself) to embrace such occurrences, if not with enthusiasm, then at least with tolerant acceptance. When such cumulative disappointments do bring an end to love, again we should probably conclude that love was inadequate in the first place, or the conception of either love or the lover was too ethereal, too uncompromising. So, too, if love leads to *dis*illusionment, it is not because love is an illusion or deluding but because one's concept of love, or at least that specific experience of love, was overidealized to begin with.

One aspect of love that does surely wane is the frequency and intensity of sexual desire. A man's sexual physiology is said to "peak" at eighteen, leaving for the rest of life—which for most of us is our entire sexual life—a slow decline. The anxiety and anticipation of the first sexual encounter rarely last even to the second, and the thrills of several early weeks or maybe months necessarily diminish as not only the novelty but the uncertainty wear thin and sex becomes predictable and expected if not taken for granted. But anxiety is certainly not a positive experience, and the fact that sex becomes more predictable and secure is not exactly unpleasant or undesirable. Familiar sex, comfortable sex and knowing sex do not mean boring sex, empty sex, unromantic sex. Quite the contrary, it is in sex free from the performance and anxiety of "proving oneself" that romantic expression is most readily available, with room for the most personal variation, play and eccentricity. The fact that the frequency and frenzy of sex may wane has little to do with the persistence or diminution of romantic love.

But to hear some sad couples tell it, the change in sexual frequency and/or intensity is not one of gradual waning and familiarity but of utter collapse. One of two vital and healthy married friends will confess to you with mixed sadness, anger and embarrassment that they have not had sex together for many months or years. Candid letters to the advice columnist of a daily paper complain bitterly about a husband who is "demanding and insatiable, like an animal," or about a wife who "thinks that twice a year is enough." One is reminded of the split-screen scene in *Annie Hall*, where Annie objects to her boyfriend's insatiability —"Constantly. I'd say three times a week!"—while Alvy Singer complains "Hardly ever, three times a week." But differences in desires and preferences aside, the waning of lust is not the same as the waning of love. Neither, of course, is it entirely irrelevant. "When a marriage goes on the rocks, the rocks are right here," screams Big Mama in *Cat on a Hot Tin Roof*, slapping the bed. A decrease in frequency and frenzy in sex is to be expected, but the virtual termination of sex is almost always a signal of some deeper decision or disillusionment, a part of a play for power or a cry for attention and help.

One of the reasons often given for the waning of love is that "beauty fades," but this is at best an analogy rather than an explanation. The fact is, as we've said, that beauty becomes less important as a relationship goes on; indeed, it may become less important even at the very beginning. One does not have to spend very much time with a person before personality takes precedence. If one were just in love with beauty, it *would* make sense to suppose that love will wane as the beauty diminishes— or as one gets more used to the partner's beauty and takes it for granted. But love is not aesthetic appreciation; it is an emotion of shared identity. A lover looks beautiful because of the way he or she looks at and relates to you. Nietzsche once quipped that one should think of marriage as a long conversation. Personality doesn't wane, it gets better with age, more practiced, more confident, more individual, and two personalities together get more synchronized, more reciprocally fluent, more comfortable but also—in the best of cases—more understanding and mutually inspiring. It is tragic that we are so encouraged to cultivate the features of first attraction—like physical beauty—while the primary advice we get concerning matters of personality and communication is simply the unhelpful, even cynical, "Just be yourself." Granted, particularly in love, one should not affect false personality traits, but character and personality are learned, not "natural." Getting along, falling in love, forming a relationship and developing love are mastered with experiment and experience, and they—not the charms of initial attraction—are responsible for lasting love. Whether or not beauty fades, personalities grow closer together, and it is that closeness, the shared identity that comes of a life together, that explains and supports love that lasts a lifetime.

The waning of love can be attributed, in many cases, to lack of attention—lack of attention to the other person, lack of attention to the relationship itself. In the early phases of love, paying attention is virtually guaranteed by the novelty of the situation and the newness of the other person. There is so much that one doesn't know; there is so much that may be unexpected. It is not that the novelty wears off (which, of course, it must) that explains love's waning, but rather that, with familiarity, one too easily starts to take the other person and the situation for granted. One simply assumes instead of paying attention. The relationship goes on automatic pilot and once-attentive answers turn into such mechanical replies as "Uh-huh" and "Great"—recited without enthusiasm. It is sometimes argued that such neglect is "natural"; it comes along with comfort, familiarity and knowledge. But this is laziness, not nature, and one might well reply that lack of interest in what is closest to us isn't natural, it is perverse. But it is nevertheless a fact that we tend to take for granted what is closest to us—whether what is "closest" to each of us is our own minds, our own selves, those we love or our very souls. It was Nietzsche who reminded us that we seem furthest from that which is closest to us, and the inattention we sometimes give to the love of our lives is certainly an apt and tragic instance of this. Love consists of the interaction of the two "halves" of a shared self, but these two halves form a whole only by virtue of the attention lavished upon them. It is *thinking* that accounts for shared identity, not the pseudo-physical origins imagined by Aristophanes nor even the very real physical sharing that is manifested in sexual intercourse, for that, however graphic, still leaves entirely open the question whether the relationship is love or not. Love is bound to wane when those two selves cease to see themselves as "two halves," as bound together, and this can become the case with lack of attention just as surely as it can when two people fail to share, to care and to communicate. Attention is not only the main demand of love—sexual desire, too, demands attention, and the excitement of new sex is at least as much the consequence of intense attention as it is the sensations themselves. Sexual desire is also the need to be attended to; it is the desire to be desired as well as desire as such. And attention, unlike sex and the brain's physiology, and many of the various surprises that plague us through life, is quite thoroughly within our own domain and control. Inattention—and consequently the waning of love—is very much our own doing. Mutual romantic attention, not just in the beginning but throughout a relationship, is always the key to lasting love.

Not all attention is conducive to love, needless to say. Some couples watch their love not wane but get gobbled up or nibbled to death by small objections and complaints. And, as in inattention, they do it to themselves. In part, of course, such nagging and niggling can be a reaction to the lack of attention—a petty punishment, a perverse demand, a frustrated effort to make the other take notice even if only through indignation or annoyance. Thus inattention and such critical attention often go together, which forces us to qualify our insistence on the importance of attention by asking "Attending to what?" Not just to the other person, but to the attractions and the virtues of the other person —the ones that presumably brought us together in the first place. And not just attention to the relationship itself—which may be largely a matter of maintenance and compromise rather than romance as such. Indeed, excessive attention to the relationship, to the exclusion of care and concern for the other as an individual, leads to possessiveness and throws off the balance of shared self and autonomy. Attention must be paid to love itself, to the circumstances in which it may flourish (including, most important, time alone together). Talking a relationship to death, while surely a proof of paying attention, is hardly conducive to love and is dangerously conducive to just the nagging and niggling and mutual recriminations that tarnish and obliterate love and turn a relationship into a source of constant conflict instead of romance. Stendhal and Gide's notion of "decrystallization" here seems to be suffering from yet a third stage of degeneration—we might call it "encrustation"—where a relationship starts to build up so much crud that it takes on a dull and dirty, cheerless look, attracting only more crud, refusing to reflect any brilliance or flattering light.

The three most devastating reasons for the waning of love,

however, have to do with our faulty notions about love. The first is that we think of love too readily in terms of just its initial stages. The second is that we think of love in terms of its options. The third, the most serious, is that we tire, not so much of the other person or the relationship, but of ourselves.

One: we have to get over the distinction, so familiar to us that we do not question it, between new love and old love, between love that is "romantic" and love that is "conjugal" (or "companionate" in the ugly new coinage). Not, of course, that there isn't old and new—the very existence of time demands a chronology. But we tend to think of these as two distinct *types* of love, the former passionate and sensual, the latter dull but durable and comfortable. There is the obvious, of course—that love—most loves—that begin with a flair and fireworks soon dwindle to domestic comfort or worse, but we should be careful in analyzing this change and, most important, we should resist any theory that makes it sound inevitable. For instance, there are the new neurochemical theories that attribute romantic love to amphetamine-type chemicals—whose "high" is inevitably (by physiological necessity) followed by a "crash." Such theories must be rejected. The excitement of first love may be no more than that—excitement, as much fear and anxiety as love. And it is cruel to insist that longtime love, which may be just as enthusiastic as new love, is less passionate because it is less physiologically explosive. The structure of love, new and old, is the same, though the circumstances are certainly different.

Here's a different way of thinking about it: remember the last time you moved to a new city or neighborhood. At first you were all curiosity and exploration. You visited every new shop or museum, were entirely open to new people, the possibility of new friendships. After a while you settle in and get comfortable, as it all becomes familiar. Indeed, many of the old explorations now seem not worth the bother, and new friendships, while nice if they happen, no longer seem so necessary. It's not that the city changes or even that your life in it changes. The difference is between discovery and familiarity, between looking forward to and enjoying. It is not that it changes—it's that it stays *the same*. So, too, with relationships. That first eagerness to learn and explore does not change but solidifies. There is still enthusiasm, but it is the same. In the same way, sex at first may be a thrill—just the idea of doing it, the impulse of performance. But the enthusiasm increases with familiarity, and partners fall into a ritual, *not* negative or meaningless but the opposite. Rituals have meanings that first explorations do not. Of course if the love goes bad, then the sex can be intolerably boring or worse, no matter how "good." ("I had an orgasm every time," she said with contempt.) And sex, of course, can be separated from love—in other words it isn't so much an expression of love as an expression of other passions, and it may not be satisfying even if the love is intact (though sexual dissatisfaction is often confused with the love itself losing its spark). For men or women who think of love primarily as power and conquest, as "proving themselves," familiarity and intimacy will not be welcome, even if they also love the person. But again, let's be very cautious about attributing this to the decline of love. What is just as likely is that some other desire isn't getting satisfied.

There is, of course, one typical consequence of romantic love and relationships that does indeed change everything, and that is—children. The problem is not just the inevitable explosion of domestic duties, household chores, sleepless nights and lack of leisure time. It is rather the fact that a couple is suddenly never alone, and so lacks that precondition of intimacy that, until now, has been so readily available. Much has been made in social psychology of "triangulation theory," which is, simply put, the dramatic changes that enter into interpersonal relations when there are three people rather than only two—even if the third consciousness is infantile. A baby makes demands, offers smiles and signs of affection, and even this is enough to deflect the once exclusive attention that the couple could pay to each other. But, on the other hand, children are not only the product but the personification of the notion of shared selves. They may, as such, become the ultimate bond of love, but it cannot be simply assumed (as it so often is) that this will be the case.

Two: one reason why love tends to wane is the happy fact that we have so many options. So many marriages today end in divorce and unhappiness that we are tempted to conclude, without warrant, that when divorce was more difficult or impossible there must have been all of these miserable and loveless marriages. But this is unduly pessimistic and tacitly self-consoling. The truth is that when there were no options for escape there were not nearly so many reflective pressures working *against* love. The question "Am I fulfilled?" went unasked—which does not mean that people were unfulfilled, and the question "Do we really still love each other?" went unasked as well—without indicating that couples did not love one another. Enforced marriages had their own benefits, one of which was the protection of love, not love as an *issue*, perhaps, but love as a more or less steady and stable state of affairs. The psychologist John Money writes:

> Even if it's a relatively poor match, it can last as long as two years—
> that's about the natural history of the high flame of a love affair—and
> then it begins to burn lower. But nature is very clever. She gives you
> long enough to create a pregnancy and have the baby, and then the
> bond of the lovers has to enlarge to include the baby, and it becomes
> a three-way bond.

When you know that you are in love and marriage for life, everything changes. It is not that there is no choice left about it. The decisions just become bigger and riskier. But one is not forced to consider options at every stage of the way. What we find so intolerable (because we can easily imagine ourselves out of it), our grandparents could accept with mere annoyance just because they knew they were in it for life.

Love is often said to last by virtue of a couple's making a "commitment." We have already cast some doubt on the importance of this familiar notion in love by pointing out that this quasi-legalistic conception is quite opposed to the emotional intransigence and resolution that explain lasting love. This is not to say that some conscious and mutual decision to "make it work" is not important and, in times of crisis, effective in holding a relationship together. Nor is it to say that commitments are irrelevant to romance; indeed, marriage in particular has recently evolved as the culmination of romance, and marriage is perhaps the greatest commitment that most of us ever make. But commitment as a legal entity lacks teeth today. It is easier to get a divorce than it is to get a chauffeur's license in many states. As social expectation, it is empty; our friends are less surprised by an impending divorce than they were by the wedding announcement. And as a personal resolution or a promise, we all know how easily commitment can melt when one no longer sees the point of it. Indeed, that is the problem (if it is a problem): the fact that we insist on being able to ask whether we want it anymore, with one available and easy-to-act-upon answer always being "no." The lesson that one should fall in love with the best possible person has changed from the noble idealization of one's lover to the constant search for something better, and the new absurdity of "wanting it all" seems to be dictating the desirability of marriage- or romance-hopping as a way to social success in much the same way that ambitious young executives go job-hopping on their way up the corporate ladder. With such an attitude, it is no wonder that love tends to wane in the face of ever-present options and constant competition.

Three: love is considered to be an emotion of respect if not awe for the *other* person, not an emotion that is largely concerned with oneself. Accordingly, we tend to view the waning of love as some sort of loss of respect for the other, or perhaps some lack of commitment or generosity on our part. Of course there are many marriages and relationships that break apart because one does lose respect for the other, or because one is no longer willing to put up with disappointments or betrayals that have ignored too many warnings, too many opportunities to correct themselves. But the most dramatic and devastating reversal of love takes place within oneself and toward oneself, in the development of contempt and even a sense of betrayal for what one oneself has become. We may well project this sense of resentment and betrayal outward and blame the person we once loved, but we know that we have done it to ourselves, albeit slowly, over time, and we can't even begin to retrace the steps of our own self-degradation. Simply put, loves comes to an end because we can no longer stand what we ourselves have become. In the development of a shared identity, we chose (we were never forced) to choose the wrong role. A woman thinks that she is acting out love by taking on the domestic duties she has always despised—and then years later finds that she has become those duties; her husband assumes and depends on them; she measures her success and failure on their basis. Consequently, she feels that she is a failure and has contempt for herself, resentment of her husband and little room for love. A man tries to treat his wife to a life of luxury and attentiveness, only to find that, years later, he has reduced himself to no more than a servant, not a lover, and he despises himself. A man prides himself on his strength and domination of a relationship, but then starts to realize that he views himself—as his wife views him—as a conceited and insensitive bully, and though he condemns himself, he starts to complain that his wife will not stand up to him, as if this were not a role that he endorsed from the very beginning. Or a woman who wanted a man who is strong and assertive starts to realize that she has put herself in a position of continuing abuse and defensiveness, and when she finally has had enough of love, it is explicitly because she doesn't ever want to be (i.e., put herself) in that position again.

Love finally comes down to a matter of selfhood, and the waning of love turns out to be a question of what kind of self we want to be—attentive to love or neglectful of its demise. We all want to be loved "for ourselves," but the truth is that few of us have the nerve to ask whether we have a self worth loving. One of the most frequent reasons why love wanes—though no surprise to any third party—is that the self that we expect to be loved is quite a boring and flawed self, in contrast to the adventurous, charming and elegant self that we first presented when we were trying to get into love. There may be no fixed standards for lovability: one person is loved for his or her casual inelegance while another is adored for sophisticated fashionability. One person is loved for his or her animal insight and alertness while another is adored for educated ethereal brilliance and articulateness. But whatever the reasons why we love or are loved, those reasons can be betrayed. If one presented oneself as a lover of the arts, it would be a betrayal to admit indifference or philistinism later on. If one went courting as a charming élégante, one should not be surprised if love fails to survive increasing gruffness and slovenliness. Love is a match of selves to form a new self, and as one becomes less self-conscious or self-aware, it can be expected that a dull self that shows no interest in improvement will provide little continuing sustenance for love. And yet so many of us act as if love, once earned, is assured or even guaranteed for life, unconditionally. As if the show we first put on will suffice and somehow remain the center of focus long after that apparent self has disappeared.

Love wanes because of neglect, not because of any natural process. And yet the danger of this neglect is already inherent in love, for it is the comfort and familiarity that love engenders that breeds the assumptions and lassitude that lead to inattention, then resentment, then bitterness and encrustation. But there is nothing inevitable about this, and if there is anything hopeful about the general waning of love it is the realization that we are doing it to ourselves—through carelessness, through taking it (or the other person) for granted, through neglect of ourselves. This is not to say that love never begins wrong, or to deny that many relationships are bound to destruction through poor choices, given the almost complete freedom most people now have to make their own mistakes. But the waning of love is not something that happens or even something that we let happen. It is something that we do—though too often we become aware of what we have done only when the destruction is irreversible. The advice in the magazines, most of which consists of re-creating romantic scenarios or experimenting with some novel mode of seduction, are actually not off the mark. These are all devices to remind us to attend to what we have and what we stand to lose, to admire once again the attractions and virtues of a person whom we have long thought "the most wonderful in the world."

Critics have too often challenged love for its "blindness" and its unwillingness to recognize faults in one's lover, but the other side is that it is just such idealization and the ability to see past the faults and fully appreciate the beauty of someone else that keeps love alive. It is no triumph of realism that a couple together after fifteen or twenty years sees each other's faults and blemishes and no longer fantasizes or celebrates or exaggerates virtues. The alternative to criticism is not "blindness," it is loving, paying attention and being full of appreciation for this other person with whom you are spending so much time, with whom you have spent so much time, with whom you plan to spend so much more time. Indeed, if I had to pick out a single trait that seems to characterize those couples who continue to love the most after many years, who keep sex and romance alive, it is the very opposite of those compulsive efforts at continued glamour and sexiness, those serious sessions of therapy and therapeutic tasks aimed at mutual understanding. It is, in a phrase, a mutual sense of humor. It is the ability to be *amused* by each other, to find faults as charms—often so easy in the first weeks of an affair but so soon infuriating when the efficiency demands of a relationship begin. For all of the advice in the magazines on "How to Keep Your Love Alive," the salvation of love is not the prolongation of sexual desire but the shared lifelong cultivation of a romantic lightheartedness that softens conflicts and anxieties and focuses our serious attention even as it undermines seriousness as such. It's hard to fall out of love so long as you're laughing together.

REINVENTING LOVE

I have an idea that love is a lot more exclusive than popular songs have led us to believe. . . . These days, certainly, folks seem more concerned with furthering careers than with furthering romance.

—T O M   R O B B I N S , *Still Life with Woodpecker*

Being in love is not a momentary passion but a process, and so, in a sense, there is no point in asking how to make love last. Love has time built right into it, and the right question, perhaps, is why so often love doesn't last, doesn't develop, doesn't take full advantage of the foundation of shared identity that it has built for itself. Sometimes, of course, the obvious answer is that two people were "wrong" for one another, but I am more and more convinced that such an answer will not do. It is the very nature of love that it aims at the impossible fusion of two very different personalities. So, in this sense, we are all "wrong" for one another and there is no perfect Aristophanic fit for any of us. Nor is it the case that the "degree" of fit is an adequate explanation, for the passion of love is often proportional precisely to its difficulty, and the most difficult relationships are those that invite and demand the most devotion, the most attention, the most care—and may last the longest. Love doesn't last because—contrary to our abstract celebrations and initial enthusiasm—we do not take it sufficiently seriously. We conceive of it falsely—as a feeling, as novelty, as bound up with youth and beauty. We fall into domestic habits and routine relationships and assume that love will take care of itself, which, of course, it will not. We expect an explosion at the beginning powerful enough to fuel love through all of its ups and downs instead of viewing love as a process over which we have control, a process that tends to *increase* with time rather than wane. But the most important feature of all, in making love last, is our appreciation of the fact that love, no matter how pervasive in our society, is in fact a very recent and incomplete invention, that we are all, in every relationship, reinventing love for ourselves.

There is no such thing as "true" love, if by that phrase one means a single form of relationship or affection that eclipses all possible others. There is nothing more "true" about a comfortable lifelong marriage than a series of tumultuous affairs, nothing more right or "natural" about a married couple with children than a childless unmarried couple, nothing healthier or better about a couple who hum along effortlessly than a couple whose love is punctuated by forced battles and passionate lovemaking. There is nothing authoritative about monogamy, or sexual exclusiveness, nothing ultimately written about what should be possible or tolerable. This is not to say that "anything goes," but only that there are no absolute authorities or standards. There are still a thousand ways of getting it wrong—or not getting it at all—but where love is concerned, whatever "works" is enough. And it is the very structure of love—not just the techniques that keep a couple together—that are in question here. There are no longer rules for love. There are only love and relationships and the many ways of working them out and making them work.

We still place too much confidence in the expectations and guidelines that were deemed appropriate for our grandparents (the sexual revolution notwithstanding) and too readily accept the idea that love endures by staying within the lines instead of taking risks and continually testing and renewing itself. Despite a sexual infidelity rate that some researchers estimate to be 70 percent or so (for women as well as men), there are still many couples who see a casual affair not as a complication or a crisis but as simply "The End." Despite the fact that two-job couples now make up an enormous proportion of the work force, old sexual stereotypes of work-and-home behavior persist nonetheless, casting men and women in romantic roles no longer appropriate to their daily lives. Despite the fact that people are not just getting divorced more often but marrying more often too, we still tend to praise "first love" in terms of novelty and innocence instead of giving full recognition to an emotion that gets mastered only with time and probably after many mistakes. In the twelfth century, Andreas Capellanus drafted a list of rules for courtly love that seem little but amusing to us now. Just a century ago there were strict rules of love and courtship, many of which we now see as heartless and barbaric. Our lack of historical sympathy aside, what becomes obvious is that today we have to make up our own rules for love.

One doesn't have to deny biology or the Zeitgeist to insist that, no matter what our built-in biology or the established rules of the culture, it is up to us what to make of what we are and shall become. The facts of biology are ours for the taking, from the exquisite skills of lovemaking to the glorification or denial of sexual differences. Well-entrenched social expectations are ours to use to our own satisfaction; romance becomes a personal adventure, marriage becomes a personal statement. The timetables of love, while they cannot be denied, may yet be manipulated— from the momentary schedule of sensual excitement to the long-term questions of fidelity and continuing romance. Twenty years ago there was an explosion of creativity in the realm of multiple romances, "open" marriages and self-authored marital contracts, but it was not just the exhilaration of the sixties that provoked such a widespread rebellion. We conceive of love and relationships as personal and private, depending on the mutual agreement of the two "consenting adults" involved. There will always be conservative arguments proving to us that only monogamy is "natural," that sex before or outside of marriage is immoral, that it is psychologically impossible to love more than one person at once. But the fact is that what is "natural" is in our hands and what is moral is determined by a negotiable set of demands. What is psychologically possible is a subject for experimentation and not pontification.

The need to make up one's own rules in love has nothing to do with youthful rebelliousness. Indeed, it is older couples who find themselves facing the necessity of inventing love anew, first because the guidelines for long-term love are woefully inadequate (lack of role models, the idea that most rules for long-term love provide prohibition rather than stimulation, the "happily ever after" delusion), and second because the rules of romance are so youth- and seduction-oriented that any couple over the age of forty is bound to find them largely irrelevant. We think of youth as rebellious and age as tradition-bound, but the fact seems to be that young love unwittingly follows the rules of romance even as it pretends to rebel against society, while the elderly and older couples are forced to invent their own rules. There are rules of etiquette, if not morality, governing proper behavior on a first date, on the morning after, following an engagement and at the wedding. But there are no rules or even hints about how to behave when the kids go off to college, when you get divorced at fifty-five or when you date someone who's recently had a heart attack or kidney troubles. First love is never unique—no matter how miraculous it may seem to the hitherto uninitiated. Love the second or third time around, no matter how entrenched it may be in old romantic habits, is always of necessity creative. The first time one follows the "rules." After that one has to respond to one's own illusions and mistakes.

One of the themes in this book is the multiple modes of love, from obsessive being "in love" to tender but tolerant loving to friendship and the formal commitments of marriage. What this means is that there is a *choice* between modes of love, and to "get involved" with someone does not in itself dictate any particular path or passion. A relationship can be a friendship—with or without sex—with minimal demands and expectations regarding the amount of time to be spent together or what is permitted or expected in time apart. Or it can be exclusive and openly obsessive, with a number of explicit and implicit arrangements and rules and an absolute prohibition on any other even vaguely romantic relationships. Couples have spent a lifetime together in separate apartments with separate sequences of lovers. One thinks immediately of the celebrated lifelong love affair between Jean-Paul Sartre and Simone de Beauvoir, whose lives and careers were intimately intertwined while they lived in separate residences, carried on a variety of affairs and friendships together and separately and lived a life that (quite conscientiously) defied bourgeois categories of love and marriage. And while one would not expect such a complex social and sexual arrangement to be without its fights and resentments, all of them eloquently documented for the world in both literature and philosophy, pointing out such difficulties is not moral censure or the instructions of "nature."

The idea of "making up one's own rules" is almost always interpreted along a single dimension—that of free-wheeling sexuality. The inference is that, by making up one's own rules, one gets permission to "play around." But sex, while essential, is hardly the critical issue, and the (usually male) claim to autonomy as an excuse for sexual irresponsibility is not at all what I have in mind here. Nena and George O'Neill's best-selling book ten years ago, *Open Marriage*, disappointed many readers and reviewers just because it never said (what many of them wanted to read) that extramarital sex was okay and even healthy for the marriage. Their concern, and mine, was much more involved

with the substance of the relationship, questions about time together and time apart, questions about obligations and intentions, questions about kids and careers, questions about all of
those felt responsibilities, demands and attachments that
threaten and deaden a relationship and make it suffocating instead of supportive. Questions about sexual fidelity may be the
most tantalizing and traumatic, but sex, like most other aspects
of love relationships, is a matter of interpretation and what
counts for one couple as infidelity and betrayal might for another
be no more than a mutually entertaining interlude. And, more
important, the decision to practice sexual fidelity is just as much
a matter of personal choice and commitment in love as the decision to play around. One might try to point out that the traditional rules have always insisted on marital fidelity, but a
thousand years of literature and experience show that our actual
expectations are quite otherwise.

None of this is to say that "making one's own rules" is done
easily or should be done glibly, simply out of the spirit of rebellion. It is one thing to decide that one will deviate from the norm
—continue a passionate relationship without sexual satisfaction,
for instance, or continue a live-in sexually passionate relationship without fidelity or any future expectations. It is something
else to carry on a relationship in the face of not only personal
resistance and intransigence but also social disapprobation and
censure. The timetables and expectations of love are not just
"out there," in the opinions and sanctions of society; they are "in
us," internalized with the rest of our language and our culture,
our expectations about what is fair and what is "natural." There
are severe limits to how far we can go, in each of us and even
more so between the two of us. And yet the inadequacy and
contradictoriness of our established rituals and expectations
make it not only possible but desirable, maybe even necessary,
to make up our own rules as we go. Perhaps every couple in
some sense does so anyway—no matter how much they may
think that they are merely "normal" and following the estab-

lished rules. Love is nothing less than the (re-)creation of one's own most personal identity. It would not be surprising if there turned out to be a wealth of personal creativity and eccentricity as well.

The need to rethink the rules of love and reinvent love for ourselves is in fact one of the most powerful inspirations of love. Love thrives by being thought about; it is not just a feeling that goes on its way whether we pay attention to it or not. Hegel, among other philosophers, developed the notion that there are at least three levels of consciousness, the last and the highest being what we might call "reflection" (he calls it "reason"). This is not just self-consciousness but "self-awareness." It is not just a sense of self but a perspective on oneself, the attempt to *think* about oneself and to comprehend who one is and what one is doing. The much-touted experience of "first love" is rarely more than mere romantic self-consciousness (barely even that!), for there is little understanding, or for that matter even questioning. In later love, however, there is some perspective, not only confusion but an attempt to understand, an attempt to grapple with the other person and, more important, to wrestle with one's own expectations and self-image, as reflected by and in the other. This in turn feeds into the love itself and turns it into not only a rebellious but a revolutionary force in one's life, filled with philosophy as well as enthusiasm. Hegel argued that reflection is essential to freedom, but Marx added, importantly, that reflection makes freedom possible, for it allows us to change the very features that we now understand as making up our essential selves. In first love we follow the rules of love, even if unwittingly. In later love, when we might think that we are being more conservative, we make them up. Indeed, we could not do otherwise, for we have evolved ourselves to such a level of sophistication that the old expectations are no more than nostalgia and fond memories. Love must be reinvented, but it is being so right now, by all of us, two at a time.